Contents

Acknowledgements

Text and diagrams reproduced by kind permission of:
Biological Sciences Review; Blackie Publishers; Blackwell Scientific Publications Ltd; British Agrochemical Association; Cambridge University Press; Chapman & Hall Ltd; Dover Publishers; Edward Arnold Publishers; Field Studies Council; FMA; Granada; Harper and Row Publishers; John Moores University; Journal of Zoology; Liverpool Polytechnic; Longman Publishers; Manchester Metro; Mauna Lou Observatory, Hawaii; National Rivers Authority; Nature Conservancy Council/Game Conservancy; New Scientist; Open University; Open University Science Foundation; Oxford University Press; Reed Business Publishing; RSPB Conservation; The Daily Mail; The Guardian Newspaper; The Observer Newspaper; Thomas Nelson Publishers; University Tutorial Press; W.B. Saunders Co. Ltd; Wiltshire Trust for Nature Conservation; World Wildlife Fund.

Every effort has been made to contact the holders of copyright material, but if any have been inadvertently overlooked the publishers will be pleased to make the necessary arrangements at the first opportunity.

The publishers would like to thank the following for permission to reproduce photographs
(T = Top, B = Bottom, C = Centre, L= Left, R = Right):

Anglian Water Services Ltd 29L; John Bebbington FRPS (Field Studies Council) 82; John Birdsall Photography 75R, 142TR; The Bodleian Library, Oxford (MS Eng. D 2528, Fol. 1B) 6T; D Allan (B.A.S) 49; P Bucktrout (B.A.S) 55; C J Gilbert (B.A.S) 58; British Sugar plc 137TL; Broads Authority 30; Bruce Coleman/H Lange 8BL, J Burton 8TR, N Blake 9T , J Murray 12, J Taylor 17, Fr. J Erize 42C, A Potts 43, J Johnson 93, J L G Grande 133; Collections/Roger Scruton 88TR; R J Corbin 148; Environmental Images/P Ferraby 29R; Greenpeace 46T; Leslie Garland 19R; Tony Waltham/Geophotos 36; Ronald Grant Archive 42B, 92; Professor Don Grierson 164; Hedgehog House, New Zealand/ T de Roy 46C,

C Monteath 46R, 57, P Broady 54B, G Rowell 54T, G Kooyman 56L, K Westerskov 56R; Holt Studios International/ N Cattlin 109, 111, 118, 119, 123L, 124, 127, 135, 138, 139, 141, 143C, 146, 150, 156B, 162, 167; R Anthony 112; P Karunakaren 107; A Morant 121; A Burridge 128, 137TR; Holt Studios 151BR; B Gibbons 155L; W Harinck 98B; I Spence 153; Horticultural Research International – Wellesbourne· 163; Imperial War Museum, London 115TR; John Innes Centre/ Dr D M Lonsdale 166; Institute of Hydrology 87R ; FLPA Ltd/D P Wilson 89, P Reynolds 98T; Magnum Photos Ltd/S McCurry 73; Network Photographers/H Logan 31R; NHPA/S Kraseman 9CR , S Dalton 18, 44, H Palo Jnr 25, D Woodfall 26, 61, 62, 68, 70, 87L, P Parks 28 35, L Campbell 31L, A Bannister 33L, B Wood 33R; NRA 67, 74;

OSF/A & S Carey 6C, T Ulrich 6L, A Walsh 15; Panos Pictures/B Press 114; Photos Horticultural 159; Popperfoto/Reuters 88L; Margery Reid, School of Biological & Molecular Sciences, Oxford Brookes University 77, 81; Cleland (SAC) 78; Science Photo Library 1, 47, 129, 155R, 156T; Still Pictures/M Edwards 23L, 72, 76 102, 103TR, H Mason 64, T Raupach 95, S Dawson 96, D Dancer 103BL, R Morton 143B, M Milligan 165; Tony Stone Images 105, 125, 142L, 147, 151TL; C & S Thompson 115L, 116; Woodfall Wild Images 19L, 21, 23(inset), 32, 60, 75L, 85, 99, 122, 123R, 131, 161;

Cover photograph supplied by Science Photo Library.

To the student

This book aims to make your study of advanced science successful and interesting. The authors have made sure that the ideas you need to understand are covered in a clear and straightforward way. The book is designed to be a study of scientific ideas as well as a reference text when needed. Science is constantly evolving and, wherever possible, modern issues and problems have been used to make your study interesting and to encourage you to continue studying science after your current course is complete.

Working on your own

Studying on your own is often difficult and sometimes textbooks give you the impression that you have to be an expert in the subject before you can read the book. I hope you find that this book is not like that. The authors have carefully built up ideas, so that when you are working on your own there is less chance of you becoming lost in the text and frustrated with the subject.

Don't try to achieve too much in one reading session. Science is complex and some demanding ideas need to be supported with a lot of facts. Trying to take in too much at one time can make you lose sight of the most important ideas – all you see is a mass of information. Use the learning objectives to select one idea to study in a particular session.

Chapter design

Each chapter starts by showing how the science you will learn is applied somewhere in the world. Next come learning objectives which tell you exactly what you should learn as you read the chapter. These are written in a way which spells out what you will be able to do with your new knowledge, rather like a checklist – they could be very helpful when you revise your work. At certain points in the chapters you will find key ideas listed. These are checks for you to use, to make sure that you have grasped these ideas. Words written in **bold type** appear in the glossary at the end of the book. If you don't know the meaning of one of these words check it out immediately – don't persevere, hoping all will become clear.

The questions in the text are there for you to check you have understood what is being explained. These are all short – longer questions are included in a support pack which goes with this book. The questions are straightforward in style – there are no trick questions. Don't be tempted to pass over these questions, they will give you new insights into the work which you may not have seen. Answers to questions are given in the back of the book.

Good luck with your studies. I hope you find the book an interesting read.

Mike Coles, Series Editor
University of London Institute of Education, June 1995

Webs and pyramids

In 1921 Charles Elton took part in an expedition to Spitsbergen in the Arctic and made an ecological survey of the animal life there. Before this, most expeditions had been interested in botany.

Charles Elton was a remarkable man who was responsible for developing many of the concepts of the science we know now as ecology. In 1927, he wrote his classic work *Animal Ecology* in just 3 months! It set out important ecological principles such as food chains, food webs and the pyramid of numbers. Discovering these principles was the result of close observation of animals.

He established the Bureau of Animal Population at Oxford, where much of his work was directed towards controlling the numbers of rodent pests. How can the study of different animals and their interrelated feeding habits help us control animal populations? Can understanding feeding relationships also help us make our food production more efficient?

A Canadian lynx stalking prey.

Population sizes in Canada

Rabbit population

Numbers (thousands)

Lynx population

Year

1820 1840 1860 1880 1900 1914

1909

Source: data taken from Hewitt, 1921, based on fur returns of Hudson's Bay Company

A Canadian snowshoe hare. After his work in the Arctic, Elton studied changes in the population numbers of fur-bearing animals in Canada.

1.1 Learning objectives

After working through this chapter, you should be able to:

- **recall** that ecosystems contain biotic and abiotic components;

- **use** food chains, food webs and ecological pyramids to illustrate feeding relationships;

- **explain** how energy is gained, used and lost as it passes through the trophic levels of a community;

- **investigate** the efficiency of primary and secondary production;

- **solve** energy budget problems;

- **explain** the energy relations of environments at different stages of succession;

- **relate** the energy relations of different ecosystems to potential use by humans.

Collins Advanced Modular Sciences

Food, Farming and Environment

Damian Allen and Gareth Williams

Series Editor: Mike Coles

Collins Educational
An imprint of HarperCollinsPublishers

Northern
Modular Science Scheme

Published by CollinsEducational
An imprint of HarperCollins*Publishers* Ltd
77–85 Fulham Palace Road
Hammersmith
London
W6 8JB

First published 1997
Reprinted 1997

ISBN 0 00 322391 4

British Library Cataloguing in Publication Data
A catalogue record for this book is available from
the British Library.

Design by Ewing Paddock at Peartree Design

Edited by Eva Fairnell

Picture research by Caroline Thompson

Illustrations by Barking Dog Art, Russell Birkett,
Tom Cross

Production by Mandy Inness

Printed and bound by Scotprint Ltd, Musselburgh

1.2 Ecology

Charles Elton introduced a clear purpose and scientific method to the study of natural history. He had a **quantitative** approach to his studies, rather than the **qualitative** approach of many earlier natural historians. A quantitative approach is concerned with the numbers of organisms in an area, while a qualitative approach studies the characteristics of the organisms. For example, Elton did not just observe that there were lynx and snowshoe hares present in Canada. He also found out how many individuals of each species were present.

Elton was interested in how living organisms interact with each other and their **environment**. The environment of an organism is made up of all the conditions that affect it. This includes other living organisms and the physical surroundings.

Ecology is the study of how organisms interact with each other and with their environment. These interactions are **dynamic** because they can cause changes in the organisms and the environment that lead to new interactions and more changes.

Living organisms, together with their environment, form an **ecosystem**. Ecosystems are made up of **biotic**, the living, and **abiotic**, the non-living, components, and the interrelationships between them.

The abiotic part of an ecosystem provides the conditions needed for plants and animals to exist, such as oxygen, light and nutrients. These conditions are the characteristics of the **habitat** of particular organisms. A habitat is the place a particular organism lives, for example a rocky stream bed or a grass plain.

The biotic part of the ecosystem is made up of the plants and animals that live in a habitat. This is called the **community** (Fig. 1). Each community is made up of different **populations** of plants and animals. A population is a group of individuals of the same **species**. A species is a group of organisms with similar features that can interbreed to produce fertile offspring.

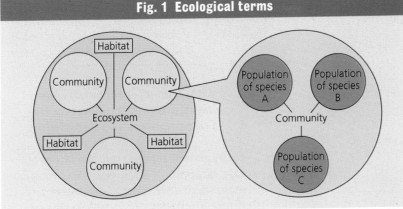

Fig. 1 Ecological terms

1 Explain the differences between:
 (i) ecosystem and habitat;
 (ii) population and community.

1.3 Food chains and webs

Elton used feeding relationships to classify organisms. A plant can be eaten by an animal that in turn may be eaten by another animal, that in turn may itself be eaten. This sequence of events is called a **food chain.** A food chain highlights a sequence by which food, and therefore

energy, passes from one organism to another.

Each stage of a food chain is called a **trophic level**. The arrows show the transfer of food from one trophic level to another. A trophic level indicates an organism's feeding relationships with other organisms.

Oak leaves → slug → thrush → sparrowhawk
Producer → primary consumer → secondary consumer → tertiary consumer

Organisms are either **autotrophs** or **heterotrophs**. Autotrophs are able to make their own **organic** food, by using **inorganic** mineral ions and a source of energy. Organic nutrients always contain carbon and hydrogen atoms. Inorganic nutrients do not always have carbon. Green plants make their food by photosynthesis, using light as the energy source. Others, mainly chemosynthetic bacteria, derive their energy source from chemical reactions. Autotrophs are **producers**. Producers ultimately provide food for all other members of the community.

Heterotrophs cannot make their own food; they have to take food into their bodies ready made. As a result they are called **consumers**. All consumers are ultimately dependent upon producers for food. **Primary consumers** are herbivores, they feed upon green plants. **Secondary consumers** are carnivores, they feed upon primary consumers. **Tertiary consumers** are carnivores that feed upon secondary consumers, and so on. Elton noticed that any one food chain rarely exceeded five links.

Some food chains are based on living organic matter.

Diatom (algae)	→ blackfly larva	→ stonefly larva → trout
Phytoplankton (tiny aquatic plants)	→ barnacle larva	→ arrow worm → herring
Hazel leaf	→ moth caterpillar → robin	→ tawny owl

Other food chains are based on dead and waste organic matter. **Detritivores** are primary consumers that contribute to the process of decomposition. They feed upon fragments of dead organic matter called **detritus**. Detritivores break down detritus into finer particles. Detritivores include earthworms and woodlice in the soil, and freshwater shrimps and hoglice in rivers and streams.

Once the detritus has been broken down by detritivores, **decomposers** feed upon the dead or decaying plants and animals. The main decomposers are bacteria and fungi. These microorganisms cycle nutrients used in plant growth. In doing this, they themselves obtain a source of energy.

A pike catching a ten-spined stickleback. Pike are ferocious carnivores, at the top of many freshwater food chains.

Detritus	→ midge larva	→ leech	→ perch → pike
Leaf litter	→ woodlouse	→ shrew → weasel
Dead animal	→ blowfly maggot → frog	→ adder

 2 Explain the differences between:
   (i) autotrophs and heterotrophs;
   (ii) decomposers and detritivores.

Elton also observed that predators are usually larger than their prey. So organisms increase in size with each successive link of the food chain. An exception to this occurs when parasites are involved. In this case the top consumers will consist of many smaller organisms.

| Primrose leaf → snail → hedgehog → flea |

Communities seldom consist of a single food chain. The feeding relationships between different trophic levels are likely to be more complex and this can be shown by a **food web** (Fig. 2). Each animal does not feed on just one prey item, frogs would get pretty fed up feeding only on maggots! The food web shows the interweaving food chains and gives a better picture of the complexity of feeding relationships.

Plenty of earthworms is a sign that the soil is healthy. Keen gardeners encourage worms to help make good quality compost.

On Bear Island, Spitsbergen, the number of species was so few that food webs could be worked out easily. This puffin has a beak full of sand eels.

The following feeding relationships may be observed on a rocky British shore, some when the tide is in, others when the tide is out:

- limpets grazing on diatoms attached to the rocks;
- dogwhelks eating barnacles and mussels;
- crabs consuming detritus and dead mussels in crannies in the rocks;
- barnacles feeding on zooplankton (tiny aquatic animals);
- mussels feeding on phytoplankton diatoms;
- flat periwinkles feeding on diatoms attached to seaweeds;
- gulls feeding on dead crabs;
- turnstones (birds) feeding on dogwhelks, limpets and periwinkles.

3a Sort the organisms above into primary consumers, secondary consumers and tertiary consumers.
b Construct one complete food chain from the list.
c Could you construct any other food chains? Is this ecosystem better described as a series of food chains or as a food web? Explain why.

Fig. 2 The food web on Bear Island

Nitrogen → Protozoa
Skua / Glaucous gull
Kittiwake / Guillemots / Fulmar petrel / Little auk / Puffin / Northern eider / Long-tailed duck / Red-throated diver
Bacteria → Dung
Mineral salts
Collembola / Diptera / Mites / Hymenoptera → Spider
Dead plants
Arctic fox
Marine animals
Plants → Ptarmigan
Worms
Dung / Seals
Geese
Purple sandpiper
Diptera (adult)
Snow bunting
Polar bear
Algae → Protozoa
Decaying matter → Lepidurus
Diptera (immature)
Entomostraca / Rotifera
Algae
Entomostraca / Rotifera / Tardigrada / Oligochaeta / Nematoda
Protozoa
Freshwater plankton
Moss
Freshwater bottom and shore

Source: Summerhayes and Elton, 1923.

On the 1921 Spitsbergen expedition, Elton carried out a survey of all the animal life. He pieced together the feeding relationships of the different organisms, such as the Arctic fox.

Key ideas

- Ecology is the study of the interrelationships between organisms and their environment.
- An ecosystem is a dynamic system made up of abiotic and biotic components that interact.
- Communities are made up of populations of different species in a particular habitat.
- The dynamic feeding relationships within a community can be recorded by food chains and food webs.
- Food chains and food webs show how energy passes from one trophic level to another.

1.4 Ecological pyramids

Food webs describe the feeding relationships that exist within a community, but they give no indication of the numbers of individuals involved. They are not quantitative. It takes many plants to support a few herbivores, which in turn support even fewer carnivores (Fig. 3).

In his book *Animal Ecology*, Elton noted that 'animals at the base of a food chain are relatively abundant while those at the end are relatively few in number, and there is a progressive decrease in between the two extremes.' This was the original basis upon which the **Eltonian pyramid of numbers** was proposed.

Pyramids of number are constructed by first sampling the organisms in a particular

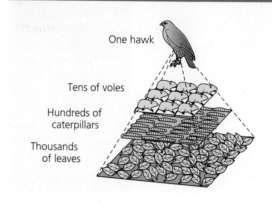

Fig. 3 Feeding numbers

One hawk

Tens of voles

Hundreds of caterpillars

Thousands of leaves

community and placing them in their correct trophic level. This is usually done by observing their feeding behaviour or by examining their gut contents. Pyramids of number are essentially bar charts plotted horizontally. The area of each bar is proportional to the number of individuals at that trophic level. The producers are placed at the base of the pyramid, with each successive consumer level above them. In general, as you go up a pyramid:
- the numbers of individuals decrease;
- the sizes of individuals increase (Fig. 4).

However, when comparing different pyramids this method does not take account of the relative size of different organisms. For example, one beech tree will provide food for far more consumers than one grass plant. And parasites can produce a top-heavy pyramid (Fig. 4).

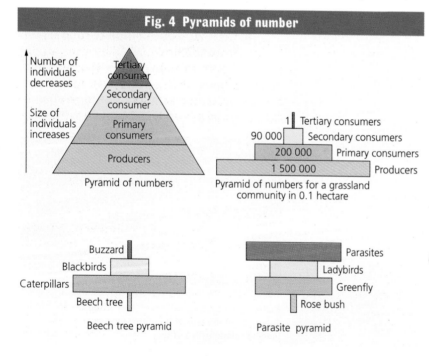

Fig. 4 Pyramids of number

Number of individuals decreases

Size of individuals increases

Tertiary consumer
Secondary consumer
Primary consumers
Producers

Pyramid of numbers

1 Tertiary consumers
90 000 Secondary consumers
200 000 Primary consumers
1 500 000 Producers

Pyramid of numbers for a grassland community in 0.1 hectare

Buzzard
Blackbirds
Caterpillars
Beech tree

Beech tree pyramid

Parasites
Ladybirds
Greenfly
Rose bush

Parasite pyramid

Q 4 a Using Fig. 5, how many more people could be supported on a diet of frogs rather than trout?
  b How many more people could be supported on a diet of grasshoppers rather than frogs?

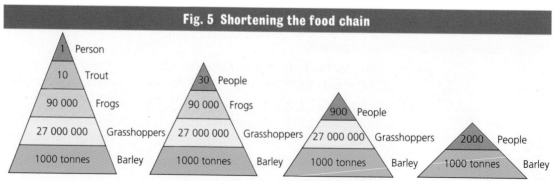

Fig. 5 Shortening the food chain

1 Person
10 Trout
90 000 Frogs
27 000 000 Grasshoppers
1000 tonnes Barley

30 People
90 000 Frogs
27 000 000 Grasshoppers
1000 tonnes Barley

900 People
27 000 000 Grasshoppers
1000 tonnes Barley

2000 People
1000 tonnes Barley

Pyramids of biomass overcome the problem of size of organisms. They show the **biomass**, which is the total mass of all living organisms per unit volume or area, at a particular time. This is also know as the **standing crop**. To obtain a measure of the standing crop, a representative sample of the organisms at each trophic level is weighed. This is known as the **wet mass**. The wet mass is then multiplied by the estimated number of the organisms in the community (Fig. 6).

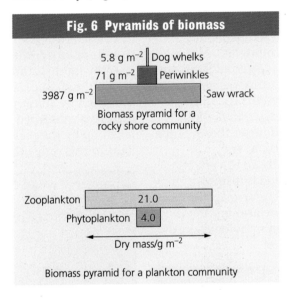

Fig. 6 Pyramids of biomass

5.8 g m^{-2} | Dog whelks
71 g m^{-2} | Periwinkles
3987 g m^{-2} | Saw wrack

Biomass pyramid for a rocky shore community

Zooplankton | 21.0
Phytoplankton | 4.0

Dry mass/g m^{-2}

Biomass pyramid for a plankton community

The water content in organisms can vary, so **dry mass** measurements are more reliable. Obtaining the dry mass involves heating the sample in an oven at 110°C to a constant mass. This is often neither practicable nor desirable because it kills the plants and animals being studied.

Productivity is the rate of production of organic material per unit area or volume per unit time. Biomass pyramids have drawbacks because they give no indication of the rate at which materials are produced or used up per unit time.

Phytoplankton are very small aquatic plants. **Zooplankton** are very small aquatic animals that feed on phytoplankton. Phytoplankton grow very quickly and so have a high productivity. However, they do not have a large biomass so at a particular point in time an inverted pyramid can still appear (Fig. 6).

5 **The biomass of an individual may also vary with the time of year. For example, an oak tree has far more biomass in June than in December. Why is this?**

Pyramids of energy show the productivity or the rate of energy flow at successive trophic levels in a given area or volume, over a fixed period of time (Fig. 7).

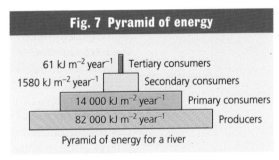

Fig. 7 Pyramid of energy

61 kJ m^{-2} year^{-1} | Tertiary consumers
1580 kJ m^{-2} year^{-1} | Secondary consumers
14 000 kJ m^{-2} year^{-1} | Primary consumers
82 000 kJ m^{-2} year^{-1} | Producers

Pyramid of energy for a river

Energy pyramids reveal the efficiency of energy transfer from one trophic level to the next, and because only a proportion of that energy is passed on they are never inverted. They also make it possible to compare the productivity of different communities accurately. However, it can be difficult to gather data to draw energy pyramids. It involves burning known masses of organisms from each trophic level to establish their energy values.

6 **What are the advantages and disadvantages of the following types of ecological pyramids:**
(i) pyramids of number;
(ii) pyramids of biomass;
(iii) pyramids of energy?

1.5 Energy flow through an ecosystem

Elton realised that in order to study ecosystems, it is important to study all the dynamic relations between all the different parts of the ecosystem. This includes all the interconnections between all the populations in a community in a habitat over a period of time. One dynamic relationship is feeding. Another is energy flow.

The concept of a dynamic ecosystem assumes the transfer of energy from one trophic level to another. As energy flows through an ecosystem, interrelationships change. Energy can be transferred from one form into another but cannot be created or destroyed. The sun represents the ultimate energy source. Solar energy enters the producer level during photosynthesis. Some of this energy is passed on to the consumers, but eventually all the energy that passed into the plants is lost from the system as heat (Fig. 8). The arrows in food chains and webs therefore also represent the **energy flow** between individuals in the community.

Energy flow through producers

All living organisms depend directly or indirectly upon **primary production**. Primary production is the production of biomass by photosynthetic autotrophs, the producers. However, only about 0.1% of the total solar energy reaching the surface of the Earth becomes incorporated into plant biomass. This relatively low figure can be partly explained by the fact that much of the Earth's surface is too cold, too dry, too dark or too poor in plant nutrients to sustain photosynthesis.

Only light within the wavelengths 380 nm (red) and 720 nm (blue) can be **absorbed** by chlorophyll and other plant pigments. Absorbed means the energy is taken up by the plants and used. It is the light in this range that can be used for

Fig. 8 Energy flow

Energy used for respiration, etc.

Tertiary consumers

Secondary consumers

Primary consumers

Producers

Dead remains, faeces, etc.

Dead remains, etc.

Energy lost as heat

Decomposers

Energy input

Sun

Green plants and photosynthetic bacteria are the only living organisms on our planet able to convert solar energy into energy in chemical bonds in biomass.

photosynthesis and is termed **photosynthetically active radiation** (PAR). About 45% of solar energy falls within the PAR waveband.

Photosynthetic efficiency is a measure of how well a plant captures energy.

$$\text{Photosynthetic efficiency} = \frac{\text{amount of energy incorporated into newly formed carbohydrate}}{\text{amount of light energy falling on the plant}}$$

Even under ideal conditions the overall efficiency of energy conversion in photosynthesis is as low as 8%. In reality, ideal conditions are rare due to seasonal and daily fluctuations in light and temperature, lack of nutrients and plant dormancy.

Photosynthetic products accumulate as **gross primary production** (GPP). A great deal of this is used up in plant respiration, but the remainder is called **net primary production** (NPP). NPP represents the potential food available to primary consumers.

$$\text{Net primary production (NPP)} = \text{gross primary production (GPP)} - \text{respiration}$$

The efficiency of energy transfer from sunlight to net primary production is relatively low. Subsequent transfers between trophic levels are at least ten times more efficient. Some energy will be transferred from the plant when it dies and when it sheds its leaves or loses fruits and seeds. This will benefit decomposers, who derive energy from dead plant material.

7 a **Use the data in Fig. 9 and the equation above to work out the photosynthetic efficiency for the crop plant.**
  b **What percentage of the solar energy absorbed by the chloroplasts is 'lost' from photosynthetic reactions? Account for these 'losses'.**

Fig. 9 Photosynthetic efficiency

The amount of solar energy intercepted by green plants depends a great deal on geographical location. In Britain this is estimated as approximately 1×10^6 kJ m^{-2} year^{-1}, but at least 95% of this is unavailable to plants for photosynthesis.

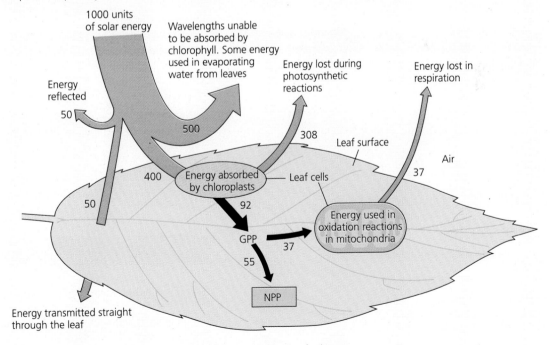

The photosynthetic efficiency of a crop plant, based on 1000 units of solar energy

Source: adapted from Open University Science Foundation course and data taken from ABAL, Cambridge University Press

Different ecosystems have different NPP values, due to the different abiotic and biotic characteristics.

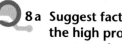

8 a Suggest factors that contribute to the high productivity in the two most productive ecosystems in Table 1.

b Suggest factors that reduce productivity in the two least productive ecosystems.

c Figures like those in the table can be obtained by collecting the above-ground vegetation at the end of the growing season and making dry mass measurements. What inaccuracies may occur in the use of this technique?

Table 1. NPP values	
Ecosystem	NPP/kJ m^{-2} year^{-1}
Extreme desert	260
Desert scrub	2600
Subsistence agriculture	3000
Open ocean	4700
Areas over continental shelf	13 500
Temperate grasslands	15 000
Temperate deciduous forest	26 000
Intensive agriculture	30 000
Tropical forest	40 000

Source: Open University Foundation Science Course

Energy flow through consumers

The transfer of energy from producers to primary consumers (plants to herbivores) also involves a loss. Energy conversion into the bodies of consumers is termed **secondary production**. This time the efficiency of energy transfer is approximately 10%. So, for every 100 g of plant material, 10 g ends up as new herbivore biomass. Reasons for the inefficiency of this energy transfer are:

- some of the plant material is not digested and passes out of the body in the faeces;
- a great proportion of the energy is used in herbivore respiration;
- some energy passes to decomposers in dead animal remains.

Similar losses of energy occur between each subsequent trophic level, although carnivores are able to achieve as much as 20% energy conversion because they are able to digest their high protein diets very efficiently.

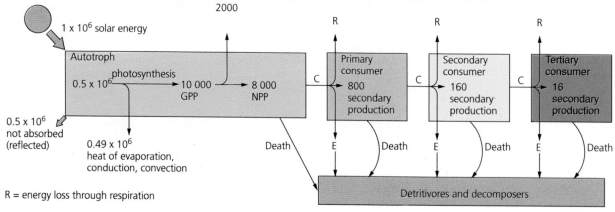

Fig. 10 Energy flow through a grazing food chain

R = energy loss through respiration

E = energy lost from grazing food chain to detritivores and decomposers through excretion (e.g. urine) and egestion (e.g. faeces)

C = consumption by organisms at the higher trophic level

Energy flow though a grazing food chain, such as a grazed pasture. Figures represent kJ m^{-2} year^{-1}

Source: Green et al., Biological Science 1 & 2, Cambridge University Press, 1994

Q 9 a From Fig. 10 what percentage of the solar energy absorbed is available for photosynthesis?

b Write down an equation to show how the figure for NPP production is arrived at.

c What percentage of the energy consumed is used for secondary production in:
(i) the primary consumer;
(ii) the secondary consumer;
(iii) the tertiary consumer?

d Which animal in this food chain makes the most efficient use of the food it eats?

e In what ways is energy lost from the food chain?

Energy budgets can be very useful to farmers when they have to consider the feeding requirements of their stock, whether the stock is cattle, sheep, llamas or any other species! These llamas were bred in the UK.

Table 2. Freshwater stream data

	GPP	Respiration	NPP
Plants	9.0×10^4	5.0×10^4	x
	Food assimilated	Respiration	Production
Primary consumer	12.0×10^3	10.3×10^3	1.7×10^3
Secondary consumers	1.5×10^3	1.3×10^3	0.2×10^3
Tertiary consumers	10.0×10^1	6.0×10^1	4.0×10^1
Decomposers	2.0×10^4	1.8×10^4	0.2×10^4

All values are kJ m^{-2} year^{-1}

Source: Open University Science Foundation Course

Energy budgets

If the amounts of energy entering, being used up and leaving an animal are measured, an **energy budget** can be worked out for it.

Of the food consumed (C) by an animal, a proportion of it is used up or **assimilated** (A) and the rest passes out as faeces (F).

Consumption = assimilation + faeces
$$C = A + F$$

This assimilated energy is of great significance to the energy budget of domestic animals, because it represents the proportion of the food that is used by the body's metabolism. The proportion of assimilated food to consumed food is known as the **assimilation efficiency**.

Of the food assimilated, much will be used up during respiration (R) to provide energy for chemical reactions in the body or for movement. A further proportion will go towards producing new body tissues (P). The remainder is excreted as metabolic waste in urine (E).

Assimilation = respiration + production + excretion
$$A = R + P + E$$

Fig. 11 Food web of a freshwater stream

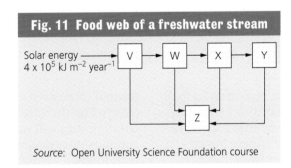

Solar energy
4×10^5 kJ m^{-2} year^{-1}

Source: Open University Science Foundation course

Q 10 a Calculate the missing value *x* from Table 2.

b Identify the trophic levels V to Z in Fig. 11.

c Compare the overall respiration with the GPP. Does this ecosystem show a net gain or a net loss of energy? Assume that the total biomass is constant and that the total amount of detritus remains constant.

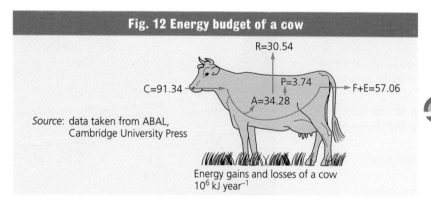

Fig. 12 Energy budget of a cow

R=30.54
P=3.74
C=91.34
A=34.28
F+E=57.06

Source: data taken from ABAL, Cambridge University Press

Energy gains and losses of a cow
10^6 kJ year^{-1}

For every square metre of grass it eats, a cow obtains 3000 kJ of energy. It uses 100 kJ for production (P), 1000 kJ are lost as heat from respiration (R),and 1900 kJ are lost in excretion (E) and faeces (F).

 11 a What percentage of the energy in one square metre of grass:
   (i) is used in production;
   (ii) passes through the gut and is not absorbed?
b Work out the assimilation efficiency of the cow using Fig. 12.
c Cows spend a great deal of their time grazing. With reference to the energy budget, say why you think this is.
d If beef has an energy content of 12 kJ g^{-1}, how many square metres of grass are needed to produce 100 g of beef?

Taking the components of assimilation separately, the overall energy budget is as follows.

Consumption = respiration + production + excretion + faeces
C = R + P + E + F

Key ideas

- Ecological pyramids can be used to show the feeding relationships of an ecosystem.

- Energy is transferred from one organism to another in an ecosystem.

- Ecological pyramids can be used to show the flow of energy through different trophic levels.

- Energy is lost between each trophic level because the efficiency of transfer varies between different organisms.

- Primary and secondary production is related to the efficiency of energy transfer.

- Energy budgets can be used to determine the feeding requirements of organisms.

1.6 Succession and energy relations

Elton was one of the first ecologists to look at plant and animal associations within communities. He observed that plant and animal communities are closely linked. With time the number of species in a community increases, the feeding relationships become more complex and the total biomass increases. Some types of community, such as grassland, are replaced by a series of different communities until a stable community develops. This is usually a forest. The process is called **succession** and the final community is called the **climax community**. The climax community ages but does not change into a different type of community. Some forests in Europe are thousands of years old.

Animal succession and plant succession are affected by the same factors. Simple communities will mature into more complex ones depending on abiotic conditions.

But what about the energy relations of the community? With increasing maturity, food chains in a community become longer as a consequence of the greater number of species. In a relatively new or young community, there will be fewer individual species and consequently shorter food chains. NPP increases with succession, as grassland progresses to herb and then shrub stages. When the forest stage is reached, however, production becomes stable. Biomass, in contrast, still continues to

Fig. 13 Production to biomass ratio

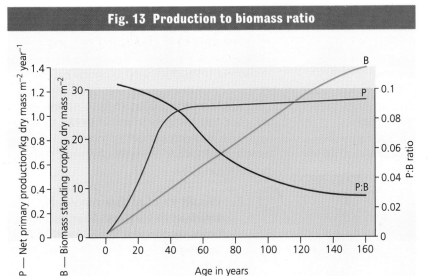

Annual above-ground net primary production (P) and standing crop biomass (B) and production to biomass ratio (P:B) in forest succession following fire on Long Island, New York (data of Whittaker and Woodwell 1968,1969)

Source: Begon et al., Ecology, Blackwell Science, 1986

Table 3. Different ecosystems

Characteristic	Ecosystem condition	
	Less mature	More mature
Structure		
Biomass	Small	Large
Species diversity	Low	High
Energy flow		
Food chains	Short	Long
Primary production per unit of biomass	High	Low
Individual populations		
Fluctuations	More pronounced	Less pronounced
Life cycles	Simple	Complex
Feeding relations	Generalised	Specialised
Size of individuals	Smaller	Larger
Life span of individuals	Short	Long
Population control mechanisms	Abiotic	Biotic
Exploitation by humans		
Potential yield	High	Low

Source: Adapted from Krebs, Ecology, Harper and Row, 1986

increase in the climax community (Fig. 13). The energy in a complex, mature community tends to be used by plants to maintain non-photosynthetic and supporting tissue. The energy in plants in young communities is used to generate photosynthetic structures and little support tissue.

For this reason, in the early stages of succession, the production:biomass ratio (P:B) is high. However, with time, the transition to a forest community means that the P:B ratio declines.

Mature and less mature communities can be compared in terms of their biomass and **species diversity** (Table 3). Species diversity is the number of different species living in the same community. An understanding of the ecology of an ecosystem, including the use of energy and the interrelationships of the different organisms, means the effect of disturbing them can be worked out.

Elton introduced the idea of measuring data from ecosystems quantitatively. Some of Elton's studies, at the Hudson's Bay Company and the Bureau of Animal Population, were to try and work out why some animal populations fluctuate greatly over time. By observing the animal populations and collecting quantitative data, he was able to show patterns in the periods of fluctuation. This meant it could

Regrowth of plants after a forest fire uses solar energy to produce as much greenery as possible. The P:B ratio is high until the climax community is established again.

be possible to predict years of abundance of animals wanted for the fur trade, or years of plagues of pests. In more complex ecosystems, with more interrelationships between the greater number of species, population sizes are less likely to fluctuate.

Different environments, such as those disturbed by human activity, new environments that have been formed as a result of human activity, and older, more stable environments, have different levels of productivity. The whole community has to be studied to understand how one species is affected by a change in its ecosystem. Productivity depends on the efficiency of energy transfer between the different trophic levels. Studies of energy transfer can be used to indicate the most efficient way of producing food in different environments for our own growing population.

Between the two world wars, Elton carried out an extensive survey of Bagley Wood, near Oxford. He estimated the size of populations of bank voles and woodmice. This was the first such investigation of its kind and showed that population sizes rose and then fell. Such cyclical changes were also found when, during the Second World War, Elton and his co-workers at the Bureau of Animal Population studied the populations of pest rodent species in an attempt to protect the country's food reserves.

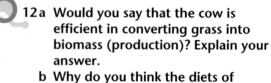 12a Would you say that the cow is efficient in converting grass into biomass (production)? Explain your answer.
 b Why do you think the diets of people in underdeveloped countries tend to be made up mostly of plants?
 c From what you have learnt in this chapter, what does it suggest to you about the number of people that can be sustained on a vegetarian diet?
 d With the huge increase in the world's population, explain the change in human diet that may occur in the future.

Key ideas

- Energy relations change as communities undergo succession.

- Succession can lead to a climax community, with a less hostile abiotic environment and greater species diversity.

- The diversity of organisms in an ecosystem indicates the stability of the ecosystem.

- The ratio between net primary production and biomass (P:B) is an important measure of succession in a community.

- Understanding energy relations means ecosystems can be used by humans more efficiently.

Cycling nutrients

" Call for cash to reclaim derelict land "

500 hectares of derelict land should be reclaimed with money from the government. 'This land has become so damaged by industrial development that it is incapable of beneficial use without treatment' said a National Park representative. This dereliction has been produced as a result of coal mining and the dumping of colliery waste over the last 150 years.

" Plan to turn pitland over to recreation "

Derelict land resulting from mining activities in the past is to be levelled and reclaimed for recreational use.

The land has had an offensive and depressing effect upon the local community, deterring industrial and housing development. Restoration of the site will provide attractive amenity grassland and playing fields.

The actions of humans can affect the nutrient balance of an ecosystem. Derelict land is usually lacking in many of the nutrients needed by plants. If plants cannot survive, no animals, nor humans, will be attracted to the area. We can try to repair damaged land by using fertilisers. How easy is it to return nutrients and so reclaim waste sites? And what effects can our actions have on the nutrient supply of aquatic environments?

The site could look like this after reclamation! This is an exhibition at the National Garden Festival at Gateshead in 1990.

2.1 Learning objectives

After working through this chapter, you should be able to:

- **explain** that ecosystems depend upon the action of abiotic and biotic factors to provide a source of nutrients;

- **recall** that plants require a range of nutrients for healthy growth;

- **describe** how nutrients are absorbed by organisms, transferred through trophic levels and released back into the environment;

- **describe** the role of decomposers and detritivores in the cycling of nutrients;

- **explain** how in aquatic ecosystems nutrients have to return to the surface from the depths to maintain primary production;

- **explain** why eutrophication can cause environmental problems;

- **demonstrate** that the balance between input and loss of nutrients can affect productivity.

19

2.2 Nutrients

All living organisms need energy. Energy enters ecosystems as sunlight, which is trapped by plants and photosynthetic bacteria, and transferred through the community to be released eventually as heat.

Living organisms also need organic and inorganic nutrients to survive. These nutrients can be obtained either from other organisms, the biotic environment, or from soil and the atmosphere, the abiotic environment. Like energy, nutrients are absorbed by organisms and transferred through the trophic levels. Absorbed means

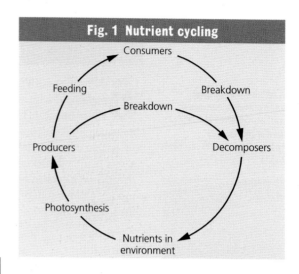

Fig. 1 Nutrient cycling

the energy and nutrients become part of an organism. But unlike energy, nutrients are released back into the environment in a form that can be reused (Fig. 1).

There is a fixed amount of nutrients on Earth and they move perpetually in a cycle from the atmosphere, water and soil into living organisms and back again. **Nutrient cycles** show the use and reuse of nutrients in the environment. The nutrients cycle between the biotic and abiotic environments.

The energy lost as heat at each trophic level cannot be reused by other organisms. All other organisms depend on the primary production by producers for their food and energy supply.

Q 1 a What is primary production?
  b Why is it that nutrients can be cycled through ecosystems, but energy cannot?

The nutrients taken up from the soil by green plants in large amounts are called **macronutrients** (Table 1). Nutrients that are needed in smaller quantities are called **essential trace elements**, and include iron, manganese, boron, copper, zinc and molybdenum.

Rainwater can drain very easily through the heaps of waste left by coal mines, called **colliery waste**. Any nutrients in the colliery waste can be washed away by the rainwater. This is called **leaching**.

Table 1. The essential macronutrients of green plants			
Element	**Taken up by plants as**	**Needed for**	**Deficiency symptoms**
Nitrogen	Nitrate NO_3^-	Making amino acids and proteins Important for growth and development of leaves and indirectly photosynthesis	Stunted growth and chlorosis, (yellowing) especially of older leaves
Phosphorus	Phosphate PO_4^{3-} Orthophosphate $H_2PO_4^-$	Encourages rapid and vigorous growth of seedlings and early root formation	Poor root growth
Potassium	K^+	Protein synthesis and photosynthesis Increases plant vigour and resistance to disease	Yellow and brown margins of the leaves and premature death
Sulphur	Sulphate SO_4^{2-}	Synthesis of proteins and other organic compounds like coenzymes	Chlorosis
Calcium	Ca^{2+}	Cell wall development	Stunted growth and poor root development
Magnesium	Mg^{2+}	Part of chlorophyll molecule important for photosynthesis	Chlorosis

If any nutrient is in short supply the growth of the plant will be limited. The nutrient is then called a **limiting factor**. A limiting factor reduces the rate of a process. The most common nutrient that can limit the growth of plants is nitrogen. Other important macronutrients are phosphorus, often limiting in acid soils, and to a lesser extent potassium. Deficiencies of the other plant nutrients are far less common. In derelict land the amounts of nitrogen and phosphorus are often too low to support healthy plant growth.

Different factors limit plant growth on different types of derelict land. For colliery waste, limiting factors include lack of water, lack of nutrients, high temperature, low pH and a high concentration of **toxic** elements. Toxic elements are poisonous. The addition of major nutrients to derelict land does not always produce improved plant growth if one of the other factors is still limiting.

Natural regeneration of hawthorn scrub on an old mining site. Before regeneration the content of the waste will have had an effect on the land and the water environment.

2 a Suggest the effect nitrogen shortage will have on the growth of plants on colliery waste.

b What steps might be taken to correct nutrient shortage on colliery waste?

Fig. 3 Adding organic nutrients

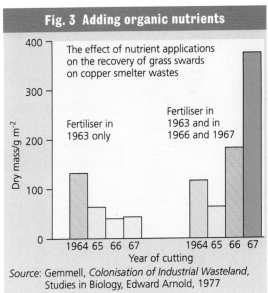

The effect of nutrient applications on the recovery of grass swards on copper smelter wastes

Source: Gemmell, *Colonisation of Industrial Wasteland*, Studies in Biology, Edward Arnold, 1977

Fig. 2 Adding inorganic nutrients

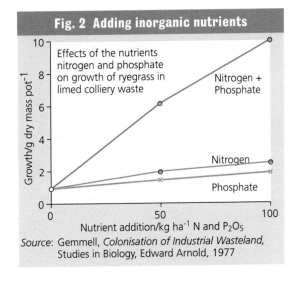

Effects of the nutrients nitrogen and phosphate on growth of ryegrass in limed colliery waste

Source: Gemmell, *Colonisation of Industrial Wasteland*, Studies in Biology, Edward Arnold, 1977

Chemical inorganic fertilisers can be used to correct nutrient deficiencies (Fig. 2). Ammonium nitrate can be used as a source of nitrogen. Calcium phosphate and basic slag from steel works can be used to add phosphorus, while potassium sulphate corrects potassium shortage.

The level of organic matter in most colliery waste is usually so low that organic fertilisers also need to be applied every year until a reasonable amount of **humus** can form. Humus is decaying organic matter that acts as a pool of nutrients that plants can use (Fig. 3). Humus also improves the water-holding ability of the soil.

Abiotic sources of nutrients include rainwater and the action of weather on rocks. As rocks break down into smaller bits, nutrients are released. Soil with plenty of humus can keep the nutrients from rainwater and rocks in a form plants can use.

Colliery waste has a low pH, i.e. it is acidic. At low pH large amounts of iron and aluminium form iron and aluminium phosphate. Since the phosphate has formed compounds with the iron and aluminium, it cannot be used by plants, so there is phosphate deficiency. A few species of grass can survive in acidic soils. On colliery waste they will become dominant because there will be few plants competing with them. Their growth will be limited by lack of phosphates. The pH can be raised by adding lime to the spoil, and in the short term extra phosphate can be added. More plants will then be able to grow on the colliery waste.

3 a Why does the nature of colliery waste make it prone to nutrient shortage?
  b Some species of grasses are tolerant to conditions on colliery spoil tips. Suggest what conditions the tolerant species can survive in.

Key ideas

- Nutrients cycle through trophic levels and are released back to the environment to be reused.

- Nutrients are essential for primary production in plants and ultimately secondary production in animals.

- If nutrients are in short supply, they can become limiting factors that prevent the growth of plant populations.

- Nutrients can be added to derelict land to encourage the growth of plants.

2.3 Carbon cycle

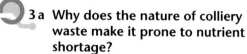
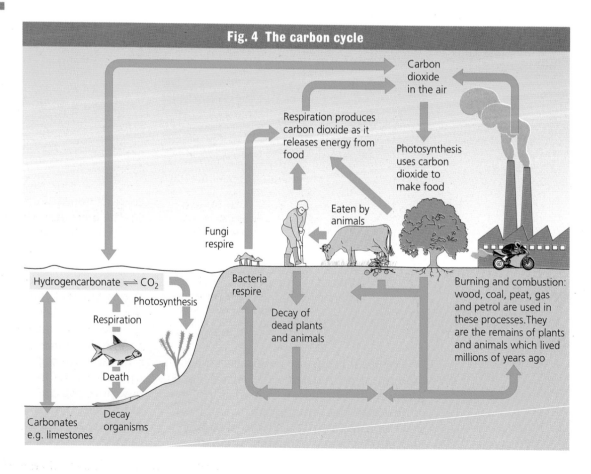

Fig. 4 The carbon cycle

Carbon dioxide in the air

Respiration produces carbon dioxide as it releases energy from food

Photosynthesis uses carbon dioxide to make food

Eaten by animals

Fungi respire

Bacteria respire

Decay of dead plants and animals

Burning and combustion: wood, coal, peat, gas and petrol are used in these processes. They are the remains of plants and animals which lived millions of years ago

Hydrogencarbonate $\rightleftharpoons$ CO_2

Photosynthesis

Respiration

Death

Decay organisms

Carbonates e.g. limestones

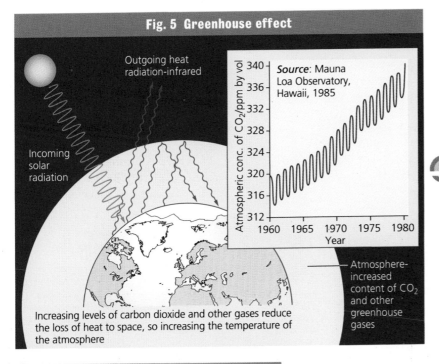

Fig. 5 Greenhouse effect

Outgoing heat radiation-infrared

Incoming solar radiation

Source: Mauna Loa Observatory, Hawaii, 1985

Atmospheric conc. of CO_2/ppm by vol

340
336
332
328
324
320
316
312

1960   1965   1970   1975   1980
Year

Atmosphere-increased content of CO_2 and other greenhouse gases

Increasing levels of carbon dioxide and other gases reduce the loss of heat to space, so increasing the temperature of the atmosphere

Atmospheric pollution from industry, such as this scene in Poland, sends vast quantities of carbon into the atmosphere.

The burning of rainforest trees to enlarge cattle ranches in Brazil releases carbon dioxide into the atmosphere. Furthermore, ploughing of the land after the trees have been felled results in a rapid release of carbon dioxide due to the decomposition of organic material. The loss of trees also reduces the rate of photosynthesis.

Organic compounds, compounds containing carbon, are the building blocks of life. The processes of photosynthesis and respiration dominate the carbon cycle. Photosynthesis fixes atmospheric carbon dioxide into an organic form. Respiration effectively does the reverse. Carbon dioxide is highly soluble in water so it can also be transported from one place to another in freshwater and seawater.

Q 4 a Using Fig. 4, by what processes does carbon enter and leave plants?
b List the ways carbon enters and leaves animals.
c Explain two ways in which carbon can be taken out of the cycle for long periods of time.
d Which organisms play a vital role by breaking down dead material and making carbon available to plants?

Increasing levels of carbon dioxide and certain other gases in the atmosphere reduces the loss of heat to space, so increasing the temperature of the atmosphere (Fig. 5). These gases act in a similar way to the glass in a greenhouse and have a warming effect upon the Earth. Therefore it is known as the **greenhouse effect**.

Q 5 Explain the pattern shown in Fig. 5 and suggest what might be causing the carbon dioxide level to rise.

Over the last century, the amount of carbon dioxide in the atmosphere has increased by 30% to 350 ppm. This is thought to have raised the Earth's temperature by 0.75°C. This is known as **global warming**. The rise may not seem much, but the rate of warming is increasing and could lead to polar temperatures rising above 0°C. This could melt the Arctic and Antarctic ice caps, leading to a catastrophic rise in sea-level and flooding of low-lying areas.

The reasons for the rise in atmospheric carbon dioxide include:
- combustion of oil and coal in power stations and factories;
- the burning and ploughing of tropical rainforests;
- damage to plant life, including phytoplankton.

23

2.4 Nitrogen cycle

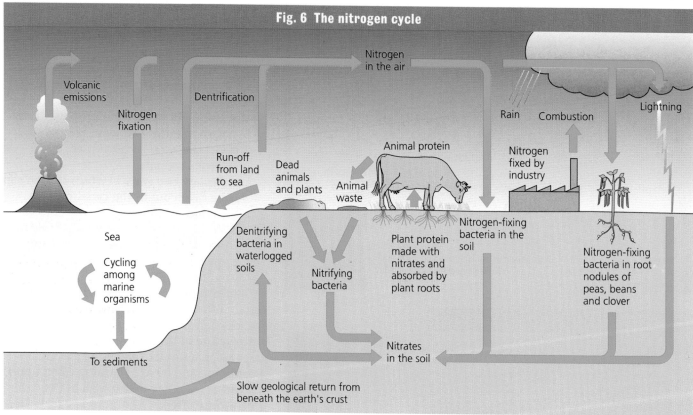

Fig. 6 The nitrogen cycle

Nitrogen is an unreactive gas that makes up nearly 80% of the air. Nitrogen is also an essential element in proteins. Animals and plants need to take in nitrogen if they are to make new proteins. The main way in which plants get their nitrogen is by taking up nitrates from the soil. Colliery waste is short of nitrogen, so the size of plant populations is limited. This reduces primary production.

6 a From Fig. 6 how does nitrogen get into animals?

b In what ways is nitrogen returned to the soil by plants and animals?

c List the ways in which nitrogen can be lost from the soil.

d How do humans ensure that nitrogen shortage does not reduce crop yield?

Bacteria and fungi are able to break down large, complex molecules in dead plants and animals, faeces and urine into smaller, simpler molecules. The bacteria and fungi then make use of the nutrients and energy in

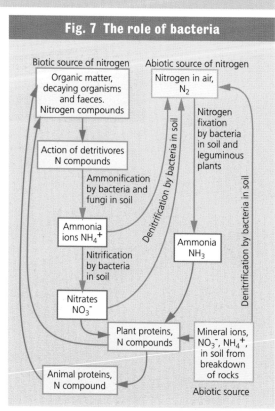

Fig. 7 The role of bacteria

the dead and excreted material. This is known as decomposition. The nutrients the bacteria and fungi have released from the dead organic matter are also available to organisms in higher trophic levels. Decomposition dominates the nitrogen cycle.

Bacteria and fungi break down dead and waste organic matter to form ammonium ions. This is called **ammonification** (Fig. 7).

Many of the ammonium ions produced are then converted by other bacteria into toxic nitrite ions, which are then converted into nitrate ions. These bacteria are called **nitrifying** bacteria and the process is know as **nitrification**. The energy released by the process of nitrification is used by the bacteria.

Some bacteria are able to extract nitrogen gas from the air and convert it into a form that can be used by other organisms. This is known as **nitrogen fixation**. Free-living microorganisms such as *Azotobacter* and cyanobacteria such as *Nostoc* are responsible for 90% of the nitrogen fixation that occurs

in the soil. Other bacteria, such as *Rhizobium,* are able to form **symbiotic** relationships with leguminous plants such as peas and clover. In symbiotic relationships, one organism usually provides a habitat for another, different organism. *Rhizobium* are found in the root nodules of the leguminous plants and supply a source of nitrogen to the plants. The bacteria receive carbohydrate from the host plant. Because both organisms benefit, the relationship is called **mutualistic**.

Both nitrates and ammonium ions can be converted back to nitrogen gas by **denitrifying** bacteria. This is know as **denitrification**. It occurs most rapidly in oxygen-poor conditions, for instance in water-logged soils.

 7 a Why do you think that water-logged soils might result in reduced primary production?

b In what ways does bacterial activity affect the nitrogen cycle?

2.5 Decomposition

Fungi are essential for the decomposition of wood and other plant materials, as they are able to secrete cellulases, enzymes that break down cellulose. This breakdown allows other decomposers to gain access to the nutrients.

Fragments of decomposing material are called detritus. The numerous small invertebrates that feed upon detritus are known as detritivores. These animals shred up dead organic material, making it easier for decomposers to use the material. It is easy to confuse detritivores and decomposers. Detritivores are the small animals that start off the breakdown of organic material in the soil or in the water. Decomposers are the bacteria and fungi that complete decomposition and allow the release of organic and inorganic nutrients and energy, that in turn can be taken up by green plants.

In order to reclaim derelict land, the soil has to contain nutrients for plants. The actions of the decomposers and detritivores on organic and inorganic waste will release the nutrients back into the cycle. The interaction between detritivores and decomposers affects the rate of decomposition.

Temperature and humidity affect the rate of decomposition. It is much more rapid in tropical rainforests, where the temperature and humidity are high, than it is in temperate forests. Due to the lower rate of decomposition, there is a thick leaf litter and high humus content in the soils of beech or oak woodland. In contrast, the soils of rainforests have low humus and little leaf litter is present. The local climate conditions will therefore also have to be taken into consideration when planning to reclaim land.

8 Would the nutrients in temperate or tropical forests be more easily lost if the ecosystem was disturbed? Explain your answer.

Table 2. The size of soil organisms	
Mesh size/mm	Organisms that can enter the mesh
7.0	Decomposers, detritivores
1.0	Decomposers and detritivores except earthworms
0.5	Decomposers and small detritivores such as mites, springtails and enchytraeids
0.003	Decomposers only

Nylon bags with different mesh sizes were used to prevent access by decomposers and detritivores to buried pieces of oak leaves.

Source: Phillipson, *Ecological Energetics*, Studies in Biology, Edward Arnold, 1966 (in Simpkins and Williams, Collins Educational)

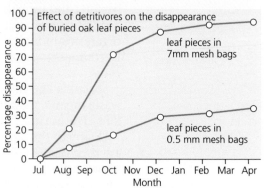

Fig. 8 Decomposition

Effect of detritivores on the disappearance of buried oak leaf pieces

leaf pieces in 7mm mesh bags

leaf pieces in 0.5 mm mesh bags

Source: Phillipson, *Ecological Energetics*, Studies in Biology, Edward Arnold, 1966 (in Simpkins and Williams, Collins Educational)

9 From Table 2 and Fig. 8, evaluate the contribution of the following to the breakdown of the buried oak leaves:
(i) earthworms;
(ii) other detritivores;
(iii) decomposers only.

Key ideas

- Photosynthesis and respiration are important in the carbon cycle.

- Nutrient cycling relies upon the activities of decomposers and detritivores.

- Bacteria and fungi break down large molecules in an ecosystem so that carbon dioxide and mineral ions can be reused by organisms.

- Mutualistic relationships between bacteria and plants enable nitrogen from the air to be used in an ecosystem.

- The human impact on the carbon cycle could be leading to global warming.

2.6 Nutrient budgets

Two or three days of heavy rain are required before burning heather, so that the peat becomes soaked. This ensures that the fire does not damage the heather roots, as new shoots will grow from these in the next year. The burning takes place in the late autumn or early winter to allow better new growth of heather the following spring.

Balancing the input and output of nutrients of an ecosystem provides the **nutrient budget**. This can be used to manage ecosystems. Moorlands have to be managed because burning, although needed to encourage new shoots for young grouse to feed on, causes nitrogen loss from the ecosystem.

The heather moorlands in Britain are an environmentally and economically important ecosystem, with distinctive plants and animals. The moorlands are managed to provide good feeding and breeding conditions for grouse. Most

Table 3. A nutrient balance sheet for a moorland heath						
	Na	K	Ca	Mg	P	N
Output, loss in smoke	1.5	8.3	12.5	4.0	2.2	173.1
Input, 12 years by rainfall	305	14	56	67	0.12	62
Difference, gain/loss	+303	+5.7	+43.5	+63	−2.08	−111

Source: from Chapman 1967 in Gimingham, *Ecology of Heathlands,* Chapman and Hall

moorlands are naturally deficient in phosphorus because they are acidic. Phosphates are prominent in the young shoots upon which grouse feed. These phosphates are important for the production of good quality eggs.

The moorlands are traditionally managed by burning the heather. But what happens to the nutrients contained in the heather stems and leaves when they are burnt? Does the burning deplete the soil of nutrients? Are nutrients carried away in drifting smoke or do they re-enter the soil when the ash dissolves in rainfall?

The loss of most mineral nutrients appears to be counterbalanced by the input from the ash that is washed back into the soil by rain (Table 3). However, burning does produce deficiencies of nitrogen and phosphorus. This progressively reduces the fertility of the moorland. The regeneration of the new heather as a result of burning also creates a demand for nitrogen that is far greater than the input from rainfall can supply. Managed moorland soils often therefore show signs of nitrogen deficiency. The application of nitrogenous fertilisers results in an immediate increase in the growth of heather.

The concept of a nutrient budget can be applied to any ecosystem. It is possible to identify the inputs and outputs of nutrients in the ecosystem and perhaps diagnose deficiencies, as in the case of moorlands and derelict land, or surpluses, as in the case of some lakes. Working out the nutrient budget of derelict land can indicate how the land should be managed to encourage species to return to it. As the diversity of species increases, the nutrient budget will stabilise and human intervention will be needed less.

Table 4. Flow of nutrients in an ecosystem	
Input	**Output**
Precipitation	Run-off and stream outflow
Particles in the atmosphere	Particles removed by wind
Biotic sources	Biotic losses
Fixation from the atmosphere	Release to the atmosphere
Weathering of soil and rocks	Loss by leaching
Fertiliser application	Human harvest

Source: Begon, Harper and Townsend, *Ecology,* Blackwell, 1986

 10 Apply the pattern shown in Table 4 to a community that is the result of human activity, for example a colliery tip or a motorway verge. Use a diagram to summarise your ideas.

2.7 Nutrient cycling in aquatic systems

Organisms in aquatic ecosystems also need nutrients. Abiotic factors, such as rainfall and breaking down of rocks on the sea or river bed, add nutrients to the water. Biotic sources of nutrients depend on decomposition, as on land. But in aquatic ecosystems the nutrients have to be circulated from the source to where primary production takes place.

Phytoplankton, tiny aquatic plants, only occur where there is enough light for photosynthesis. So primary production in bodies of water is in the upper sunlit layers.

The same processes of decomposition take place in freshwater and seawater. Dead organisms and other organic matter sink in water and decomposition takes place on the sea bed or at the bottom of a lake. The area where decomposition takes place is therefore separated from the area of production. Water currents carry the nitrates and phosphates released by decomposers back to the surface. Anything that circulates the water column will also redistribute nutrients.

In lakes and oceans this circulation of water does not happen throughout the year. There are times of nutrient shortage

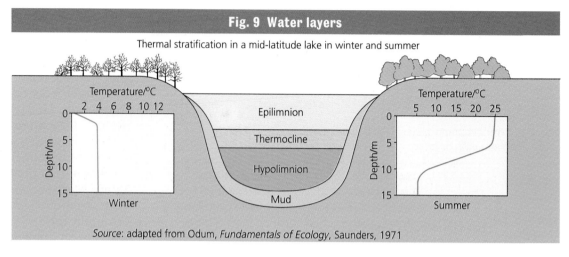

Fig. 9 Water layers

Thermal stratification in a mid-latitude lake in winter and summer

Epilimnion

Thermocline

Hypolimnion

Mud

Temperature/°C (Winter: 2 4 6 8 10 12)

Temperature/°C (Summer: 5 10 15 20 25)

Depth/m

Winter

Summer

Source: adapted from Odum, *Fundamentals of Ecology*, Saunders, 1971

Diatoms are unicellular photosynthetic organisms that play an important part in the primary production of aquatic ecosystems.

and therefore periods when there is a reduction in the primary production of the phytoplankton. The main reason for this interruption in nutrient supply is the formation of a **thermocline**. In temperate waters in summer, the surface waters warm up and so become less dense. They form a separate layer, floating on top of the colder, denser water beneath. The less dense, warmer upper layer is known as the **epilimnion**, the colder, denser water below is the **hypolimnion**. Where the two bodies of water meet a thin layer is formed. It is characterised by a rapid fall in temperature; this is the thermocline (Fig. 9).

The thermocline forms a barrier between the epilimnion and hypolimnion. The two bodies of water do not mix, so nutrients cannot return to the surface layers. Phytoplankton production decreases

sharply, even though there is plenty of light and warmth. Any nutrients in dead organic matter sink through the thermocline and cannot be carried back to the surface by vertical mixing of the water column, until the thermocline breaks down.

In autumn the epilimnion cools, its waters become more dense, and they sink. So the thermocline breaks down and vertical mixing of the water column is re-established. Nutrient-rich water is brought to the surface from the depths, and primary production increases for a short time until light and temperature limit photosynthesis.

11 a Using Fig. 10, what limits phytoplankton production in the winter and in the summer?
b What prevents the rapid increase in phytoplankton production in the spring continuing?
c What causes the second increase in the phytoplankton in the autumn?
d Why is this increase less than the spring increase?

Lakes that contain few nutrients are called **oligotrophic**. Over long periods of time, as inorganic nutrients such as nitrate and phosphorus are released, lakes become more rich in nutrients. This is called **eutrophication**. Eutrophication is a natural process and is caused by:
- erosion of the bedrock by rivers and streams;
- dead leaves falling into the water;
- run-off from the surrounding land.

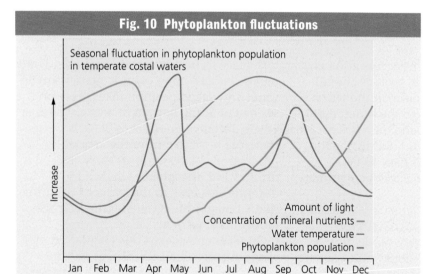

Fig. 10 Phytoplankton fluctuations

Seasonal fluctuation in phytoplankton population in temperate costal waters

Increase

Amount of light
Concentration of mineral nutrients —
Water temperature —
Phytoplankton population —

Jan Feb Mar Apr May Jun Jul Aug Sep Oct Nov Dec

Toxic algae plague off Britain's coast

Plagues of toxic algae are erupting around Britain's coast as a result of pollution from farms and sewage works. The main culprit is nitrogen, mainly in the form of nitrate from farm waste, sewage works and the run-off from arable land. Britain puts 73 000 tonnes of it into the North Sea alone every year.

The whole of Britain's eastern and southern coasts from Dundee to Cornwall are at risk from nitrate pollution. Blooms of various kinds of toxic algae have been observed near Berwick upon Tweed,

Sunderland, the Humber and Thames estuaries, and off the coasts of Cornwall, Dorset and Devon. Infestations of unpleasant but non-toxic algae, which form foam and scum, have been found off the Mersey, Dee and Thames estuaries and the Dorset and Devon coasts.

Mr Andrew Lees, Friends of the Earth's water and toxics campaigner, said: 'The government has repeatedly discounted evidence of widespread ecological problems due to nitrate pollution in UK waters.'

Source: Observer

However, human activities can result in artificial, rapid eutrophication. The use of chemical fertilisers in agriculture has increased substantially over the past 40 years. Urban sources of nutrients include domestic sewage and industrial wastes. Once they enter bodies of water, if other conditions, such as light and temperature, are not limiting, they increase plant growth.

As eutrophication takes place, and nutrient levels increase, aquatic plant populations, including phytoplankton and algae, can grow. When these organisms die, they sink to the bottom of the lake where decomposition takes place. The increase in dead organic matter means the populations of bacteria and fungi can grow. As they increase in number, they use up the oxygen in the water as they respire.

Low levels of oxygen in the water means fish such as trout and invertebrates such as mayfly, stonefly and caddis larvae cannot survive. Only organisms that can tolerate low oxygen levels, such as midge larvae and the annelid worm *Tubifex* will remain.

Q 12a **Explain the effect on algal cell numbers of the phosphate concentration upstream and downstream as indicated in Fig. 11.**
b **What could be the ecological consequences downstream?**

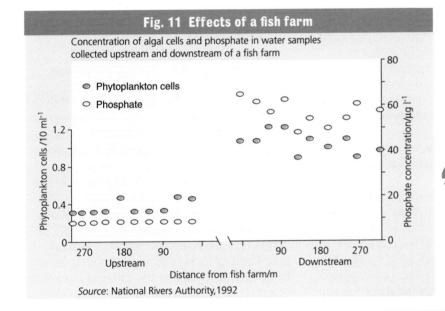

Fig. 11 Effects of a fish farm

Concentration of algal cells and phosphate in water samples collected upstream and downstream of a fish farm

○ (shaded) Phytoplankton cells
○ Phosphate

Source: National Rivers Authority, 1992

Windsurfing on Rutland water is only enjoyable and safe when the water is clean and healthy.

Blue-green algae in high concentrations in shallow water at Rutland Water, in the UK. These algae can be toxic when present in large quantities.

This mud pump sucks out dead algae that have sunk to the bottom of the broads. This stops the broads from becoming shallow, and helps prevent oxygen depletion. Conservationists also sow plant species that provide a home for invertebrates that eat algae.

fish and aquatic invertebrates. Rooted plants that have leaves above the water, like reeds, may increase in growth, resulting in a narrowing of river channels, making navigation difficult.

Excessive eutrophication has occurred in the Norfolk Broads, probably due to run-off of agricultural fertilisers. Attempts have been made to reverse the effects of eutrophication, by controlling the input of nutrients and cleaning up the affected areas.

 14a Make a flow diagram to show the sequence of events that take place during eutrophication in a lake.
 b What problems could eutrophication of fresh water cause humans?

In summer, growth of phytoplankton and cyanobacteria can produce temporary **algal blooms**. These give the water a characteristic 'pea soup' colour and an unpleasant taste and small. Some of these algae release toxins into the water that can poison marine and land animals.

13 Suggest why algal blooms are an indication of eutrophication.

Dense phytoplankton growth also results in an increased **turbidity**, or cloudiness, of the water. Consequently less light can penetrate to the rooted plants living at the bottom, leading to reduced photosynthesis. If these plants die, there will be a reduction in habitat and food for

Eutrophication is an example of how nutrients in an ecosystem have to be balanced. Adding fertilisers thoughtlessly to an ecosystem can do more harm than good. When reclaiming derelict land, for example by building an artificial lake, it is important not to over-fertilise. If nutrients are no longer limiting the growth of plants, other factors will affect the size of plant populations, which will affect the size of other species' populations and species diversity. Analysing the nutrient budget and limiting factors of a habitat that need to be managed means the greatest diversity of species can be encouraged.

Key ideas

- The abundance of a species is affected by abiotic and biotic limiting factors.

- Aquatic and terrestrial ecosystems depend on abiotic factors to provide a source of mineral ions.

- Soil must contain nutrients that can be absorbed by plant communities.

- Primary production in aquatic ecosystems relies upon the circulation of nutrients from the depths.

- Nutrient budgets can identify the input and output of nutrients in an ecosystem.

Something to grouse about?

" To shoot or not to shoot "

Landowners are up in arms at Forestry Commission recommendations to plant conifers over 1.8 million hectares of upland over the next 50 years. They claim that increasing areas covered with forest, together with over-grazing by sheep, reduces the numbers of grouse available for shooting. This makes the grouse shooting uneconomic. Conservationists and some animal welfare groups, normally opposed to grouse shooting, support the landowners' claims.

The red grouse is important to naturalists, sportsmen and environmental scientists. Their different interests in the same bird can cause conflict over managing the bird's habitat. However, grouse shooting may be something that all three groups want to see continued.

If farmers cannot make money from moorland by grouse shooting, they may not be able to play a part in conserving the landscape. If the value of their land falls farmers may have to let it be used for commercial forestry instead. Opponents of field sports want to ban grouse shooting, but this might have a disastrous effect on moorland conservation. More farmers may have to plant conifers to make a living. So is it better to allow shooting to preserve the moorland habitat?

3.1 Learning objectives

After working through this chapter, you should be able to:

- **define** population dynamics and population density;

- **explain** the relationship between birth and death rates and immigration and emigration;

- **explain** biotic potential, carrying capacity and environmental resistance;

- **explain** how limiting factors affect the size of a population;

- **interpret** survivorship curves;

- **identify** and describe stages of population growth and distinguish between S- and J-curves;

- **explain** what is meant by fluctuation and regulation in population numbers;

- **describe** examples of population cycles, predator/prey interactions and competition;

- **explain** the differences between density-dependent and density-independent factors affecting populations.

3.2 Economics of the red grouse

There are roughly 1 million hectares (ha) of grouse moor in Britain, which play an important role in the economics of rural communities and estates. In northern England and Scotland an average of 400 000 grouse are shot each year, generating a gross income in the order of £10 million. Landowners have to pay rates based on previous numbers of grouse shot on their land. This means that if the numbers of grouse being bred fall, the activity becomes uneconomic. This leads to the loss of shooting rights and increases pressure for **afforestation**. Afforestation means the land is planted and then managed as forest. There are tax incentives for landowners to use their land for afforestation. Often the tree species planted are conifers. The replacement of moorland

Managed heather moorland is a characteristic feature of parts of the British Isles, and supports distinctive plants and animals, including the red grouse. Heather moorland is a habitat of international as well as national importance.

Fig. 1 Conifers and grouse

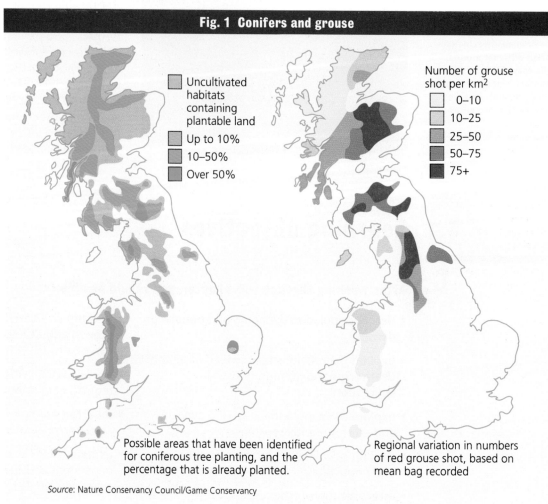

Uncultivated habitats containing plantable land

Up to 10%

10–50%

Over 50%

Number of grouse shot per km²

0–10

10–25

25–50

50–75

75+

Possible areas that have been identified for coniferous tree planting, and the percentage that is already planted.

Regional variation in numbers of red grouse shot, based on mean bag recorded

Source: Nature Conservancy Council/Game Conservancy

with Sitka spruce and lodgepole pine will affect the area's environment and landscape value, and affect human communities.

 1 **From the maps in Fig. 1 what can be concluded about the distribution of coniferous forestry and the incidence of grouse shooting?**

Ecologically, afforestation can increase the density of perching birds such as tits and chaffinches, which are already common. It also decreases the density of many specialised birds, including waders such as golden plovers, birds of prey such as peregrine falcons, and ground-dwelling birds such as the red grouse.

 2 **Why do you think an increase in coniferous planting would lead to an increase in the numbers of perching birds?**

Red grouse populations have been studied over the last 30 years by two research organisations, the Institute of Terrestrial Ecology, a government agency, and the Game Conservancy, a group initiated and funded by a group of interested landowners.

Population ecology is the study of populations in their environment. The Institute of Terrestrial Ecology has studied grouse population ecology through field observations and experiments on the numbers, behaviour and nutrition of wild grouse. It has also studied the moorland habitat, moorland management, predation, the effects of ticks and parasitic worms, grouse genetics, and the impact of human activity on grouse.

The research by the Game Conservancy has looked at the factors influencing breeding production and the development of new management techniques to improve production.

 3 a **Account for the different work by each research team.**
   b **Comment on how some people might view the results of each research team.**

Central to the long-term future of the grouse and the management of its habitat is an intimate knowledge and understanding of its **population dynamics**. Population dynamics is the study of the factors influencing changes in a population.

3.3 Population dynamics

Many animals gain protection, for example from predators and weather conditions, by living together in vast numbers, such as herds of antelope and shoals of fish.

An individual organism living in isolation may be able to gain important requirements such as food, shelter and light from a particular habitat. However, there are benefits from living in a population, for

example more successful breeding and rearing of young.

 4 **What is a population?**

There are also disadvantages to living in a population. Overcrowding can lead to competition for food, space, light or some other resource. Some individuals will not survive this competition.

Fig. 2 Population dynamics

Populations gain individuals when young are born (B)

Populations gain individuals when new members join the group from other populations. This is known as **immigration** (I)

Gains

B — Births

I — Immigrants

Population — Spatial boundary of population

D — Deaths

E — Emigrants

Losses

Populations lose individuals when members die (D)

Populations lose individuals when members leave an area to join another population. This is known as **emigration** (E)

In a stable population there is no increase or decrease in number over a period of time

Population numbers / Time

B + I > D + E — Birth rate + immigration greater than death rate + emigration *Increasing population*

B + I = D + E — Birth rate + immigration = death rate + emigration

B + I < D + E — Birth rate + immigration less than death rate + emigration *Decreasing population*

Populations are always changing, in other words they are dynamic (Fig. 2). These changes may be seasonal, for example due to breeding, or may result from other pressures, such as predation.

Immigration and emigration are most common in mammals, fish, insects and birds that are mobile. A **territory** is the area that an individual occupies and defends from others. Male grouse that cannot establish territories in autumn emigrate to other moors or die.

The rate at which young are born over a period of time is the **birth rate** of a population:

$$\text{Birth rate} = \frac{\text{number of births}}{\text{number of adults in the population}}$$

The rate at which death occurs is the **death rate** of a population:

$$\text{Death rate} = \frac{\text{number of deaths}}{\text{number of adults in the population}}$$

Both rates depend on features of the organisms concerned, such as how long they live, and abiotic and biotic environmental factors.

 5 **Suggest some biotic and abiotic factors that could affect the numbers of individuals in a population.**

3.4 Population density

The number of individuals per unit area in a population is the **population density**. The density of a population can vary over time (Fig. 3).

The population density is controlled by three factors:
- the biotic potential of the population;
- environmental resistance;
- the carrying capacity of the environment.

The **biotic potential** of a population is the maximum rate at which it can reproduce, if it has unlimited essential resources. Populations seldom if ever achieve their biotic potential because of **environmental resistance**. Essential resources within the habitat, such as food,

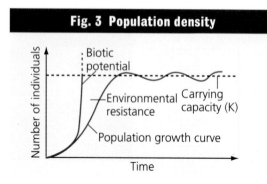

Fig. 3 Population density

Number of individuals / Time

Biotic potential

Environmental resistance

Carrying capacity (K)

Population growth curve

water and space, may become scarce. They then become limiting factors and the population cannot increase. Environmental resistance is the total of all the abiotic and biotic environmental factors that prevent a population from growing indefinitely.

6a What is a limiting factor?
b Suggest why humans and elephants have lower biotic potentials than bacteria and mice.

Availability of nutrients may be a limiting factor in the growth of grouse populations. Young heather shoots provide essential nutrients for growth in grouse. The amount of young green shoots declines with the age of the heather stand (Fig. 4). As a result the moor supports fewer grouse.

Fig. 4 Protein content of heather

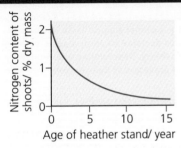
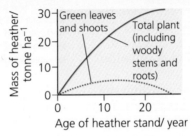

Source: Gimmingham, *An Introduction to Heathland Ecology*, 1975

Lack of shelter can act as a limiting factor. Lack of shelter can mean animals are more likely to die from predation or extremes of climate. Although grouse prefer young shoots for food, these plants tend not to be very tall and so provide poor cover from predators. During severe winters, as much as 70–80% of grouse will not survive to breed the following year. Therefore a balance of old and new heather plants is needed to provide both shelter and food. That is why heather moorland is managed by being burnt.

Predators are consumers that eat other animals, their **prey**. They usually kill and then eat their prey straight away. The most damaging predators of grouse are those that take entire egg clutches, such as foxes and crows. Foxes may even kill the sitting hen.

Parasites, on the other hand, are organisms that feed off another species, the **host**. A successful parasite will not kill the host straight away, but will use it as a source of live food for a long time. A viral disease of sheep and red grouse, called 'louping ill', can increase the death rate of grouse populations. The virus is carried by the insect parasite *Ixodes ricinus*, which is a sheep tick. In addition to the sheep tick, grouse can suffer a heavy infestation of the parasitic gut worm *Trichostrongylus tenuis*, which can reduce the breeding success of the bird and eventually lead to death. The more dense a population, the more quickly infections can spread.

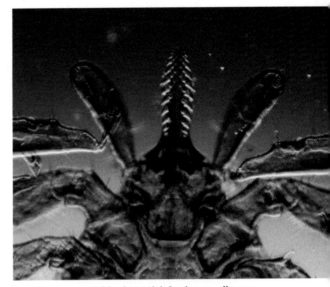

Parasites, such as this sheep tick *Ixodes* sp., disease and predators can all contribute to environmental resistance.

The **carrying capacity** of the environment is a measure of the maximum number of a species that can be supported in a habitat. Carrying capacity is often abbreviated to K. K is determined by the availability of essential resources within the habitat, such as nutrients, water and space. The population density of a species may vary due to changes in abiotic and biotic limiting factors. However, an ecosystem can only support a certain population density of a particular species at a particular time.

If the carrying capacity of the environment is improved by an increase in food or a decrease in predation, then the population density of a species can increase. Species with a high biotic potential can take advantage of a new opportunity sooner than those with a lower biotic potential. As the population density increases, other factors become limiting, and the population size may decline or **crash**. After a population has crashed, the

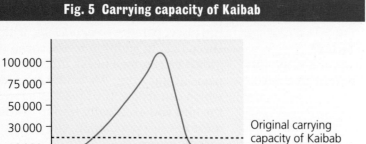

Fig. 5 Carrying capacity of Kaibab

Original carrying capacity of Kaibab
New carrying capacity of Kaibab

The carrying capacity of some environments is lower than others because there are fewer resources. The Kaibab plateau is a wild area near the American Grand Canyon. Because it is dry it cannot support large numbers of herbivores. It was declared a nature reserve at the turn of the nineteenth century. Deer hunting was forbidden, and coyotes, natural predators of Kaibab deer, were killed.

carrying capacity may be lower than it was before. This was the case with the Kaibab mule deer of Arizona in 1906 (Fig. 5). Because their predators were removed, their numbers rose well above the carrying capacity of the environment. This led to overgrazing and a subsequent population crash.

The accuracy of the data regarding the size of the Kaibab deer population has been questioned. In order to draw meaningful conclusions from population data, the size of the population must be estimated as accurately as possible. If the carrying capacity of the environment, or the effect of predators on their prey, is misinterpreted, then the management of the habitat could be ineffective or destructive.

3.5 Patterns of survival

A **survivorship curve** can be used in the study of population dynamics. A group of individuals, such as a thousand, is identified at birth. At regular intervals, the number of survivors from this thousand is plotted, and the curve drawn. The curve shows the different death rates of individuals of different ages. It therefore shows at what age an individual is most likely to die. This can be used to direct studies of the causes of change in the size of the population.

Q7 a Plot a survivorship curve using the data in Table 1. Assume that the number at age 1 represents 100% and convert the other numbers to a percentage. Plot the figures on logarithmic graph paper.
b At what age would it be most important to find the cause of death if larger populations of kestrel were to be encouraged?

Some populations produce a vast number of young, the majority of which die. An example is the cod. They will show quite a different survival curve from populations where there are few young and a long life expectancy, such as humans in a developed country.

Table 1. Ringed kestrel chicks										
Age	1	2	3	4	5	6	7	8	9	10
Number of kestrels alive	245	119	70	36	22	14	10	5	4	2

Source: Open University

Fig. 6 Survivorship curves

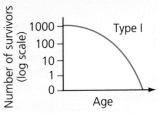

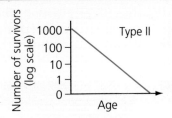

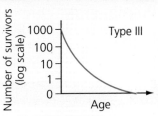

The death rate is concentrated in older age groups; the probability of death increases with age; the population probably has few natural predators

The death rate decreases gradually with time; the probability of death is constant with age

The death rate is concentrated in younger age groups; the probability of death decreases with age

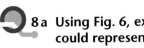 **8 a** **Using Fig. 6, explain which curve could represent a cod population, and which a human population.**

b **Suggest an example for the third curve.**

3.6 Patterns of growth

Some populations also show predictable patterns of growth and decline. Growth patterns can be represented as **growth curves**.

Algae can undergo rapid increases in numbers when environmental factors like light, temperature and nutrients are in unlimited supply. Growth starts off slowly and then increases rapidly. This is called **exponential growth**. An algal bloom is the result of exponential growth when environmental conditions are favourable. However, as the nutrients are used up and

become a limiting factor, the population size can fall as quickly as it rose. This type of 'boom and bust' situation produces a **J-shaped** growth curve (Fig. 7). Pest species that have many generations in one year often have J-shaped curves.

However, if a population encounters environmental resistance, such as little shelter, as it starts its growth, the curve slopes more gently to form an **S-shaped** curve (Fig. 7). These curves are typical of species that are in new habitats. The population growth increases slowly as the

Fig. 7 Growth curves

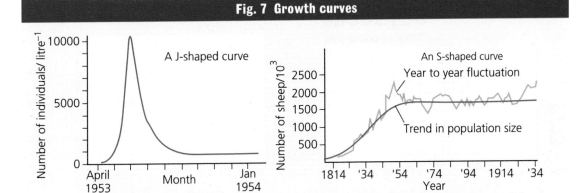

Changes in the population size of a brown alga

Changes in the population size of sheep following their introduction into Tasmania

Source: Adapted from Rowland, *University of Bath Science 16–19: Biology*, Nelson, 1992

species adapts to the habitat, and then can level off and become stable. If a factor then becomes limiting, the population will decline. S-shaped growth curves can therefore be divided into distinctive phases (Fig. 8).

Fig. 8 S-shaped growth curves

In the **lag phase** growth is slower than that which is theoretically possible. The organisms may be growing to maturity, or becoming accustomed to new conditions

In the **logarithmic** or **exponential phase** the population increases by repeated doubling in the sequence 1, 2, 4, 8, 16, 32, etc. This is exponential growth and there are consistently more births than deaths. **Arithmetic growth** is when the rate remains constant, i.e. 2, 4, 6, 8, 10, etc.

Lag phase | Logarithmic or exponential phase | Stable or equilibrium phase | Decline phase

Number of organisms

Extinction

Time

In the **stable** or **equilibrium phase** the growth rate slows down, e.g. due to a shortage of food or a build up of waste. The birth rate is balanced by the death rate and the population size remains constant.

In the **decline phase** the growth rate starts to fall as the death rate begins to exceed the birth rate. This could be due to increased competition for resources or accumulating toxins. Eventually a point is reached when the last individual has died, this is called the **extinction** point.

9 a A bacterium cell can divide every 20 minutes. Starting with one bacterium, plot a graph of cell number against time for the first 2 hours, assuming no deaths occur.
  b Describe the shape of the graph you have drawn.
  c For each graph in Fig. 9, suggest the limiting factor and explain its effect on the population's growth.

Fig. 9 Population growth

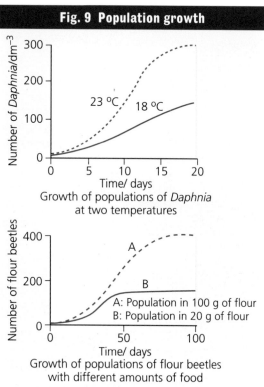

Growth of populations of *Daphnia* at two temperatures

A: Population in 100 g of flour
B: Population in 20 g of flour

Growth of populations of flour beetles with different amounts of food

Source: Sands, Problems in Ecology, Bell and Hyman, 1978

Key ideas

- Population dynamics is the study of changes in the numbers of organisms in a population and the factors influencing those changes.

- The size of a population is increased by birth and immigration and decreased by death and emigration. Population sizes can vary over time.

- An ecosystem can only support a certain population size of any particular species.

- The biotic potential of a species is the maximum limit the population size could be.

- The environmental resistance is all the limiting factors, abiotic and biotic, that prevent a species reaching its maximum population size.

- The carrying capacity is the limit on the population size the environment can support.

- Different populations have different patterns of survival.

- Different populations have different patterns of growth and decline. These can be shown as J-shaped or S-shaped curves.

3.7 Population cycling

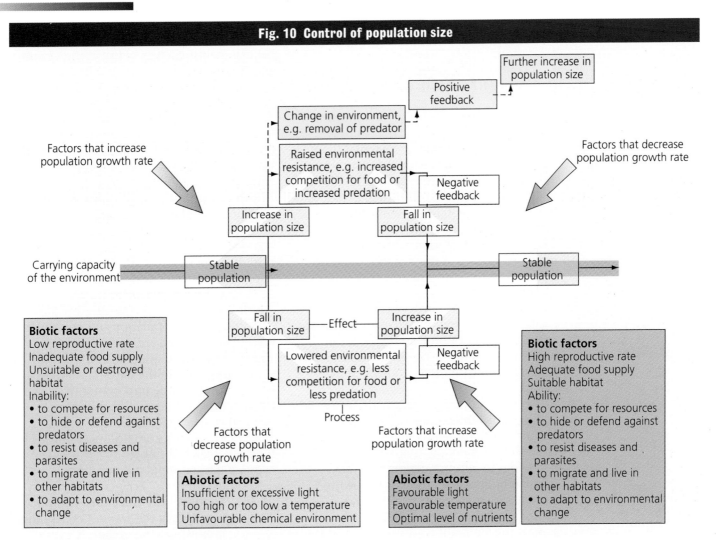

Fig. 10 Control of population size

Once a population has become established in a habitat, its density may show fluctuations above and below the carrying capacity (Fig. 10).

Some species show regular cyclical, seasonal or even daily fluctuations. Mammals such as foxes, mice and voles often have well-defined, predictable changes in population density. They may have physiological mechanisms that suppress the birth rate when the population density exceeds a certain level.

Records of the number of grouse shot show that their populations exhibit a cyclical pattern, peaking every four to five years (Fig. 11).

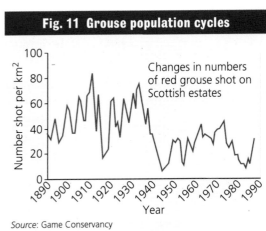

Fig. 11 Grouse population cycles

Changes in numbers of red grouse shot on Scottish estates

Source: Game Conservancy

The cycling of the grouse population density could be caused by interactions between grouse and their:

- food supply;
- predators;
- parasites.

It could also be caused by behavioural changes associated with changes in territory size.

Food supply is probably not a limiting factor because grouse typically eat only 2–3% of available heather. The quality of the heather does not seem to be the reason either. Experiments have been carried out in which the heather was fertilised, therefore increasing the protein content of the grouse's food supply. The numbers of grouse did increase in line with the increased quality of the heather, but their numbers still declined after a peak was reached.

Ecologists do not believe the cause is predators. Common predators such as foxes, crows and birds of prey do not occur in sufficient numbers to cause the decline. The predator populations are controlled by gamekeepers.

Research from the Institute of Terrestrial Ecology links the cycling of the grouse population to its behaviour. It has been shown experimentally that territorial behaviour in autumn determines the number of breeding birds the following spring. The more aggressive the male grouse, the bigger their territories, the greater the emigration rate and the lower the number of breeding pairs (Fig. 12). This model simplifies what really happens. Other considerations include changes in the sex ratio and the immigration and emigration rates.

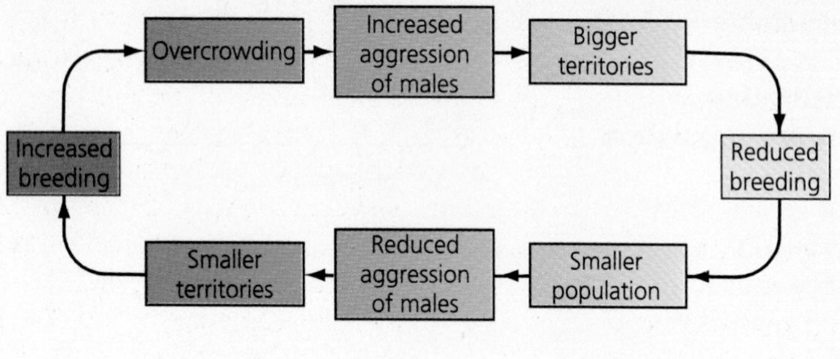

The territoriality of grouse is an example of **intraspecific interactions**. Intraspecific interactions take place between individuals in the same species.

Ecologists from the Game Conservancy believe the interaction between the grouse and its parasites affects grouse population cycling. *Trichostrongylus tenuis* reduces growth of grouse populations by decreasing breeding rates. The rate and intensity of infection by the parasite both increase as the population density of their host increases. Evidence for this view comes from studies that show:

- both grouse and *T. tenuis* have similar cyclical population densities;
- higher levels of parasite infection match greater losses from the grouse population;
- application of anti-parasite drugs increases grouse breeding and survival because the link between the two species is broken.

Some grouse populations do not have many parasites and are not cyclical. The cyclic grouse populations live in wetter areas, where the parasite survives better. However, the importance of temperature and rainfall on parasite survival is unclear.

As both models contain uncertainties further research is needed to confirm the cause of grouse population cycling.

Q 10 **Suggest how researchers could investigate the Game Conservancy model that the cycling is caused by parasites.**

Interspecific interactions take place between individuals of different species. The interactions between parasites and their hosts and predators and their prey are examples of interspecific interactions. Predators act as a limiting factor on the population growth of the prey species. But the numbers of prey will, in turn, affect the predator population. If the numbers of prey increase, then the increased food supply may mean that the predators will thrive and their numbers increase. But if the numbers of prey fall, predator numbers will inevitably fall because of the less abundant food supply. Although there is usually some kind of balance between

Fig. 12 Intraspecific interactions

Overcrowding → Increased aggression of males → Bigger territories → Reduced breeding → Smaller population → Smaller aggression of males → Smaller territories → Increased breeding → Overcrowding

the two populations, this balance is rarely stable and may show periodic fluctuations. The Canadian lynx and snowshoe hare populations are an example of this.

11a Represent the interaction between predator and prey population growth as a flow diagram.
b What factors do the two graphs in Fig. 13 have in common?
c Suggest why there is a delay between the peaks of the interacting populations.

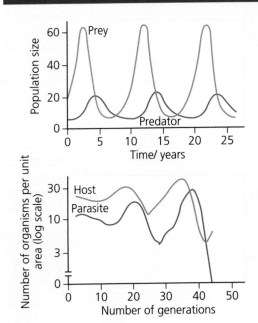

Fig. 13 Interspecific interactions

3.8 Competition

When environmental resources such as food, light and space are in short supply individuals have to compete with one another for the limited resources. Competition reduces the growth rate and lowers the reproductive capacity of a population.

Intraspecific competition is competition between individuals of the same population. Individuals of the same species require the same resources so will compete for any that are in short supply. If more offspring are produced than the habitat can support, intraspecific competition will become much more intense.

12a What is the relationship between the number of seeds sown per pot and the number of seeds per plant (Fig. 14)?
b What are the advantages and disadvantages of sowing at a high density?

Interspecific competition occurs between individuals of different populations. Interspecific competition can be more intense between populations that

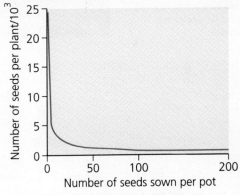

Fig. 14 Intraspecific competition

Source: Palmbald, *Ecology*, Vol. 49, pp.26–34, 1968

exist at the same trophic level in a community than between populations at different trophic levels in a community. Weeds such as wild oats compete with crop plants such as wheat for light, water, nutrients and space. Successful weeds often germinate, grow, flower and set seed before the crop has attained its full height. Different species of animals can compete for the same food resources. Predatory animals such as owls and weasels compete for shrews. Nesting sea birds like gannets compete for territory, shelter and nesting sites.

Q 13 a Describe and interpret what is happening to each species in Fig. 15 when they are cultured together.
b What resource are both species of *Paramecium* probably competing for?
c What explanation other than competition could account for the success of one species at the expense of the other?

At this kittiwake and guillemot colony in the gulf of Alaska, the two species of sea bird are competing for the limited space available.

Fig. 15 Interspecific competition

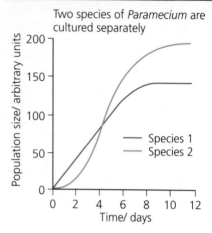

Two species of *Paramecium* are cultured separately

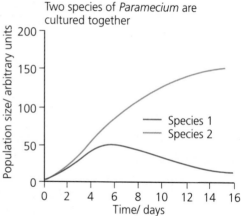

Two species of *Paramecium* are cultured together

Source: Gause, *The Struggle for Existence*, Dover Publications, 1971

The **competitive exclusion principle** states that no two species in an ecosystem can occupy the same part of the habitat at the same time. Similar species may adapt in slightly different ways to the same habitat in order to reduce interspecific competition.

There are two common species of barnacle native to England, *Semibalanus balanoides* and *Chthamalus montagui*. *Chthamalus* tends to be found higher up the shore than *Semibalanus* because it is more tolerant to water loss. Lower down the shore *Semibalanus* tends to out-compete *Chthamalus* for space because it has a faster growth rate. If areas of rock are cleared of *Semibalanus*, *Chthamalus* is able to settle and flourish because there is no competition.

The Cruel Sea. The Australian barnacle *Elminius modestus* arrived in England on the hulls of ships during the Second World War.

An Australian barnacle also lives on English shores. In many situations, *Elminius modestus* is able to out-compete both *Semibalanus* and *Chthamalus* for the following reasons:

- *Elminius* can withstand lower temperatures than *Chthamalus*;
- *Elminius* can withstand higher temperatures than *Semibalanus*;
- *Elminius* is more tolerant to low salinity, so does well in estuaries;
- *Elminius* has a faster feeding rate and rate of growth than either of the two native species.

 14 a **What does this suggest about the biotic potential of each of the three barnacle species?**
  b **What factors may limit the growth of *Elminius* populations?**

The decline in the numbers of red squirrels in Britain is thought to be another example of competitive exclusion. The native red squirrel used to be found throughout this country until the introduction of the larger grey squirrel from North America. The two squirrels appear to be so similar that only one species can survive in any one habitat at one time.

 15 **Suggest what factors the two species of squirrel are competing for.**

This red squirrel was photographed in Thornley Woods, Tyne and Wear, although the species is largely confined to upland coniferous forests in Scotland, the Lake District and isolated parts of Wales. The more successful grey squirrel is a broad-leaved generalist and is now found over a much larger range than the red squirrel.

3.9 Density-dependent and density-independent factors

Populations of species can be affected by many factors, leading to changes in population sizes. Some of these factors depend on the density of a population. The factor will only have an effect on certain population densities. These are called **density-dependent** factors. The environmental factors causing density-dependent population changes are always biotic, for example competition for food and space.

In red grouse, when adult populations are high, competition between males for territories is high. The size of the territories that each male can get will be smaller. This will result in less food for each female, which then produces fewer eggs. There is less food for the chicks, and so many will die.

 16 **How will this help regulate population density?**

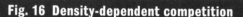

Fig. 16 Density-dependent competition

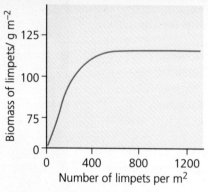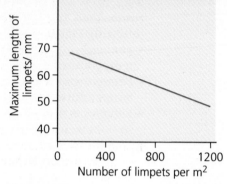

Number of limpets per m^2 Number of limpets per m^2

Source: Branch, *Journal of Animal Ecology*, Vol. 44, pp.263–281, 1975

In limpet populations, high-density populations of limpets have many small and few large individuals. In low-density populations, limpets have many large individuals and few small individuals (Fig. 16).

> **17 a** Suggest which resources the limpets are competing for.
> **b** Explain how the density affects the outcome of the competition.

The size of the nuthatch population in a particular area is affected by density-dependent and density-independent factors.

Density-independent factors do not depend on population density. They affect populations whatever the density of the population. For example, a severe winter will affect every grouse, whatever the population density was in the autumn. Density-independent factors may be abiotic, like low temperatures, or biotic, for example variation in the availability of food.

Density-dependent and density-independent factors can affect a population at the same time. When the density of nuthatches in an area is high, the immigration rate is low. The immigration rate is density-dependent. When the beechnut crop is bad, the immigration rate is even lower. The beechnut crop is a density-independent factor that also affects the immigration rate. The immigration rate of the nuthatch population is therefore regulated by a density-dependent factor, but this is influenced by a density-independent factor.

> **18 a** What would happen to the immigration rate of nuthatches if there was a glut of food, i.e. the beechnut crop the year before had been very good?
> **b** If the immigration rate increased although the number of nuthatches in the area was high, what factors may become limiting?
> **c** Would these limiting factors have a density-dependent or density-independent effect?

The dynamics of a population depend on interactions between individuals of the same and other species. These interactions can be interspecific, intraspecific, density-dependent or density-independent. All these abiotic and biotic processes and factors form the environmental resistance that usually prevents a population from exceeding the carrying capacity of the environment.

If an ecosystem is changed, perhaps by human activity, the carrying capacity of the environment for different species may be affected. Species with different biotic potentials will adapt differently to change, and the population dynamics of the species could change considerably.

Forest plantations tend to fragment the populations of moorland birds, reducing their density. Plantations also provide refuge for predators, and prevent management practices such as heather burning because of the risk of fire spreading to the trees. All these factors will affect grouse populations. A fall in grouse populations will also affect other species.

Conservationists, planners and others increasingly argue that forest plantations should be sited away from areas of moorland of nature conservation interest.

Conservationists are interested in protecting habitats to maintain the diversity of species. Understanding the way populations change in one habitat may help scientists to manage other habitats.

Grouse moors, if managed correctly, could provide a healthy industry based on sheep farming, shooting and tourism, and maintain the diversity of species. Farming, shooting, tourism and afforestation all have an effect on the moorland habitat. If shooting is profitable for farmers, the moorland will be managed in a way that also benefits tourism and conservation. Smaller populations of grouse will be just one result of the changed habitat due to afforestation.

 19 **Think back to your view about grouse shooting at the start of the chapter. Has it changed since then? Explain why.**

Key ideas

- Interspecific and intraspecific interactions and competition affect population size.

- Established populations fluctuate in size above and below the carrying capacity.

- Intraspecific reactions between members of the same species can cause changes in population sizes.

- The interactions between predators and prey and parasites and their hosts are examples of interspecific reactions that affect population sizes.

- Competition for food and space between the same and different species affects population sizes.

- The factors that affect population sizes can depend on the density of the population involved, or can act independently of the population density.

- Density-independent and density-dependent abiotic and biotic factors interact to affect population size.

4 Life at the edge

Until recently Greenpeace had a permanent base at Cape Evans in Antarctica, monitoring the activities of other nation's research bases.

A rubbish dump burning at McMurdo Station, Ross Island, Antarctica.

Paradise Bay, on the Antarctic Peninsula.

Antarctica is by far the largest area of wilderness on Earth. Yet despite its remoteness, the continent has not escaped the effects of human activity. In 1966 residues of the pesticide DDT were found in the tissues of marine food web predators such as Adelie penguins. Migratory birds will have introduced the residues into the Antarctic food web, thousands of kilometres from the nearest point of use of DDT. The uniqueness of the continent and the potential for long-lasting damage led to many calls for Antarctica to be designated a World Park, free from economic and mineral exploitation. After much lobbying by protesters and a sudden change of heart by Australia and France, Antarctica did become a World Park. In autumn 1991 a comprehensive new Antarctic Treaty was agreed that prohibits mining and exploration by any nation until 2041.

Do you agree that Antarctica should not be exploited for economic and mineral reasons? What are the benefits to humans to keep it unharmed? What can we learn from studying the organisms that have adapted to live in such a harsh environment?

4.1 Learning objectives

After working through this chapter, you should be able to:

- **explain** what factors determine where an organism lives;

- **define** the term niche and distinguish between fundamental and realised niches;

- **describe** the nature of temperature tolerance and how it is affected by certain factors;

- **distinguish** between the different terms used to classify the regulation of body temperature;

- **explain** the importance of water availability in determining the distribution and survival of organisms;

- **illustrate**, with reference to examples, ways in which organisms are adapted for survival in a given niche;

- **explain** the relationship between species diversity and the stability of an ecosystem.

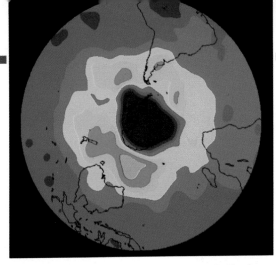

A map of the total atmospheric ozone concentration in the southern hemisphere on 8 October 1995. The ozone hole is at the centre.

4.2 Colonisation

The discovery of a seasonal drastic thinning of the ozone layer, 'the ozone hole', is perhaps the most well-known example of Antarctic research. Deep ice cores provide invaluable records of the Earth's past environmental record. These studies provide information about changes in atmospheric concentrations of carbon dioxide, methane and nitrous oxide, as well as temperature.

The plant and animal communities that survive in the Antarctic have adapted to a very harsh environment. Studying the species and their adaptations provides information that can be used to understand how communities **evolve** to survive severe abiotic conditions. Evolution is the process by which living organisms change over time to adapt to changing conditions.

 1 **Explain the difference between the terms colonisation and dispersal.**

Once a species arrives in a new habitat, individual organisms can only survive if they can tolerate the abiotic and biotic environmental conditions there. The combination of environmental factors may form conditions that are new to the species. For example, strong winds can reduce body temperature and increase the rate of water loss. Plants are often less tolerant of cold or drought in windy habitats. Species may only be able to tolerate a habitat at certain stages of its life.

For a species to continue to survive in a new habitat, it must be able to obtain sufficient nutrients and energy so that it can breed and rear healthy offspring. Some species may have very specific adaptations which mean they cannot adapt very easily to a new habitat. Plants that need the presence of certain insects to pollinate them cannot survive in habitats where the insects do not exist. Other species can adapt more easily to new conditions. Some wind-pollinated plants, including many grasses, can colonise new habitats very quickly.

Animal species may adapt their behaviour so that they can use new habitats. For example, mammals, such as antelope and seals, may rear their young in different habitats from where they feed and breed as adults.

In harsh environments, the geographical distribution of a species is limited by abiotic factors, such as temperature and the availability of water. If very few species can survive there, the communities will be small.

Fig. 1 Colonisation

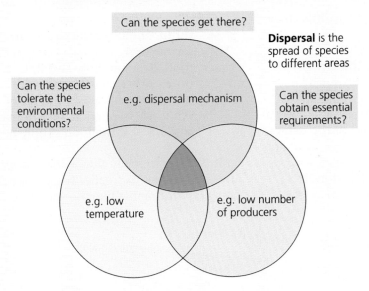

Colonisation is when a species survives in a habitat that is new or different to its normal one

Can the species get there?

Dispersal is the spread of species to different areas

Can the species tolerate the environmental conditions?

e.g. dispersal mechanism

Can the species obtain essential requirements?

e.g. low temperature

e.g. low number of producers

Optimal conditions, i.e. the organism is ideally adapted to the new habitat and can colonise it

For communities to exist in a particular habitat, species must first arrive there (Fig. 1). This may depend on the behaviour of the species and chance. For example, a bird may be blown off its normal route and arrive in a new habitat.

Over long periods of time, more species may be able to colonise the habitat, and the abiotic factors may become less severe. The plant and animal communities will undergo succession, leading to climax communities, if the abiotic and biotic factors are favourable.

As more species colonise a habitat, the community becomes more complex. As the community develops the biotic factors, such as competition, predation and the effect of parasites, become more important in limiting a species' geographical distribution than the original abiotic factors.

Every species has a particular set of requirements that have to be met so that it can live in a particular habitat. For example, abiotic factors such as temperature, water and mineral supply must be within a suitable range, and there must be an adequate food supply and space for its activities, like nest building. The part of the habitat and the particular environmental factors within a habitat that a species uses is called the species' **niche**.

Each species will become adapted for survival in a particular niche. For different species to coexist in the same habitat, they must occupy different niches.

 2 **Distinguish between the terms habitat and niche.**

Competition occurs where the niches of two species overlap. The part of the habitat that a species will use in the absence of any competitors or predators is termed its **fundamental niche**. The part that it actually uses in the presence of its competitors and predators is termed its **realised niche**. The extent of a species' fundamental niche can only be discovered if all its competitors and predators are removed in an experimental situation.

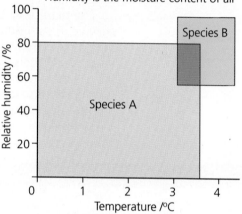

Fig. 2 Overlapping niches

Temperature and **humidity** tolerance of two subantarctic species of mite

Humidity is the moisture content of air

3a **Using Fig. 2 identify which species can survive:**
(i) **at 20% humidity and 2 °C;**
(ii) **at 90% humidity and 4 °C;**
(iii) **at 70% humidity and 3.2 °C:**
b **What will happen at 70% humidity and 3.5 °C if the food supply falls?**

It is easier to study the overlap of species and their niches in smaller communities in harsh environments like the Antarctic.

Key ideas

- Abiotic and biotic factors determine the geographical distribution of species.

- Within a habitat a species occupies a niche, determined by availability of food and the effect of abiotic factors.

- Species coexisting in the same habitat must occupy different niches.

- Species that can survive in a habitat form communities that may undergo succession to reach a climax community.

4.3 Temperature

The two major abiotic factors that influence the geographical distribution of species are temperature and water supply.

The environmental temperature affects the temperature of an organism's body, and so the rate of chemical reactions in the organism's body. In particular it affects the functioning of enzymes and the properties of cell membranes. If the chemical reactions cannot take place, because the temperature of the body has risen too high or fallen too low, then the organism will die.

Temperature also affects the solubility of gases in liquids. Gases become less soluble as temperature rises. This can affect the amount of oxygen available to aquatic organisms.

In terrestrial organisms the effects of temperature are linked with problems of water loss. At high temperatures water evaporates quickly from the surface of an organism. This evaporation is used as a cooling mechanism by many organisms, but if water is in short supply organisms could suffer from water stress.

The distribution of temperature is related to latitude. The nearer the equator, the higher the annual mean temperature. The distribution of temperature can also be affected by:

- altitude;
- slope;
- air and water movements;
- areas of land and water.

Air temperature falls by an average of 5.5 °C for an increase in altitude of 1000 m. Air and water movements can speed up or slow down temperature changes.

Water heats up and cools down more slowly than land, so large areas of water tend to restrict the temperature range around areas of land. The centre of large land areas has a much greater range of temperatures. In general, the more land-locked an area and the further away it is from the equator, the greater the annual mean range. In Antarctica there may be an annual range in temperature larger than 75 °C!

Although the total annual solar energy received at the South Pole is almost equal to the input at the equator, much of it is reflected back into space from the permanent ice cap. Antarctica is therefore the coldest of all continents. Even in summer, the water under the ice receives less than 1% of the sunlight that strikes the surface. For four months of the year the Antarctic is in total darkness.

Q 4 Explain the effect of four months of darkness on the NPP both on land and in water of the Antarctic.

Every organism has an **upper** and **lower lethal temperature**. Above the upper or below the lower temperature, the organism will die. Organisms living in colder habitats have lower lethal temperatures than organisms living in warmer habitats. Activities such as growth, reproduction and movement can only take place within an even narrower range of temperatures. Four main factors affect these temperatures during the life history of an individual organism:

- the environmental temperature at birth;
- seasonal changes of temperature tolerance;
- variation during the life cycle;
- duration of temperature extremes.

Fellfield habitats in the Antarctic are made up of communities of lichens and mosses on a stony surface. These species have to survive huge annual variations in temperature and water availability.

Every organism adapts to the temperature of the environment in which it first lives. Some organisms undergo seasonal changes in temperature **tolerance**. Tolerance describes the range that a species can survive. Some species have much wider temperature tolerance than others. Temperature tolerance can also vary between individuals within a species.

Some woody plants such as willow are more cold tolerant in winter. They can survive freezing temperatures below –15 °C, while in summer they are killed by –5 °C temperatures. In winter biochemical changes are triggered by shortening day length and lower temperatures. These changes alter the temperature tolerance.

 5a From Fig. 3 which of the fish species has the widest and which the narrowest temperature tolerance?
b Explain whether it is possible to transfer:
(i) fish species A to the temperature range of fish species C;
(ii) fish species B to the temperature range of fish species A?
c Which is most likely to be an Antarctic species?

Fig. 3 Temperature tolerance

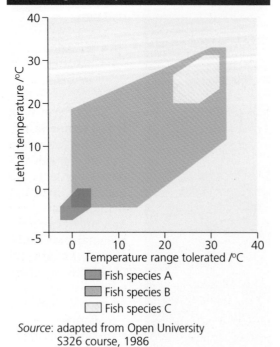

Fish species A
Fish species B
Fish species C

Source: adapted from Open University S326 course, 1986

Lethal temperatures may vary considerably during the **life cycle** of an organism. A life cycle is the series of changes that occur during the life of an organism. The stages in the life cycle of a plant that have a low water content can have a wide temperature tolerance. The stages of a plant that have a high water content can be more sensitive to temperature.

Temperature tolerance may also depend on length of exposure. The longer an organism is exposed to extreme temperatures, the more effect other environmental factors, such as humidity, may have (Fig. 4).

Fig. 4 Length of exposure

Groups of woodlice were exposed to various humidities for either 1 or 24 h, and their upper lethal temperature recorded

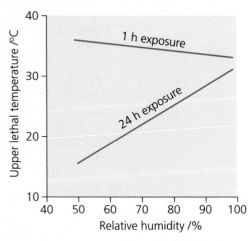

Source: Sutton, *Woodlice*, Ginn and Co.,1972

One way to prevent external temperatures from limiting an organism's survival chances is to maintain body temperature at a constant level no matter what happens outside. This body temperature control is called **thermoregulation**. **Homeothermic** animals maintain a constant core body temperature.They are able to remain active over a wide range of temperatures. Mammals and birds are homeothermic. Mammals maintain a body temperature of between 37 and 38 °C, and birds maintain a body temperature of about 40 °C.

Poikilothermic animals allow their temperatures to fluctuate with the temperature of their environment. Fish and reptiles are poikiolothermic. However, it is

Fig. 5 Body temperature

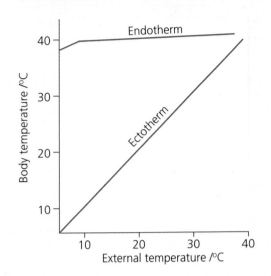

not always easy to sort animals into these two types. Many mammals have unstable body temperatures, and some reptiles are able to regulate their body temperatures within narrow limits. Animals that generate their own body heat are more accurately called **endothermic**. Animals that depend almost entirely on the environment for their body heat are called **ectothermic** (Fig. 5).

Endothermic organisms are able to colonise habitats that are too cold for ectotherms. However, they need an increased

basal metabolic rate (BMR) in order to generate the heat (Fig. 6). BMR is the minimum metabolic rate of an organism that keeps it alive. Increasing it takes a lot of energy. The BMR of an endotherm may be five times that of an ectotherm of equal size and body temperature at rest.

Another way animals can avoid unfavourable temperatures is by **migration**. Migration is the movement of a population from one habitat to another. A species migrates to find more favourable habitats in which to feed and breed. Birds can exploit habitats that are thousands of kilometres apart. The Arctic tern breeds in the Canadian Arctic during the summer there, then migrates south to the Antarctic for its summer. The round trip is 18 000 km.

Animals and plants can avoid extreme temperatures by **dormancy**. Dormancy is when an organism's BMR is reduced and growth ceases for a period of time. The organism does not use its food reserves and some species can survive months or years of drought, extreme cold or food shortage. Plant seeds, buds and storage organs can be dormant, and so can insect eggs and pupae. Mammals are dormant when they **hibernate**. During hibernation the mammal's metabolic rate decreases and its body temperature drops. Dormice and bats hibernate, but even they cannot survive long periods of freezing temperatures.

The most stressful temperature for the cells of living organisms is around the freezing point of water. The change from ice to water and back to ice is called the **freeze–thaw cycle**. In the Antarctic organisms have to be able to withstand this cycle. Some Antarctic species, both in the sea and on land, have evolved adaptations that overcome the problems of ice formation.

The rate of heating and cooling is also important. Higher cooling rates create more stressful conditions for the cells of an organism because the cell environment is changing quickly. However, some lichens in the Antarctic can survive cooling rates of 10–14 °C h^{-1}.

Fig. 6 Metabolic rate of mammals

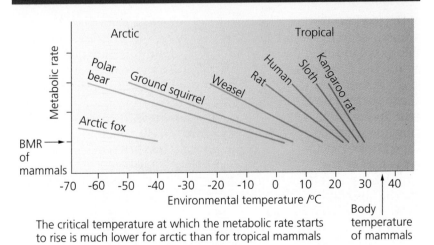

The critical temperature at which the metabolic rate starts to rise is much lower for arctic than for tropical mammals

Source: after Scholander in Roberts, *Biology a Functional Approach*, Thomas Nelson, 1986

Key ideas

- The temperature of the environment varies with latitude and is affected by other abiotic factors.
- The lethal temperatures of an organism determine the temperature range it can tolerate, and therefore the geographical area within which it can live.
- Endothermic organisms can generate their own body heat to regulate their internal temperature.
- Ectothermic organisms depend on the environment to regulate their body temperature.

4.4 Water

The availability of water has a strong influence on primary productivity and is largely responsible for determining which producers live in a habitat. As producers are the first trophic level, their presence or absence will determine what other species can colonise a habitat. Some plants such as algae, and animals such as amphibians, require water for sexual reproduction. Their abundance will therefore be limited by water availability.

Precipitation is water that forms in the atmosphere and falls to the surface of the Earth. It includes rainfall, dew and snow. It is ultimately the source of water in all ecosystems. Unlike temperature, the distribution of precipitation is not related to latitude. It depends on wind direction and the relative positions of land and oceans. Mountains modify precipitation rates around them.

Although over 70% of the world's store of freshwater is found in Antarctic ice, much of this is unavailable to organisms, even during summer, because it is frozen. In this respect the Antarctic is a desert. Animals in hot deserts like the Sahara have adapted to the lack of water and extreme hot temperatures. The kangaroo rat is a nocturnal mammal that spends the day in deep burrows away from the heat of the sun. It does not need to drink because it has very long **loops of Henle**. The loop of Henle is a tubule in the kidney that controls the amount of water in urine. High levels of sodium chloride are maintained within the loop so that water can be reabsorbed from the kidney filtrate. The longer the loop the more water can be reabsorbed because the concentration gradient of sodium chloride is greater and the filtrate takes longer to pass through the loop. The urine of a kangaroo rat is twice as concentrated as that of a rabbit.

Precipitation in the Antarctic, mostly in the form of snow, is low. In some inland areas the annual snow fall is less than the equivalent of 5 cm of rainfall, whereas in the coastal areas it may be as much as 50 cm per year. The depth and persistence of this snow is an important feature in determining biological activity.

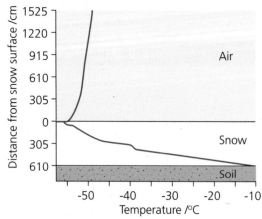

Fig. 7 Temperature gradient through snow

Source: adapted from *Ecology of the Subarctic Regions*, Proceedings of the Helsinki Symposium

 6 What do the data in Fig. 7 indicate about the environmental temperature of niches above and beneath the snow?

The seasonal timing and regularity of precipitation are usually of greater significance to organisms than the total annual value. The distribution of most organisms is influenced by their tolerance to water shortage. If an organism loses too much water from its body cells, or cannot get enough water from the environment, it will die. Mature plants are particularly affected by the availability of water because they cannot move. Plants that have adapted to survive habitats with very little available water are called **xerophytes**. Both Antarctic and desert plants have xerophytic adaptations to prevent loss of water. For example, tussock grasses have large root systems so that they can use as much underground water as possible.

Water contained in the soil and in vegetation and peat are important reservoirs that contribute to the survival of many Antarctic plants and animals. In the absence of plant cover, invertebrate life is often concentrated beneath stones where condensation keeps the soil moist.

At higher altitudes, solar energy and dry winds combine to cause water loss from the ground and snow because the water can change from solid to vapour without going through the liquid stage. This reduces the amount of water available from melting snow.

Freezing water is a major stress of Antarctic organisms. Some organisms are **freezing susceptible** and have to avoid ice formation in their cells and tissues. Other organisms are **freezing tolerant** and can tolerate the presence of ice in their body cells.

4.5 Survival strategies

If the environmental temperature and water availability allow an organism to colonise a habitat, it must then be able to find its own niche in that habitat, to avoid competition with other species.

Adaptations that allow an organism to survive in a niche can include its:
• structure;
• physiology;
• behaviour;
• life history.

Physiology includes all the processes that occur within an organism's body. Antarctic organisms often show a combination of all four adaptations. The development of these adaptations requires the simultaneous evolution of several characteristics. This may explain why so few species have adapted to life in the Antarctic.

Generally Antarctic organisms must be able to reproduce in the short summer. However, although some organisms, particularly birds, avoid the harsh winters by migrating to other habitats, where they can also breed. Plants and invertebrates may pass the winter in a dormant state. Their life cycle may also take more than one year so that they do not have to grow

and reproduce in the same short, growing season. Spreading the life cycle over a number of seasons is known as **perennation**. Some perennating plants grow underground storage organs such as **rhizomes** which can remain dormant in the soil during the winter while the above-ground parts of the plant die. All the flowering plants in the Antarctic region take more than one year to complete their life cycle and so are **perennials**. **Annual** plants take only one year to complete their life cycle.

 7 Suggest why there are no annual plants in Antarctica.

Lichens
Certain algae and fungi can live together in mutualistic relationships called **lichens**. Some lichens are very successful in the Antarctic. This is partly due to low levels of competition because there are few other lichens, relatively few mosses and virtually no flowering plants. Lichens are also able to tolerate nutrient-poor habitats and extremes of both temperature and moisture. Lichens in less severe habitats form on the surface of rocks. Antarctic

lichens have loose fungal filaments and algal cell clusters that grow between and around rock crystals, so that the lichen is embedded in the rock itself. The relative humidity in the rock may be 80% compared to 20% in the outside air, and the temperature fluctuates over a much smaller range.

Lichens such as *Umbilicaria antarctica* can tolerate a wide temperature range (−30 −35 °C) and can withstand continuous freeze–thaw cycles. They have large leaf-like structures or **thalli** with air spaces between them. The ice forms in the air spaces, restricting damage to cells. The presence of the sugars mannitol and aribitol in the cells is also thought to play a role in cold survival. They help prevent water molecules freezing.

Some lichens require 10–20 years to reach sexual maturity, but asexual reproduction can occur much earlier.

The lichen *Umbilicaria antarctica* on a rock at Cape Royds, Antarctica. Lichens are well adapted to this harsh environment and can live to be 1000 years old, with thalli reaching 30 cm in diameter!

On the subantarctic islands such as South Georgia the climate is milder than further south, although the snow-free period is still relatively short for plant growth. The most extensive plant growth is around the coast where tussock grass is dominant. Fur seals and many birds breed among these tussocks.

Tussock grass

The adaptations of tussock grass are related to temperature and nutrition. Their leaves usually curve over at night to enclose the growing shoot tip, and dead leaves are retained to form a sheath around the stem. These adaptations help insulate the plant. The temperature of the soil within the tussock may be up to 8 °C warmer than outside it. The cycling of nitrogen, phosphorus and calcium is also faster within tussocks than between them, and the root system is large relative to the shoots. By emerging as soon as possible through the snow as summer approaches, the tussocks make the most use of the short growing season. They can reach 40 cm in height and 50–60 cm in diameter in sheltered sites.

8 Suggest some of the advantages to tussock grass of having extensive underground root systems.

Arthropods

The harsh Antarctic climate means that most arthropods need to find shelter. This leads to a more or less hidden lifestyle beneath the snow. Many Antarctic arthropods have smaller wings and body size than arthropods elsewhere in the world. Because of their small size they are called **microarthropods**. A small size makes it easier for them to find protected niches in the soil, under rocks and in vegetation. The loss of wings and flight may also save energy and reduce the risk of being carried away to unsuitable habitats.

Some Antarctic flies and moths that retain their wings have to increase their body temperature in order to fly. Several species have darker bodies and wing bases than species living in less extreme climates. Because darker colours absorb more solar energy, their body temperatures increase when they bask in the sun.

Freezing-tolerant arthropods include a species of wingless midge. The larvae of this insect are able to make use of a range of anti-freezing substances that they obtain in their diet from a green alga species. These substances prevent cytoplasm and membrane damage at very low temperatures, and these insects' bodies do not freeze until about −10 °C. Below this temperature the mite can tolerate ice within its body.

A species of freezing-susceptible Antarctic mite is able to survive temperatures below −30 °C by preventing ice formation in the body fluids. This is done by emptying the gut of any substances that will cause ice crystals to form. Cooling a liquid below its freezing point without it freezing is called **supercooling**.

This Antarctic mite species is about the size of a pin head, yet is one of the largest terrestrial animals living in the Antarctic.

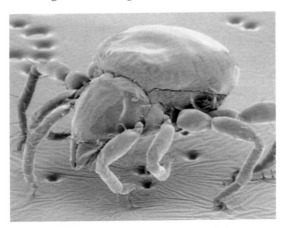

The production of glycerol at low temperatures may play a part in supercooling. Ice crystals in the body of freezing-susceptible mites will kill the arthropod.

 9 **The mite cannot feed and supercool at the same time. Suggest how it divides its time for these two activities, between summer and winter.**

In some habitats where overwintering arthropods are trapped below the ice they will experience periods of oxygen deficiency. Under these conditions some species of mites and springtails resort to anaerobic metabolism, sometimes for up to six months.

Temperate species of arthropods may have several generations per year, and some Antarctic species can complete their life cycle in one year. However, more often Antarctic species are restricted to one generation every two or more years due to the short growing season and low summer temperatures.

Different species of wolf spider live in different alpine and Arctic habitats. The life cycles of the spider species vary between 1 and 6 years. Those species in the more extreme, colder habitats have the longer life cycles. One Arctic moth species has a life cycle of 14 years.

 10 a Suggest the advantages of an Antarctic species being able to complete its life cycle in one year.
b Suggest the advantages of an Antarctic species being able to complete its life cycle over several years.

Fish

The Antarctic ocean is the coldest ocean on Earth and was thought to be uninhabitable. However, a group of perch-like fish has evolved to dominate the species present.

These fish possess two adaptations, the ability to produce compounds that have powerful anti-freezing properties and the development, in certain species, of 'neutral' buoyancy or weightlessness in water. Weightlessness means fish do not have to use energy to float.

Ice is a threat to fish because it penetrates their gills and skin. Fish are ectotherms and cannot survive if their blood temperature drops more than one degree below its freezing point. Most tropical fish freeze when their body fluids cool to approximately -0.8 °C. Some Antarctic fish only freeze when their temperature goes to -2.2 °C below the external temperature. The main anti-freezing substance in Antarctic fish can lower the freezing point of body fluids 200–300 times more than substances such as sodium chloride. The molecules are adsorbed onto tiny ice crystals and prevent their growth.

The production of anti-freezing substances needs a lot of energy. Usually fish have glomeruli in their kidney, but Antarctic fish do not so that the anti-freezing substances are not excreted.

The Antarctic Toothfish is a species that lives in mid-waters and exhibits neutral buoyancy. It is over three times larger than similar species that are bottom dwellers. It has reduced the density of its bony material by having a largely cartilage skeleton and hollow vertebrae. This species also has large amounts of lipid filling fat cells under the skin and throughout the muscle fibres. The lipid is less dense than water so aids buoyancy without excessive energy use.

Many Antarctic fish live, feed and reproduce near the sea floor. They account for 90% of the fish in the Antarctic.

Penguins

Only two species of penguin breed on the Antarctic continent itself. One of them, the Emperor penguin, is renowned for breeding on ice and rearing its chick throughout the Antarctic winter.

The Emperor penguin is the largest and heaviest penguin in the world. It is 115 cm in length and weighs 20–40 kg. Its closest relative is the King penguin, which is found 2000 km to the north in South America. The King penguin is only 95 cm in length and weighs 10–20 kg. This is an example of **Bergman's rule**. Animals of the same genus tend to be smaller in warmer regions and larger in colder regions.

The Emperor penguin is also smoother and sleeker than the King penguin. This is an example of **Allen's rule**. Parts of the body that stick out, such as limbs and facial features, are smaller in species living in colder regions.

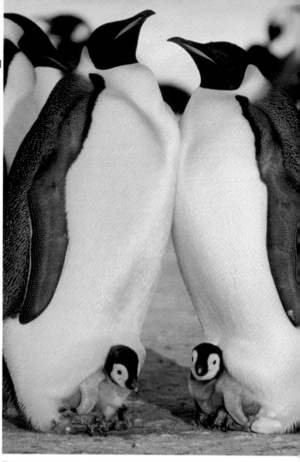

Emperor penguins do not stake out separate incubating territories like other penguins but huddle together. This is a vital behavioural adaptation that allows them to survive the Antarctic winter.

The effect of these adaptations in size and shape is to decrease the **surface area to volume ratio**. As the volume of an organism increases, the surface area increases by less, so the surface area to volume ratio decreases. A larger volume means an organism can store more heat within its body. The relatively smaller surface area means the organism has a relatively smaller potential for losing heat via conduction and radiation.

In addition to surviving temperatures as low as -60 °C and hurricane winds, male Emperor penguins must walk a distance of up to 200 km from the sea to the nesting area and back, before taking over the incubation of the egg. While incubating, male Emperor penguins spend up to four months fasting. It has been calculated that at least 25 kg of tissue should be consumed during this period, yet a large male bird of 35 kg only carries 15–20 kg in reserve. The answer to this mismatch is found in the bird's behaviour. Incubating males make use of collective thermoregulation through huddling together. This allows them to minimise their exposure to the cold and conserve energy.

Unlike other birds, penguins lack defined feather tracks and have short specialised feathers covering their body's surface. The feathers are very dense and form overlapping layers. Each layer traps a layer of air. This multi-layered sandwich of feathers and air is impermeable to water. In addition, penguins have a well-defined subcutaneous fat layer and a highly developed **countercurrent heat exchanger system** of blood vessels in the flippers and legs (Fig. 8). The heat from outgoing arterial blood is transferred to venous blood returning from exposed parts. This reduces heat loss from the body core.

The Adelie penguin is smaller and more abundant than the Emperor penguins. To conserve heat still further the nasal passages of Adelie penguins are complex in structure. They transfer heat from warm air being

On land Adelie penguins can waddle but will toboggan where possible. This uses less energy than walking.

exhaled to the cool air being breathed in. Extensive feathering at the base of the bill helps this even more. These heat-conserving adaptations are so effective that on hot days Adelies may have problems shedding heat!

The bodies of Adelies are also highly adapted to swimming. Their body shape is streamlined so they can move through water with little resistance. They have reduced wings that form strong narrow flippers. These allow rapid propulsion through the water. Their feet are short and set well back on their body and are used together with the tail as a rudder.

 11 **What advantages do Adelie penguins' body shape adaptations give them in their shared aquatic habitat?**

Seals

The Antarctic fur seal gains its name from its very effective double-layered coat. This is made of stiff, stout guard hairs together with a much denser growth of very fine under-fur fibres. The tips of the guard hairs are coated with secretions from sebaceous glands. This makes the whole coat water repellent so that the skin beneath stays dry. The trapped layer of air around the under-fur fibres acts as an insulating barrier to heat loss. In the Antarctic fur seal there are about 1350 guard hairs per cm^2, each with about 30 under-fur fibres associated with it, giving a fibre density of some 40 000 hairs per cm^2!

 12 **Suggest the reason why Antarctic fur seals were nearly hunted to extinction during the last century.**

Fig. 8 Countercurrent heat exchange

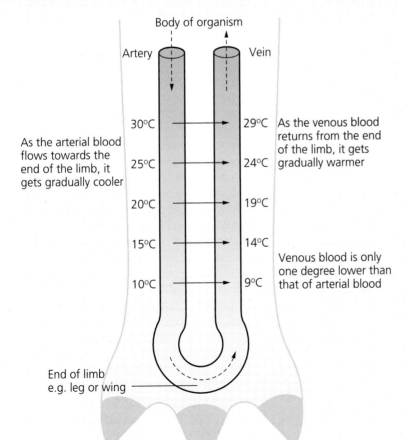

Body of organism

Artery · Vein

As the arterial blood flows towards the end of the limb, it gets gradually cooler

30°C → 29°C As the venous blood returns from the end of the limb, it gets gradually warmer

25°C → 24°C

20°C → 19°C

15°C → 14°C

Venous blood is only one degree lower than that of arterial blood

10°C → 9°C

End of limb e.g. leg or wing

4.6　A fragile wilderness

Antarctica covers about 10% of the world's land mass with an area of 13.9 million km². Ninety-eight per cent of it is permanently covered with ice and snow, confining terrestrial life to the remaining 2%. It is the coldest continent, with temperatures recorded as low as −88 °C. It is also the highest, with an average elevation of 1180 m, the driest, with an average annual precipitation of only 10 cm, and the windiest.

This wilderness harbours some of the least disturbed and most sensitive ecosystems on Earth. The organisms that live there have developed unique and complex adaptations so that they can survive.

In the past Antarctica's marine resources have been the focus of exploitation, particularly by the fishing industries. Concern about potential overfishing of some fish and tiny shrimp-like organisms called **krill** led to the establishment of the Convention on the Conservation of Antarctic Marine Living Resources in 1982. However, this convention requires all the countries that have signed it to agree before decisions can be made. This makes regulation and management difficult in practice and so over-fishing continues. The annual catch of krill has increased 30-fold over the last 20 years, from 20 000 to 600 000 tonnes.

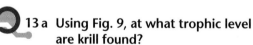

13 a Using Fig. 9, at what trophic level are krill found?

b Explain the effect of the increase in krill catch by humans on the sperm whale population.

c During the 1960s the populations of Baleen whales declined due to overfishing. What effect would this have had on the krill?

The communities that exist in Antarctica contain few species and are very susceptible to damage by human activity. Any change in species survival in lower trophic levels could have serious effects further up the food chain.

The Antarctic fur seal was hunted almost to extinction, and only a small population remained early in the 20th century. Because the seal is protected and no longer hunted, it has taken advantage of the increased supply of krill caused by the decrease in the whale populations. As a result, the Antarctic fur seal has undergone one of the most rapid population increases ever recorded for a marine mammal. In turn, the rise in the seal population has had a devastating effect on their summer habitat on Signey Island in the South Orkneys. The number of plant species has fallen, and fellfield communities have been destroyed. Seal urine and other organic waste has increased the nitrogen content of the soil and water, causing eutrophication of freshwater streams and lakes.

Within the Antarctic continent the habitats and ecosystems are even more fragile than those on Signey Island. The diversity of species is so small that any change can affect all the communities.

The variety of species in a community is called the **diversity**. A greater diversity of species can make an ecosystem more stable because more resources are available at each trophic level. For example, in a temperate woodland primary consumers, such as insects, have a choice of food sources, whereas in the Antarctic a primary consumer has very limited sources of The diversity of species in extreme environments is low, and the distribution and abundance of species is largely influenced by abiotic factors. In less severe environments, there is a greater diversity of species and their distribution and abundance is influenced largely by biotic factors.

The abiotic and biotic factors of an environment and the diversity of species and stability of an ecosystem are therefore linked. Very harsh abiotic factors mean few species can survive, so only small communities exist. Succession will be slow and the climax community may never be reached. If species diversity is low, then the ecosystem is not very stable because there are few resources. Any change, e.g. hunting a species almost to extinction, can affect the whole ecosystem.

Much of the scientific evidence to

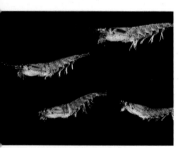

Krill are the most abundant animal in the world. They are unique because they support all the higher consumers in the Antarctic food web.

Fig. 9 Antarctic food web

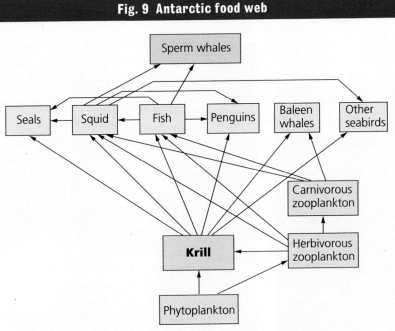

Krill form the central link in the Antarctic food web, both directly at sea and indirectly via the seabirds and the nutrients their droppings bring to the nesting sites on land

Source: Barnes, *Lets Save Antarctica*, Greenhouse Publications, 1982

support the formation of a World Park has come from studies by organisations such as the British Antarctic Survey, who carry out terrestrial and marine biological studies from a number of permanent bases around the Antarctic Peninsula.

Ecologists with the British Antarctic Survey carry out ecological, biological and environmental research. They aim to understand how Antarctic ecosystems have evolved, and why certain organisms can survive in the Antarctic environment. By relating the Antarctic findings to information from Arctic and alpine areas of the world, a general picture can be constructed, which will help our understanding of how such ecosystems function. This will allow us to adopt measures which will prevent further damage to these regions.

By keeping the Antarctic ecosystem unharmed, the effect of changes in the global system can be monitored more easily. Because the Antarctic communities are not diverse nor complex, any changes are easier to see.

Key ideas

- Precipitation is the source of all freshwater in ecosystems. The distribution of organisms is influenced by their ability to survive water shortage.

- To survive in extreme conditions, organisms evolve specific adaptations and occupy small, specialised niches.

- Behavioural adaptations include migration and dormancy.

- Structural adaptations include reduced surface area to volume ratio, streamlined bodies and tussock growth formations.

- Physiological adaptations include production of anti-freeze substances and countercurrent heat exchange systems.

- Life history adaptations include extended and shortened life cycles.

- In extreme environmental conditions, species diversity is small and food webs are simple.

- Abiotic and biotic factors and species diversity are linked.

- The higher the the diversity of species in an ecosystem, the more stable it is.

Dirty and dangerous

Treating sewage is one way we try to prevent pollution. If we did not have sewage works, just imagine the mess! Sewage treatment plants have to be kept to a high standard to make sure our waste has as little impact on the environment as possible.

Not all sources of pollution are as easy to see as this agricultural chemical run-off. The EA has to know the probable effect of different pollutants so that appropriate action can be recommended.

The National Rivers Authority (NRA) was set up in 1989 by the Government, and became part of the Environment Agency (EA) in 1996. The EA's responsibilities throughout England and Wales include pollution prevention and control, waste minimisation, management of water resources, flood defence and conservation. The EA is organised into eight regions, each of which has to deal with problems specific to the environment of their area. They have to know the likely causes of pollution in their area and monitor any pollution that does occur.

Monitoring damage alone is not a solution, however. EA scientists have to try to predict where damage will occur and then try to prevent it. But this needs a good understanding of the way pollution spreads through the environment. How easy is it to predict and how conclusive must the proof be before the EA acts to stop people doing things that may lead to environmental damage?

5.1 Learning objectives

After working through this chapter, you should be able to:

- **describe** common sources of pollutants;

- **describe** techniques used to monitor aquatic ecosystems;

- **explain** the advantages and disadvantages of chemical and biological monitoring;

- **select** and measure a range of environmental variables;

- **explain** the effect of specific pollutants on living organisms and their environment;

- **explain** how human activities can have an effect on ecosystems;

- **explain** how diversity is affected by environmental pollution.

5.2 Sources of pollutants

Pollution occurs when humans introduce substances, **pollutants**, into the environment that are likely to cause damage. Pollution effects may mimic the stages of natural processes. For example, adding organic pollution to a river resembles the processes of decay that occur in the autumn when leaves fall in a stream.

Different pollutants are released into the environment in different ways. Some are mainly from one location, for example from a sewage treatment works or landfill site. Others are from sources that are spread over a larger area, such as agricultural run-off. Pollutants can enter the ecosystem all the time, for example from sewage works. Others may occur as isolated incidents, for example as a result of an industrial accident.

 1 **Suggest which methods of release make it more difficult to monitor and clean up a pollution incident. Explain your choices.**

To investigate freshwater pollution problems, the Environment Agency (EA) needs to know the source of the pollution, how the pollutants affect the ecosystem and its organisms, and how these effects can be monitored. They may then be able to advise on the control of any further pollution and how to clean up the existing mess.

The major sources of freshwater pollution are:
- agriculture;
- industry;
- households.

All of these sources may release more than one type of pollutant. Think about the water that you use during the course of a day. As individual consumers we tend to forget that we are major contributors to waste water! Domestic waste water may contain organic matter, mineral ions in detergents and bleach, and occasionally disease-causing microorganisms.

Water flowing from a sewage plant or industrial site into a stream or river is called **effluent**. Effluents often contain more than

The liquid leaking from this muck heap is flowing into the water course and polluting it. This sort of problem can be very difficult to avoid.

one type of pollutant and there can be more than one source of effluent at various points along the length of a river.

Each pollutant may affect the river system in a different way. If two or more pollutants are present they may have a combined effect on the ecosystem that is worse than the effect of either pollutant on its own. If the overall effect is greater than the total of the individual effects, the effect is **synergistic**. For example, increased water temperature can increase the sensitivity of fish to some metal ions. Temperature changes in a river as a result of the temperature of the effluent is known as **thermal pollution**.

Alternatively, the pollutants may interfere with each other. This is called **antagonism**.

The impact of pollutants will also depend on the conditions of the ecosystems they have entered.

Dilution is making a substance less concentrated by adding more liquid. Dilution in rivers depends on the volume and flow rate of the water. In a large, rapidly flowing river even quite large amounts of pollutant can be quickly diluted to insignificant levels. The same amount being discharged into a small stream could have disastrous results. Dilution is less effective during dry periods when river flows are reduced, or when large volumes of water are being removed for drinking water. Dilution has always been an effective way to reduce the impact of a freshwater pollutant. One of the first rules set for sewage treatment was that the effluent had to be discharged into water that was at least eight times its own volume.

Flowing water is an excellent medium for transporting and distributing pollutants, particularly suspended solids such as sewage effluent. These suspended solids increase the turbidity, or cloudiness, of the water.

These rainbow trout have been killed by fuel oil pollution in a fish farm. Dead fish are often a sign the water has been polluted, but it can be very difficult to recognise the source of the pollution.

Q 2 Explain how an increase in turbidity will affect the amount of photosynthesis carried out by aquatic plants and algae.

Eventually, depending on the amount of water flow and turbulence, the particles will settle onto the river bed. This is **sedimentation**. Sedimentation removes suspended solids from the water column.

Sedimentation can help to remove inorganic substances such as **heavy metal** ions from the water by causing them to become attached, **adsorbed**, onto mud particles on the river bed. Heavy metals are metals such as lead, nickel, cadmium, zinc, copper and mercury that have an atomic number greater than 20. They can enter freshwater as by-products of industrial processes and some agricultural uses. For example, mercury is an industrial waste product and is used in pesticides.

Heavy metals and pesticides are not easily broken down and **persist** in the environment, often being incorporated into the body tissue of animals. Persistence is how long a pollutant remains in the environment. **Biodegradable** wastes can be broken down by animals and microorganisms into carbon dioxide, nitrates and phosphates. This process may be aerobic, in the presence of oxygen, or anaerobic, in the absence of oxygen. Domestic sewage and other organic waste are examples of biodegradable waste. Biodegradable waste does not persist in the environment.

In some circumstances, pollutants may undergo **chemical transformation**, which may make things worse. Discharging soluble iron salts into naturally alkaline waters can cause **precipitation** of solid iron hydroxide. Precipitation is when a substance comes out of solution or suspension to form a solid. Iron hydroxide is a bright orange precipitate that reduces light penetration of the water. It also reduces respiration in invertebrate organisms. The formation of iron hydroxide is a synergistic effect.

Chemical conditions that exist in the mud and water, for example salinity, oxygen content and acidity, may also be changed by pollutants. These changes may **mobilise** inorganic substances. Heavy metal ions that had been adsorbed onto mud particles are released from the river bed. Acid rain decreases the pH of an ecosystem, which in turn mobilises aluminium ions in the sediments.

The soluble aluminium can cause fish deaths. Substances in a river bed may also be mobilised if the sediments are disturbed, for example during dredging or due to seasonal changes in the flow of water.

Biotransformation is the transformation of chemicals by an organism, for example the biodegradation of organic wastes by microorganisms.

Fig. 1 DDT in a food chain

DDT in fish-eating birds 25 ppm

DDT in large fish 2 ppm

DDT in small fish 0.5 ppm

DDT in zooplankton 0.04 ppm

DDT in water 3×10^{-6} ppm

Source: adapted from Haywood, *Applied Ecology*, Thomas Nelson, 1992

However, some reactions that occur within an organism can convert non-toxic compounds into toxic ones. In its metallic state mercury is not very toxic to humans, even if swallowed. Some aquatic microorganisms convert mercury to meythl mercury, which is extremely toxic. This occurred in Minimata Bay in Japan. A factory at Minimata produced a range of chemical products including plastics, drugs and perfumes, many of them by processes using mercury. Between 1932 and 1968 27 tonnes of mercury-containing waste were dumped into the bay. In the 1950s, people in Minimata began to suffer from a disease of the nervous system, which included slurring of speech, uncontrolled shouting and damage to eyesight. Microorganisms were converting mercury into methyl mercury. Methyl mercury binds strongly to fish protein, and is passed on to humans because it is not destroyed by cooking. Over the years the mercury did more and more harm to the people of Minimata. In 1969 the factory stopped dumping waste in the bay, but claims for compensation were still outstanding in 1993.

Organisms can also accumulate compounds in their tissues to toxic levels. This **bioaccumulation** occurs when the concentration of the pollutant increases along the food chain. There are several well-documented cases of this phenomenon occurring with organochloride pesticides such as DDT (Fig. 1).

 3 **Suggest why it is mainly tertiary consumers such as birds of prey that are affected by DDT.**

Key ideas

- Pollution is the introduction of substances into the environment that cause harm to ecosystems.

- Sources of water pollution include agriculture, industry and households.

- Understanding pollution requires a knowledge of the nature and effects of the pollutants.

- The effects of pollutants are determined by how they are released, and their dilution, sedimentation, biodegradability, persistence, chemical transformation, biotransformation and bioaccumulation.

5.3 Monitoring water pollution

North West Water (NWW) is being investigated by the National Rivers Authority (NRA) over claims of water being polluted by sewage. The investigation was launched after residents complained their private spring water supplies had been contaminated. Dr Steve Minter, a researcher in the microbiology unit at UMIST, claims to have found massive levels of bacteria associated with human waste in samples from the site.

The NRA is investigating whether disposal of sewage by NWW on nearby moorland is responsible for the pollution. A spokesman for the NRA said: 'We are carrying out an investigation into whether NWW is responsible for this pollution.' A NWW spokesman said it was normal for bacteria to be found in raw water supplies: 'Our own tests suggest nothing abnormal.'

Source: adapted from an article by Carl Johnston, *Manchester Metro*, 1991

A tip-off to the NRA resulted in a Disley company receiving a £11,000 fine. NRA district pollution officer Les Jolley found that a large volume of effluent containing high levels of paper fibres was being discharged through the plant's outfall pipe in the river Goyt.

An application from the paper mill company for permission to increase effluent discharges into the River Goyt was recently refused by the NRA on the grounds of the company's pollution record.

Source: adapted from *The Messenger*, 1991

EA officers routinely monitor water quality to keep a check on pollution levels. They also carry out tests and investigations if they receive complaints. But by then the damage may have been done. **Chemical monitoring** involves sampling and analysing the water. It analyses the abiotic characteristics of the aquatic ecosystem.

Oxygen is the most important variable in overall water quality. Aquatic organisms need it for aerobic respiration and for the decomposition of organic matter. Electronic meters are used to estimate the dissolved oxygen content of water. This can be done at the site as well as back in the laboratory.

Microorganisms that are breaking down organic compounds use up oxygen during respiration. Therefore organic pollution, which contains organic compounds, always results in a reduction in the amount of dissolved oxygen. This means the oxygen available to other organisms is in short supply. The **biochemical oxygen demand** (BOD) is an index of water quality and a measure of microbial respiration (Fig. 2). The lower the

This NRA officer is taking samples from a river to monitor the water quality.

BOD, the less organic pollution there is in it because less oxygen has been used by microorganisms.

Fig. 2 Biochemical oxygen demand

1 Completely fill two 250 cm³ plastic flasks, A and B, with water sample. Try to close them under water to keep them free of air bubbles.

2 Record the oxygen concentration of flask A with an electronic meter.

3 Incubate flask B in the dark for five days at 20 °C. After the five days record the oxygen concentration of flask B.

4 The 5-day BOD is the flask A oxygen concentration minus the flask B oxygen concentration.

Fig. 3 Dissolved oxygen

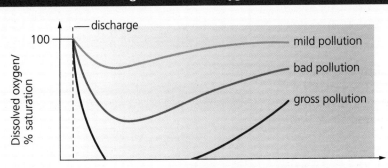

Source: Mason, *Biology of Freshwater Pollution*, Longman, 1981

Fig. 4 Filtration

1 Weigh (in grams) a filter (micropore Whatman grade 7) on a piece of foil. This is value X.

2 Take a known volume (m³) of well-mixed water sample.

3 Place the filter in a Buchner funnel. Turn on the water supply to the pump. Wet the filter with some distilled water.

4 Gradually pour the water sample through the filter.

5 Carefully remove the filter from the funnel and place it on the foil. Dry it on the foil in the oven for about 1 hour at 105 °C.

6 Reweigh the filter on its piece of foil. This is value Y.

7 The quantity of suspended solids, as g m⁻³, is:

$$\frac{Y - X}{\text{volume of sample}}$$

the gills and filtering apparatus of many aquatic species. The quantity of suspended solids can be determined by filtration and can be used as an indication of water quality (Fig. 4).

 5 Suggest sources of error when carrying out filtration.

Investigating the amount of dissolved oxygen in different rivers and at different points along a river can indicate the point where the effluent is being discharged and how bad the pollution is (Fig. 3).

4 a In Fig. 3 the point of minimum dissolved oxygen occurs below the point of discharge. Explain this observation.

b Why does the level of dissolved oxygen in the river eventually return to its original position?

Suspended solids in water can be organic or inorganic. As well as affecting the turbidity of the water, they can also clog

About 1% of human urine is sodium chloride. Sodium chloride is one of the few human excretory products to pass through sewage filtration works. A high chloride content in the water usually indicates the presence of sewage or farm drainage. Chloride can be estimated by **titration** (Fig. 5). Titration determines the strength of a solution using another, known solution.

High ammonia levels in the water can indicate recent contamination by sewage effluent. Nitrifying bacteria convert the ammonia to nitrites and then nitrates. The sources of nitrites and nitrates in water therefore include domestic and farm sewage, and also fertilisers.

Large amounts of nitrites and nitrates

Fig. 5 Salinity

1 Dissolve 27.25 g of silver nitrate in distilled water and make up to 1 litre.

2 Place 10 cm^3 of the water sample into a conical flask.

3 Titrate with the silver nitrate solution using a few drops of potassium chromate solution as indicator.

4 Swirl the flask as the silver nitrate solution is run in. The end-point is reached when the first permanent brick red colour of silver chromate occurs.

5 The volume of silver nitrate (cm^3) used in the titration is approximately equal to the salinity in g kg^{-1}.

 NB Care must be taken when doing this experiment because some of the chemicals are toxic.

Fig. 6 Flow rate

1 Measure the distance (in metres) of the sample stretch of water.

2 Choose some floats that are conspicuous and float mainly below the water surface so that they are less affected by wind. Oranges are good.

3 Time how long (in seconds) it takes the float to travel the sample stretch. On wider stretches, if possible time the floats down the middle of the water channel and near the banks.

4 Divide the average time taken by the floats by the coefficient 0.85. This allows for the fact that water flows faster at the surface than beneath it.

The velocity (m s^{-1}) is:

$$\frac{\text{distance (metres)}}{\text{time (seconds)}}$$

 NB Care must be taken when doing this activity because of the danger of working near water.

act as fertilisers and quickly stimulate the growth of phytoplankton and other algae. When the algae die, they sink to the river bottom and decompose.

 6a **How will algal growth and then decomposition affect the BOD?**
 b **What effect could this have on invertebrates that need clean water?**

Conductivity is a measure of a water sample's ability to carry an electrical current. Electricity is carried in solutions by dissolved ions. So the greater the conductivity of the water, the more dissolved ions are present. Conductivity measurements can be very accurate, but they cannot determine which ions are present. Conductivity, water temperature and pH can all be monitored with specialised electronic meters.

Another abiotic factor that needs to be taken into account when determining the effects of pollution is the flow rate of the water (Fig. 6).

7 **Explain the influence the flow rate will have on water quality.**

It is often not possible to monitor continuously for every abiotic variable, therefore samples are taken at regular intervals and tested for a limited range of pollutants.

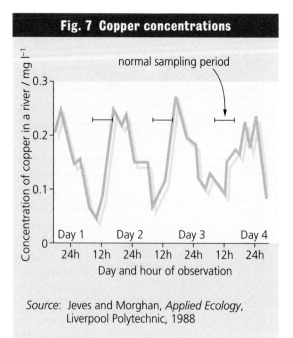

Fig. 7 Copper concentrations

Source: Jeves and Morghan, *Applied Ecology*, Liverpool Polytechnic, 1988

 8a **Explain the error of the normal sampling procedure in Fig. 7.**
 b **Suggest how it could be avoided.**

66

Much of the EA's monitoring happens in laboratories, where the samples taken are analysed in detail. The changes in species diversity and chemical characteristics of an ecosystem in response to organic pollution follow a pattern that can be recognised by EA officers.

Equipment called dataloggers can be used to monitor temperature, oxygen content, conductivity and pH continuously. If the EA has the right equipment, areas that are often polluted could be monitored continuously so that the first signs of pollution can be spotted and action taken.

Environmental pollution also affects the diversity of species in a habitat. **Biological monitoring** involves collecting and identifying the numbers and types of invertebrates and other aquatic species. Changes in water quality can show up as a change in the populations of organisms in an ecosystem. The cause of these changes can then be investigated.

There are two main methods of biological monitoring:
• biotic indices;
• diversity indices.

Biotic indices are based on the relative tolerance of invertebrates to organic pollution, in particular their response to low oxygen levels. Some organisms are very intolerant to low oxygen levels. The more tolerant a species is the lower the species' biotic index. Just the presence or absence of a species is needed. All the species' indices can be added together to give an index for the site. This can be used to compare different sites.

A **diversity index** measures the species diversity of a particular ecosystem. The Margalef index (I) is one example of a diversity index that takes account of both the number of species (S) and the number of individuals (N) of each species in an ecosystem:

$$I = \frac{S - 1}{\log N}$$

 9 a Calculate the biotic index for each of the two sites in Table 1.
   b Calculate the Margalef index for each of the two sites.
   c Comment on the differences between the two sites.

Table 1. Data from two sites					
Site 1	Biotic index	Number of individuals	Site 2	Biotic index	Number of individuals
Stonefly larvae			Mayfly larvae	4	8
Species 1	10	4			
Species 2	10	7	Snails	3	30
Species 3	10	3			
			Leeches		
Mayfly larvae			Species 1	3	1
Species 1	4	2	Species 2	3	2
Species 2	10	7			
			Fly larvae		
Cased caddis larvae			Species 1	2	30
With stones	10	2	Species 2	2	65
With leaves	7	1			
			Worms	1	120
Freshwater shrimps	6	35			
Leeches					
Species 1	3	11			
Species 2	3	3			
Snails					
Species 1	3	45			
Species 2	3	16			

Table 2. Chemical analysis						
	pH	Suspended solids/mg l⁻¹	BOD /mg O l⁻¹	Nitrates /mg N l⁻¹	Ammonia /mg N l⁻¹	Chloride /mg l⁻¹
December Before sewage fungus appeared	8.3	8	1.0	0.01	0.01	39
January After sewage fungus appeared	7.1	35	2.8	0.16	0.32	167

NB: chloride ions are present as a result of human waste and road run-off.
Source: NRA

A lot of our waste, both organic and inorganic, goes to landfill sites. If these sites are not managed they can be the cause of pollution of land and nearby water sources. At a landfill site the first reported evidence of organic pollution may be the presence of a white film called sewage fungus. This is not just a growth of fungus but a complex community of heterotrophic microorganisms that break down the organic compounds.

The advantages of diversity indices include:
• species and types need only be distinguished and not identified;
• no information on oxygen tolerance is required.

Invertebrate organisms are sometimes referred to as **indicator species** because they indicate the quality of the water. Different species are present in severely polluted water than in unpolluted water.

10 a From Fig. 8 and Table 2, what indicates that the discharge contains a large amount of organic matter?
  b Which species seem to be more tolerant of organic pollution?

Fig. 8 Indicator species

December
4105 individuals

January
10162 individuals

☐ Worms
☐ Snails (gastropods)
☐ Snails (bivalves)
☐ Midge larvae
☐ Other species

Key ideas

- Chemical monitoring analyses changes in the abiotic characteristics of the environment.

- Oxygen is the most important variable in water quality.

- Biological monitoring analyses changes in the numbers and types of species present.

- The presence and absence of indicator species provides a measure of water quality.

- Organic pollution can be detected by a variety of chemical and biological analyses.

- Abiotic factors can be measured in laboratory tests from samples obtained in the field.

- Regular sampling can be used to monitor changes in environments and indicate the presence of any pollution.

5.4 Toxic heavy metals

As well as organic pollution, the EA often has to monitor heavy metal pollution. Some heavy metals are continually released or mobilised into the aquatic environment from natural processes such as volcanic activity and weathering of rocks. Some of these, for example copper and zinc, are essential to life in small or trace amounts, but are toxic at high concentrations. Industrial processes which often use large amounts of metals have resulted in much higher levels of metal ions in the environment.

In 1955 high levels of cadmium in local foodstuffs in parts of Japan caused itai-itai-byo disease, which is very painful and gives rise to bone deformities and fractures, mainly in women over 40. The cadmium entered the food chain from irrigation water from spoil heaps of a disused mine.

The concentration of a substance affects its degree of toxicity. Toxicity can be:

- **acute**, which is a large dose of poison over a short duration and is usually lethal;
- **chronic**, which is a low dose of poison over a long duration, which may be lethal or sublethal.

Lethal effects kill an organism straight away. Sublethal affects may not kill an organism instantly but do cause harm that can lead to death. Increased or repeated doses of the poison can cause more severe effects.

The toxicity of a heavy metal depends on a number of factors:
- whether it is adsorbed to the substrate or is free in solution;

- its persistence;
- how much and for how long an organism has been exposed to it;
- how quickly it enters an organism's cells;
- any bioaccumulation that occurs.

Measurements of toxicity are usually taken from laboratory or test populations using the **lethal concentration** (LC_{50}) or **lethal dose** (LD_{50}). This is the concentration or dose required to kill 50% of the population.

 11 Compare the degree of tolerance in the two species of fish in Table 3.

Table 3. 50% lethal dose /mg l⁻¹ of heavy metals			
	Copper	**Cadmium**	**Zinc**
Stone loach	0.26 (63)	2.0 (54)	2.5 (5)
Rainbow Trout	0.28 (119)	0.017 (5.5)	4.6 (5)

Exposure time in days is in brackets.
Source: Solbe and Cooper *Water Resources*, Vol. 10, pp. 523–527, 1976

However, the application of laboratory-derived measures to field populations is increasingly being questioned by ecologists. They often fail to take account of environmental conditions such as water pH, oxygen levels, temperature and other effects produced by combinations of many factors, which can modify toxic effects. The concentration of zinc in effluent from a steel works in the East Midlands, UK, reached a value that was more than five times the 48 hour LC_{50} for rainbow trout. No fish were found immediately below the discharge point, but numbers increased further downstream.

The long-term problems associated with heavy metals arise from their persistence in the environment and tendency to bioaccummulate in food webs. If fish that survive the zinc pollution are eaten, then the consumers further up the food chain will be poisoned. The waste water from the steel works has to be treated to reduce the zinc in the effluent. Many advances in waste recycling and recovery have taken place but there is still much to be done. In the meantime agencies like the EA try to ensure industrial companies do not exceed their discharge limits.

5.5 Acid rain

Dead pine trees, such as these in South Wales, are often an indication of acid rain. The source of the acid rain may not have been the power stations near the trees, but from industrial sites much further away.

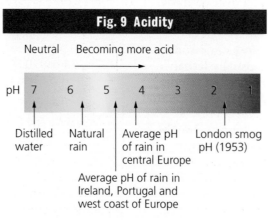

Fig. 9 Acidity

Neutral   Becoming more acid

pH 7   6   5   4   3   2   1

Distilled water
Natural rain
Average pH of rain in central Europe
London smog pH (1953)

Average pH of rain in Ireland, Portugal and west coast of Europe

Source: adapted from *New Scientist*, 5 November 1987

Some sources of inorganic pollution can have far-reaching and long-term effects. The pollution in one EA area may come from a source outside their area or even outside the country.

The name **acid rain** was first used by Robert Angus Smith, a pollution inspector in 1872, to describe the acidity of rain falling around Manchester during the height of the industrial revolution. Rain is naturally acidic due to the presence of carbon dioxide. Carbon dioxide and water combine to form carbonic acid, with a pH of 5.65. Acid rain is any precipitation that has a pH below 5.6 (Fig. 9).

Acid rain first became a public concern in the post-war smogs that plagued London and other major industrial cities. The worst example occurred in 1953 when the pH of the smog caused by factory smoke and a week-long fog fell to 1.6. This was responsible for the deaths of 4000 people. In the early 1970s, Sweden complained that the acidity of rain falling in southern Scandinavia had greatly increased since the 1950s, and that this was due to pollutants from countries such as Britain.

The acidic level of rain can be influenced by the affect of naturally occurring chemicals and processes (Fig. 10). The pollutants that are responsible for acidification are sulphur dioxide (SO_2) and the various oxides of nitrogen. These are nitrous oxide (N_2O), nitric oxide (NO) and nitrogen dioxide (NO_2), and they are collectively known as NO_x. They are emitted from power stations, vehicle exhausts and naturally from volcanic

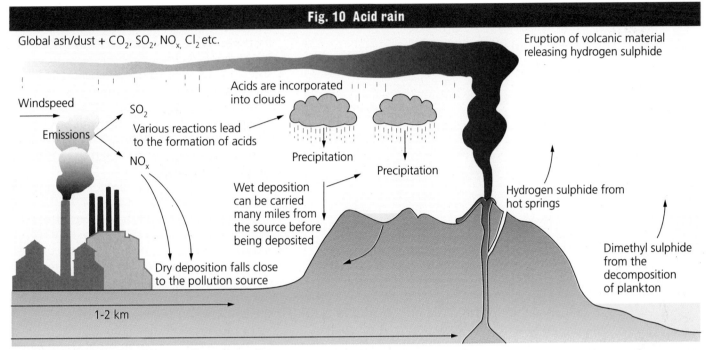

Fig. 10 Acid rain

Global ash/dust + CO_2, SO_2, NO_x, Cl_2 etc.

Eruption of volcanic material releasing hydrogen sulphide

Windspeed

Emissions

SO_2

Various reactions lead to the formation of acids

NO_x

Acids are incorporated into clouds

Precipitation

Precipitation

Wet deposition can be carried many miles from the source before being deposited

Dry deposition falls close to the pollution source

Hydrogen sulphide from hot springs

Dimethyl sulphide from the decomposition of plankton

1-2 km

100s to 1000s km

activity. They are responsible for about 85% of the acid rain that falls over Europe. Because these pollutants are spread by wind and rain, they can cause pollution many miles away from their source.

The effects of acid rain vary. Streams overlying limestone contain calcium and magnesium ions, which can neutralise the negative sulphate ions (SO_4^{2-}) in acid rain. Moorland streams flow through acidic peat with little limestone and few positive ions. There is little neutralisation and acidic waters enter the streams.

Problems in soils caused by acid rain include:
- leaching of calcium, magnesium and potassium;
- increasing solubility of aluminium, iron and manganese;
- mobilisation of toxic lead and nickel ions;
- immobilisation of some important nutrients, such as molybenium;
- inhibition of decomposition by bacteria and fungi;
- the disappearance of earthworms and molluscs, because of low calcium levels. This further reduces decomposition.

In freshwater ecosystems the damage that occurs due to a decrease in pH caused by acid rain can be dramatic. The release of aluminium ions when calcium levels are low has a number of effects, including:
- interfering with ion regulation in fish;
- reducing the efficiency of oxygen uptake by haemoglobin in fish;
- increasing mucus deposition on fish gills which reduces the efficiency of gas exchange;
- killing fish when levels become toxic;
- reducing the action of the enzyme responsible for dissolving the egg membrane of the larval stages of fish such as salmon and trout, which prevents them hatching.

Low pH can cause precipitation of phosphate in soil water. This means it does not reach the surrounding waters. As phosphate is a vital plant nutrient, phytoplankton die and their remains settle on the lake bottom. Lakes in a nutrient poor state are therefore very clear.

In a similar way to organic pollution, the best indicators of lowering pH are the distribution and diversity of freshwater invertebrates. The tolerance of freshwater organisms to acidified water varies with their requirements for calcium and the

71

Fig. 11 Plankton indicators

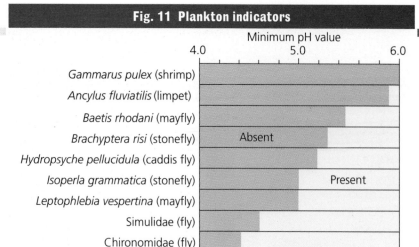

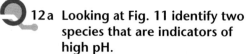

Source: Cadogan and Best, *Environment and Ecology*, Blackie, 1992

effects of aluminium. For example, in Norwegian lakes the number of species of molluscs and crustaceans decreased markedly with decreasing pH. Both of these types of organism require calcium to produce their exoskeletons. Birds such as dippers feeding on these invertebrates then produced thin-shelled eggs that did not hatch.

12 a **Looking at Fig. 11 identify two species that are indicators of high pH.**
   b **Identify two species that are indicators of low pH.**

Many rivers and lakes in Scandinavia, Scotland and Wales have pH levels below 5.5 and reduced or absent fish stocks. Acid rain is therefore a serious problem that

requires effective control. Adding lime to acidified lakes neutralises the acidity, increases the calcium levels in the soil and water, and precipitates aluminium from solution. This treatment has been tried successfully in some Scandinavian lakes. However, it is only a short-term solution and the original species may still not be able to survive there. Long-term solutions must focus on reducing or removing the causes of the gas emissions.

Most of the sulphur dioxide entering the atmosphere comes from the combustion of coal and oil. The sulphur content of coal and oil varies considerably. One way to reduce sulphur dioxide emissions is to use coal and oil with a low sulphur content or clean them to reduce their sulphur content prior to combustion. Another way is to alter the combustion methods. Recent technologies have also reduced the emissions of NO_x from internal combustion engines, for example by fitting three-way catalytic converters to new cars. The latter also reduce carbon monoxide and hydrocarbon emissions.

All these solutions are expensive and changes have been slow in some European countries. However, as the cost of the effects of acid rain start to outweigh the cost of the solutions, they are gradually being introduced.

13 **Summarise the measures that can be taken to reduce acid rain.**

5.6 Oil spills

Globally oil pollution is most dramatically and visibly evident when huge spillages occur from tankers. These pollute large areas of coastline, threatening fish, bird and other communities.

Oil tanker disasters, however, are not responsible for the largest spillages. The spill from the *IXTOC 1* oil platform blow-out in the Gulf of Mexico in 1979 held the record until the Iraqi occupation of Kuwait in 1991 (Fig. 12).

This volunteer is collecting birds killed by oil pollution after the oil tanker Braer ran aground in the Shetland Islands in January 1993, spilling 85 000 tonnes of crude oil.

Burning Kuwait oil fields. The deliberate damage to nearly 900 oil wells in Kuwait resulted in hundreds of thousands of tonnes of oil spilling into the Gulf and the desert.

Various methods are available to limit the spread of an oil spill and to break it up. These include burning, high capacity pumps like those shown here to draw off surface oil, machines to scrape up oil from the surface of the water, emulsifiers and dispersants to break the oil into droplets and help bacterial degradation. All these are methods designed to combat the short-term effects of oil pollution. The longer term effects of oil pollution are still not fully understood.

Oil pollution causes:
- suffocation of fish, as gasolene coats their gills;
- immobilisation of fish sperm, reducing fish fertility rates;
- coating the feathers of birds, reducing their buoyancy and insulation;
- intestinal irritation and pneumonia in birds which swallow the oil;
- reduction in the permeability of birds' eggs;
- destruction of certain algae and sea grasses, which are important primary producers in marine food webs.

In 1996, the Sea Empress ran aground off the Pembrokeshire coast, spilling 80 000 tonnes of crude oil. Thirty to forty per cent of mussels in the area died.

Q 14 Suggest how the local fishing industry will have been affected.

The EA does not have to deal with oil pollution of the sea, but significant levels of oil enter freshwater systems from waste motor oils. This oil may have been incorrectly dumped into domestic drains, or come from road surface run-off. It can have an synergistic effect on other

Fig. 12 Oil pollution

Kuwait 1991
1 000 000

Ixtoc 1979
(Mexico) 475 000

Amoco Cadiz 1978
(France) 223 000

Sea Empress 1996
(Wales) 80 000

Exxon Valdez 1989
(Alaska) 35 000

pollutants. The water that runs off industrial sites as they are cleaned or after rain can also be a cause of pollution.

Table 4. Factory yard run-off		
	Numbers present before yard run-off	Numbers present after yard run-off
Flatworms	2	0
Snails	1298	15
True worms	781	1008
Leeches	47	0
Freshwater shrimp	5080	2
Mayfly	2	0
Beetles	72	0
Midge larvae	337	37
Total	7691	1062

Q15 In Table 4, what indicates that this site has suffered from toxic pollution such as diesel residues rather than organic pollution? Refer to Table 1 and Fig. 8.

A single accident or careless act by humans can cause considerable environmental harm. In time, the harmful effects can be reversed if the polluting influence is removed. Knowledge of the environment and the pollutants speeds up the reversal. Monitoring normal conditions, as well as in response to pollution incidents, is therefore very important. The EA is one group that helps monitor habitats and find sources of pollution. Its role in controlling and preventing water pollution helps reduce environmental damage.

In aquatic ecosystems, how bad we think pollution is often depends on how we want to use the water. For example, water that is suitable for fishing may have to be cleaned up considerably before it can be used as drinking water.

Key ideas

• Heavy metal ions can persist in the environment for a long time, and tend to bioaccumulate.

• Acid rain can be caused by industrial pollution carried a long way from its source.

• The effect of heavy metal ions and acid rain on an aquatic ecosystem varies depending on the abiotic characteristics of the environment.

• Oil pollution, from road run-off to oil well disasters, can have devastating effects on aquatic environments, the long-term effects of which are still unknown.

When to conserve?

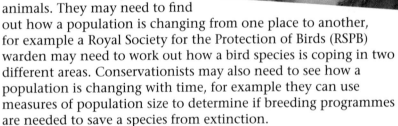

This sign is part of a woodland education scheme at a Site of Special Scientific Interest (SSSI), Roeburndale Woods in Lancashire. Before such a scheme can be set up, information about the ecology of the site has to be collected and analysed. I am collecting data on the plant communities, to find the rarest species and help work out a conservation programme.

Many ecologists need to collect data on the abundance and distribution of plants and animals. They may need to find out how a population is changing from one place to another, for example a Royal Society for the Protection of Birds (RSPB) warden may need to work out how a bird species is coping in two different areas. Conservationists may also need to see how a population is changing with time, for example they can use measures of population size to determine if breeding programmes are needed to save a species from extinction.

How can you estimate the numbers of a particular species? How do you analyse the results to see if you have discovered anything significant? How would you know if something was typical for a particular habitat, and therefore should be included in information, for example in a woodland education scheme? Whether you are a conservationist, crop scientist or environmental officer, there is little point in collecting large quantities of data if you do not know what you are going to do with it.

6.1 Learning objectives

After working through this chapter, you should be able to:

- **explain** the need to sample populations;

- **select** and use appropriate sampling techniques;

- **recall** the main measures of abundance;

- **describe** the techniques for estimating animal populations;

- **display** results in appropriate graphical forms;

- **use** standard deviation and chi-square tests;

- **explain** that conservation is the planned use of resources.

6.2 What is conservation?

Conservation is not the same as **preservation**. Preservation is keeping something the same without allowing for change. Conservation is a dynamic, ever changing, process that aims to keep ecosystems stable as environmental conditions change. The environment changes naturally, for example on a seasonal basis and through the effects of ecological succession. Human activity also changes the environment. We can change habitats for the worse, for example by causing acid rain, but we can also change habitats for the better, for example by reclaiming industrial wastelands.

In order for any conservation programme to work, the ecologists involved have to collect as much data as possible about the abiotic and biotic characteristics of the ecosystem. They must also monitor the area over time so that they are aware of

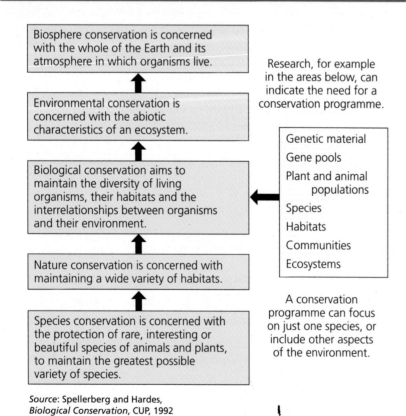

This area was originally the site of a bauxite mine. After the mining was finished, the site was seeded so that it could become reforested. A sample area of four square metres is used to monitor regularly the species composition of the area, to make sure the original mix of plants is present.

any changes to the communities and ecosystems. Often the need to conserve a species or a population or a habitat is only realised as the result of ecological research (Fig. 1).

 1 Suggest some abiotic characteristics that should be monitored in woodland habitats.

The techniques that conservationists use depend on the type of study they are carrying out. They may be:
- measuring **species composition**, i.e. what species are present;
- measuring **species abundance**, the population size of each species;
- comparing the communities of two or more sites;
- determining whether or not two species are likely to be found together.

Before they can start any monitoring or sampling, they have to plan their investigation. For example, they have to consider:
- will the technique just indicate presence or absence of species?
- are absolute numbers or the relative abundance of species needed?
- what idea is being tested?
- what sort of evidence could support or reject the idea?

Fig. 1 Conservation

Biosphere conservation is concerned with the whole of the Earth and its atmosphere in which organisms live.

Environmental conservation is concerned with the abiotic characteristics of an ecosystem.

Biological conservation aims to maintain the diversity of living organisms, their habitats and the interrelationships between organisms and their environment.

Nature conservation is concerned with maintaining a wide variety of habitats.

Species conservation is concerned with the protection of rare, interesting or beautiful species of animals and plants, to maintain the greatest possible variety of species.

Research, for example in the areas below, can indicate the need for a conservation programme.

Genetic material
Gene pools
Plant and animal populations
Species
Habitats
Communities
Ecosystems

A conservation programme can focus on just one species, or include other aspects of the environment.

Source: Spellerberg and Hardes, *Biological Conservation*, CUP, 1992

6.3 Why sample?

If conservationists, or other ecologists, are interested in a particular species, they rarely attempt to count all the individuals in a population. Could you imagine a crop scientist trying to count all the wheat plants in a field or a fish scientist trying to count all the herring in the sea! Even in far less ambitious projects, it would be extremely boring and time-consuming to count every organism. It would also disturb and damage the habitat. All ecologists have to be careful not to study environments to destruction or species to extinction.

Instead, **samples** are taken, which represent the whole population. The method of sampling chosen depends on:
- what is being sampled;
- how many samples are needed;
- where the samples will be collected from.

Conservationists have to ask themselves if the sampling technique to be used will make the best use of time and energy.

To take a **random sample**, the area to be sampled is divided into a grid of non-overlapping units of equal size (Fig. 2). Each unit is given a number, and then numbers are selected using a table of random numbers (see Appendix 1) or a calculator with a random number key. Each number must have an equal chance of being chosen. The units with the chosen numbers are the ones that are sampled.

For **systematic sampling** a grid is laid over a map of the area being studied and sampling points are located at regular intervals (Fig. 2).

A line transect or belt transect can be used to highlight changes in species composition and abundance. They can show how the species in a community can change as the habitat changes.

Fig. 2 Sampling grids

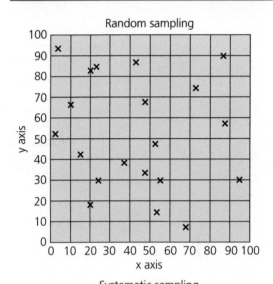
Random sampling

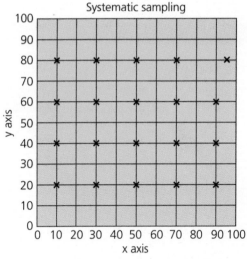
Systematic sampling

Q 2 From Fig. 2, suggest possible disadvantages to random sampling.

Transects are a type of systematic sampling. The samples are arranged in a line. Transects are useful for recording changes in species present where some sort of transition occurs, such as from water to land or from one soil type to another. For example:

estuary → salt marsh → shingle
bog → wet heath → heathland
sandy shore → fore dunes → yellow dunes → grey dunes

There are two common types of transect. The **line transect** is a quick technique. A tape is laid across the sample area, and the species that touch the tape are then recorded. The species can be recorded all the way along the tape or at regular intervals, for example every 0.5 m.

The **belt transect** is a strip (usually 0. 25 m wide) of the area of study. The strip is chosen where changes can be seen with the naked eye. With a **continuous belt transect** species are recorded within the whole of the strip. This can be very time consuming with transects over 15 m long. It is more usual to sample every metre. This gives a **ladder transect** with gaps in the coverage.

 3 Suggest why a line transect is a good way to collect samples to investigate changes along a steep rocky shoreline.

Quadrats can be used with transects. They are frames used to mark the boundaries of the sample area (Fig. 3). They are placed along the transect line or within the belt transect.

But how do you decide where to place your quadrats if you want to use them for random sampling? Throwing a quadrat over your shoulder does not achieve randomness and can damage the quadrat and perhaps other ecologists! A better way is to use a sampling grid.

All the different species in a Site of Special Scientific Interest (SSSI) may need to be sampled. The sampling technique may also need to give a true indication of the population sizes in the area. When different people are asked to study the same area using frame quadrats, they often come up with results that vary a great deal. **Point quadrats** give more objective and accurate results because they depend less on chance (Fig. 4).

4 Explain why point quadrats may be better to use than frame quadrats in a study of the abundance of a small orchid in a SSSI.

Fig. 3 Frame quadrats

Quadrats can be made from wood, wire and plastic.

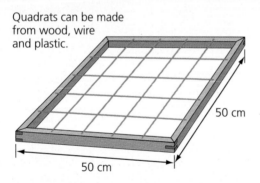

Larger quadrats, eg for sampling in woodland, can be laid out with string and pegs.

50 cm

All the species within a quadrat can be counted, or the abundance of a particular species estimated.

50 cm

A 0.5 m quadrat gives an area of 0.25 m². Wire fixed at 10 cm intervals gives 25 smaller units, to make counting easier.

Quadrats can be used in studies by crop scientists. Different crops may be grown under different conditions, and the percentage cover or presence and absence of weed species then monitored.

Fig. 4 Point quadrats

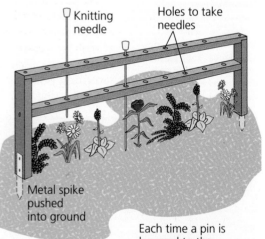

Knitting needle

Holes to take needles

Metal spike pushed into ground

Each time a pin is lowered to the ground through a hole, the number of times each species of plant is touched is recorded.

Fig. 5 Clumped distribution

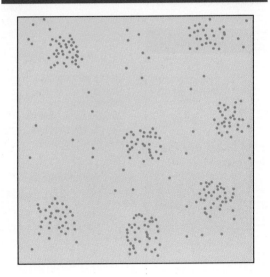

Fig. 6 Use of quadrats

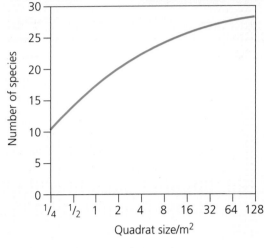

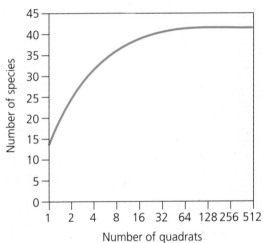

If the plants within a population were distributed randomly, then all sizes of quadrat would be equally efficient in estimating population size. However, plants are often distributed in clumps (Fig. 5).

After a certain size of quadrat, any further increase brings in very few new species. As more quadrats are used, a point is eventually reached when all the common species have been included in the sample (Fig. 6). Adding any more quadrats is not worth the extra time and effort required.

Within a SSSI, it may be discovered that two species of plant occur together more frequently than by chance. If one species occurs in 70% (0.7) of the quadrats and another species occurs in 50% (0.5), then it would be expected that the two would occur together in $0.70 \times 0.50 = 0.35$ (35%) of the quadrats. If they occur together in many more quadrats than this, then they are positively associated. The management of the habitat and any conservation programme would have to take this into account.

5 a Explain how you would decide how many quadrats should be used to provide as accurate a population estimate as possible.

b Explain how you would decide what size of quadrat should be used.

6.4 Measures of abundance

Table 1. Measures of abundance

Method	Measures	Example
Density	The mean number of individuals of a particular species per unit area	The mean number of weed plants in an organic crop
Frequency	The number or percentage of sampling units in which a particular species occurs	The frequency of orchid species within a nature reserve
Biomass	The dry mass of species in a certain area at a certain time	The hay yield from a natural water meadow
Cover	The percentage of the ground covered by a species within the sampling unit	The cover of sand dunes by couch grass

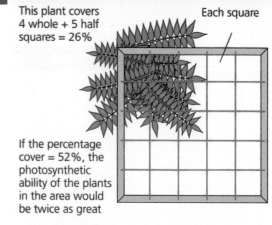

Fig. 7 Percentage cover

This plant covers 4 whole + 5 half squares = 26%

Each square

If the percentage cover = 52%, the photosynthetic ability of the plants in the area would be twice as great

To measure cover:

lay a frame quadrat over the selected area;

count the number of squares occupied by the plant species in question;

count those squares that are partially occupied;

estimate how many full squares this would represent and add it to the total.

Different methods of measurement will provide different sorts of data about the populations of species sampled. There are four main measures of abundance used in ecological investigations (Table 1).

 6 **What is the disadvantage of working out the dry biomass of a species?**

Cover estimates are important because they can be used as a measure of the photosynthetic ability of the plants in an area (Fig. 7). The percentage cover with a point quadrat is calculated as:

$$\frac{\text{hits}}{\text{hits} + \text{misses}} \times 100$$

Fifteen point quadrats were used to estimate the percentage cover of a weed in the same habitat as a rare woodland plant. The number of hits for the weed species was 20. The total number of hits and misses was 150 (15 quadrats each with 10 points).

 7 a **Calculate the percentage cover.**
b **If the percentage cover of the weed had previously been 8, what do the results indicate?**

Percentage cover values may exceed 100% when the hits for different species are added together, because the pin of a point quadrat may touch more than one species of plant on the way down. If the same species of plant is hit by the same pin more than once, then it only counts as one hit. This prevents the cover recorded for a single species exceeding 100%.

Key ideas

- Sampling can be random or systematic, using grids or transects.

- Random sampling can be used to discover the diversity and relative abundance of organisms.

- Transects are useful for recording changes in species composition and abundance along a transition zone.

- Frame quadrats provide manageable areas to sample. Point quadrats are more objective than frame quadrats.

- Quadrats can be used in studies measuring diversity and abundance.

- Species abundance can be measured as density, frequency, biomass or cover.

6.5 Animal populations

Plant and animal communities require different sampling strategies. Plants stay in one place and are easy to see, so generally pose few problems. Many animals, on the other hand, move around, hide or are only active at night, so some form of net or trap needs to be used.

A technique called **mark, release and recapture** (MRR) is used to study many animal populations (Fig. 8).

Population size can then be measured using the **Lincoln Index**:

$$P = \frac{M \times S}{R}$$

P = the estimate of population size;
M = the number captured, marked and released in the first sample;
S = the number captured in the second sample;
R = the number of marked animals recaptured in the second sample.

The method is based upon the idea that the ratio of marked to unmarked individuals in the second sample is the same as the ratio of individuals in the first sample to the total population.

One night, a warden of the SSSI took a sample of 60 moths from a light-trap. Each moth was marked with a small drop of cellulose paint. The moths were released

This mouse has been marked by clipping off some fur. This does not harm the mouse. The mouse can then be identified if it appears in a second sample.

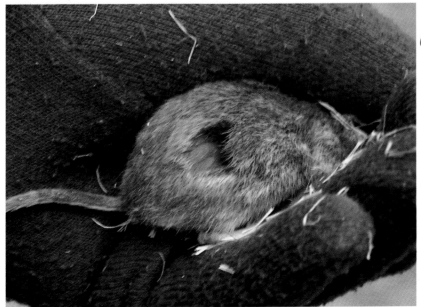

Fig. 8 Mark, release and recapture

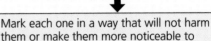

Catch a sample of the animals you want to study and count them.

Mark each one in a way that will not harm them or make them more noticeable to predators.

Release your sample back into their habitat and allow one or two days for them to mix back into their own population.

Take a second sample and count the total numbers along with the number marked from the first sample.

and left for 48 hours to mix back into their population. On the next night a second sample was taken. This time 50 moths were caught and 15 of these had paint marks.

Q 8 Estimate the population size using the Lincoln Index.

Fish scientists can also use MRR to sample populations of fish like plaice and cod. The fish are netted and plastic discs are attached to the base of the dorsal fin. Records of the time and place of release of the fish are kept. A small reward is given for the return of the discs with the details of recapture. In experiments carried out in the North Sea over 30% of tagged plaice were recaptured within 12 months of release. This percentage could be compared with the total landings of the commercial plaice fishery to gain an estimate of the total plaice population of the North Sea.

81

The Lincoln Index assumes that:
- the marked animals redistribute themselves randomly among the unmarked;
- the marks do not come off between marking and recapture;
- the marks do not affect the behaviour of the animals nor make them more noticeable to predators;
- being caught in the first sample will not increase or decrease the chances of being caught in the second sample;
- there is no movement of individuals into or out of the populations during the experiment;
- no births or deaths occur in the population during the experiment.

 9 a Suggest a species where marks are likely to come off during the experiment. Explain your answer.
b Explain how births and deaths occurring in the population during the experiment would spoil the population estimate.

In order to catch highly mobile animals such as fish or winged insects ecologists often have to use **nets**. The particular net design will depend upon its specific use (Table 2).

Samples taken with a general collecting net can be used to compare the species diversity between different streams, or different parts of streams.

10 Suggest an investigation where it will be important to quote the mesh size of the net used in the results.

Terrestrial populations can also be sampled using **traps** (Fig. 9).

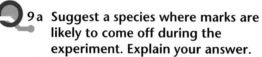

Table 2. Features of nets		
Net	**Function**	**Features**
Air nets		
Butterfly net	Catching flying insects	Short handle for ease of use, large mesh bag
Sweep net	Catching invertebrates in low growing vegetation	Long handle for brushing through vegetation, robust, small mesh bag
Water nets		
General collecting net	Sampling fresh water invertebrates	Long handle, with fitting for extension pole
Plankton net	Collecting phytoplankton and zooplankton	Robust frame to support a bag full of water, with a collecting jar at end
Dredge net	Sampling invertebrates on pond bed, can also be used on grassland	Towed by means of a harness and line
Surber sampler	Getting quantitative samples of invertebrates on sea or lake bottom	Incorporates frame for sampling 0.1 m² area, so gives more quantitative data
Drift net	Sampling invertebrate drift	Frame secured to river bed by metal rods, with sample bottle at end of net

Fig. 9 Traps

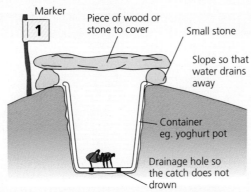

Pitfall traps can be used to trap invertebrates that are active on the soil surface or in leaf litter. 10% methanal (formalin) can be placed in the pitfall to kill predators that might otherwise kill other captives. Pitfalls are cheap and easy to use, but the number of individuals caught tends to reflect the activity of a particular species as well as its abundance.

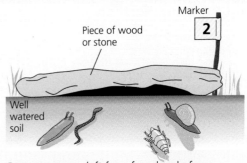

Cover traps are left for a few days before inspection. Like pitfalls they can be baited with meat, jam or potato. The catch includes slow moving animals like slugs, earthworms, snails and woodlice, rather than the faster moving invertebrates caught in pitfalls.

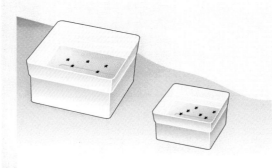

Water traps are left on open ground at different heights. Yellow coloured traps seem to attract aphids while white attracts flies. They can be made from old ice cream cartons, half filled with water. Some washing up liquid can be added to reduce the surface tension so that insects landing on the water will sink.

Source: Adapted from Wiltshire Trust for Nature Conservation

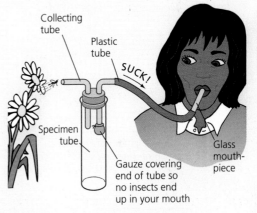

Pooters are not traps, but are useful when collecting small, easily damaged insects from small crevices in bark and stone walls.

Key ideas

- Animal populations are often studied using mark, release and recapture.

- The Lincoln index provides an measure of population size.

- Nets and traps that are appropriate for the species being studied have to be chosen.

6.6 Using the data

Fig. 10 Displaying data

Give your graph a title and label the axes clearly, including the units.

Line graphs are a simple means of showing the relationship between two variables, for example time and population size.

Line graphs are often used because any trends are quickly identifiable. It is usually best to join the points with a straight line.

Choose the scale carefully since it will determine the visual impression that the graph conveys.

It is usual to plot the dependent variable on the vertical or y axis, and the independent variable on the horizontal or x axis. The **independent variable** causes the **dependent variable** to change.

Scatter graphs plot points as dots without joining them up with a line. The pattern of dots can show a relationship between two variables. A line of 'best-fit' can be drawn to highlight the general trend of the dots.

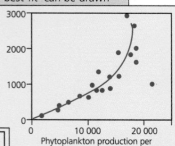

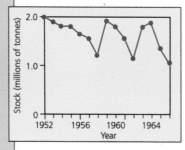

Kites are plotted as symmetrical line graphs either side of a base line. They are often used to display transect data. The higher the value, the wider the kite.

The **histogram** is sometimes confused with the bar chart, but histograms record **continuous data**, for example weight, height, time, which can include any value. In a histogram, the relative size of the data is shown by the area of each block.

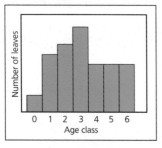

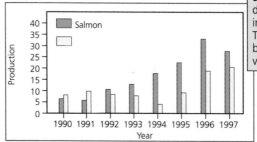

Bar charts are used to compare **discontinuous data**. Discontinuous data are data that can be grouped into convenient categories, e.g. years. The data are represented by drawing bars proportional in height to the values that they represent.

Pie graphs display the relative proportions of sections from the whole sample. The total area of a pie graph can represent the species' abundance in a sample.

Pyramids are histograms with areas proportional to the data collected for each category.

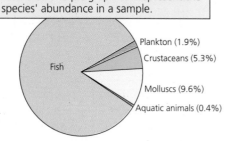

3.1 g m^{-2} Carnivores

8.3 g m^{-2} Herbivores

4727 Producers

If more than one set of data are to be displayed, then graphs may be superimposed one on the other. However, if two sets of data are to be compared, it is better to draw two adjacent graphs.

Data from the field are often disorganised and messy. Before the data can be interpreted, they need to be organised and displayed in a convenient form. Tables, graphs and diagrams can be used (Fig. 10). These can summarise data more effectively than a written account. The method used will depend on what the ecologist expects to find and how the results are to be used. The data can be displayed in a different way for the ecologists working on the conservation programme and for information panels for visitors.

Table 3. Number of duckweed plants		
Days	**Species A**	**Species B**
0	30	30
16	48	105
36	84	234
46	84	324
54	48	360
60	45	354

Duckweed grows on the surface of ponds within the SSSI. To find out how two species interact, they were grown together in a beaker (Table 3).

11a Present the data in a suitable graphical form, giving reasons for your choice.

b Suggest an explanation for the interaction between the two species.

c To be a fair test, the investigator should have also grown the two species separately. Explain why.

Table 4. The principal species of the world's fish landed in 1988	
Species	**Million metric tons**
Alaska pollack	6.6
Japanese pilchard	5.4
South American pilchard	5.0
Peruvian anchoveta	3.6
Chilean jack mackerel	3.3
Atlantic cod	2.0
Chub mackerel	1.8
Atlantic herring	1.7
European pilchard	1.3
Skipjack tuna	1.2

In order to determine which stocks need to be conserved, the size of the fisheries in Table 4 need to be analysed.

12a Represent the data in a suitable graphical form, giving reasons for your choice.

b In 1972, the Peruvian anchoveta contributed more than 12 million metric tonnes. Suggest why the size of the catch has fallen.

Foxgloves and dog rose are growing in this hedge in the Arnside/Silverdale Area of Outstanding Natural Beauty (AONB), in Lancashire.

The fruits of foxglove were collected from a mixed hedgerow. Their lengths were measured in millimetres and recorded (Table 5) to compare with previous data taken before the AONB was managed.

Table 5. Foxglove lengths							
14	18	13	16	15	16	13	17
19	14	18	14	16	15	16	19
14	15	11	19	12	19	15	19
16	19	14	21	19	18	15	16
18	17	15	13	19	20	18	20
15	15	14	12	16	15	15	20
19	17	16	15	13	18	19	15

13a Assemble the data in Table 5 to show the frequency of each length.

b Display the data in a suitable graphical form, giving reasons for your choice.

6.7 Statistical analysis

When faced with large amounts of data, it is often easier to summarise it in order to make it more manageable. The average, or **mean**, is found by adding the values together and dividing the total by the number of values. However, on its own, the mean can be misleading because it gives no information about the spread of data around it. For example, the mean rainfall for the year might be 30 mm. But this tells us nothing about how much variation there was about the mean. In one month there may have been no rainfall at all. The **standard deviation** enables us to measure the spread of data around its mean (Fig. 11). The greater the spread of the data, the less use the mean will be as a summary of it. Many calculators and computers have programs to calculate the standard deviation of samples directly from original data.

The higher the standard deviation, the greater the spread of data around the mean. The standard deviation is a better measure of this spread than the mean because it takes account of all the values in the data set.

Graphs and charts display data and may suggest a relationship between two variables. A statistical test can help decide if this relationship is **significant**. Significance is a measure of whether a result has happened by chance.

Different statistical tests require certain data. Before any ecologist begins an experiment or study, the appropriate statistical tests have to be considered. This will influence the number of samples taken.

The **chi-squared test** can be used to compare two variables (Fig. 12). It can only be used if there are at least two sets of frequency data, and the total number of observations has to be more than 20. The expected frequency in any category should not be less than five, and the observations should not influence each other.

If the null hypothesis is rejected, then there is a significant relationship between the two variables being studied. In order to

Fig. 11 Standard deviation

Number of mayfly larvae, x, in samples taken daily from a stream within a SSSI.

Sample number	x	x^2
1	12	144
2	16	256
3	17	289
4	23	529
5	26	676
6	24	576
7	16	256
8	10	100
9	7	49
10	5	25

$\Sigma x = 156$ $\Sigma x^2 = 2900$

$\bar{x} = \dfrac{156}{10} = 15.6$

$\bar{x}^2 = (15.6)^2 = 243.36$

$n = 10$

$\sigma = \sqrt{\left(\dfrac{2900}{10} - 243.36\right)} = 6.8$

x = the values
x^2 = the values squared

1 Add together all the values of x, and all the values of x^2.

2 Find the mean of all the values of x and square it.

3 Calculate the standard deviation, σ

$\sigma = \sqrt{\left(\dfrac{\Sigma x^2}{n} - \bar{x}^2\right)}$

Σ = the sum (total) of the values
$\sqrt{}$ = square root of
n = the number of values
$\bar{x}$ = the mean of the values

6.8 is the standard deviation of the data from the mean. Therefore the true mean lies within the range 15.6 ± 6.8.

Fig. 12 Chi-square

The numbers of snails found amongst four different plant species within a SSSI were sampled. The ecologist needs to know if the results are a true indication of the distribution of snails on the plants, or are a result of chance.

The **null hypothesis** is that the distribution is purely chance. If the plant species has no effect on the distribution of snails then an equal number of snails would be expected to be found on each species of plant, i.e. the number of snails found altogether (in this case 100) divided by the number of plant species (4). Therefore 25 snails would be expected on each plant species.

Plant species	Observed frequency (O)	Expected frequency (E)	$\dfrac{(O - E)^2}{E}$
1	5	25	$(5-25)^2 \div 25 = 16.0$
2	16	25	$(16-25)^2 \div 25 = 3.24$
3	23	25	$(23-25)^2 \div 25 = 0.16$
4	56	25	$(56-25)^2 \div 25 = 38.44$

1 Calculate the chi-square, χ^2:

$\chi^2 = \Sigma \dfrac{(O - E)^2}{E}$

Σ = sum of
O = observed frequency
E = expected frequency

$\chi^2 = 57.84$

2 Calculate the degrees of freedom, which is one less than the total number of categories:

   df = n − 1   df = degrees of freedom

   df = 3   n = number of test categories

3 From the graph in Appendix 2 read off the degrees of freedom (3) on the horizontal axis against the χ^2 value (57.8) on the vertical axis. The resulting point lies above the line marked 0.1 chance in 100. Therefore the probability that the data could be due to chance is less than 1 in 1000. The evidence is significantly against the null hypothesis, which must be rejected.

This is the River Rea at Calthorpe Park, to the south of Birmingham, where it flows through a human-made concrete-lined channel.

This is the East Lyn River, following a natural course through Watersmeet in Exmoor National Park.

conserve the snail species, plant species 4 has to be conserved but plant species 1 is not so important.

The work of many ecologists involves a great deal of data collection and analysis. This is vital to conservation work because the results of the data anlysis indicate the interrelationships between species and their habitats. The more that is known about a species within a SSSI, the more successful the conservation programme can be. And the more clearly the data can be presented, the easier it is to inform people of the importance of an area.

Many ecological investigations involve collecting sets of data from two study areas and comparing them. Two rivers, such as those in the photographs, may look very different. By using correct sampling techniques and presenting the results in a clear way, ecologists can show exactly how different they are. The results may be part of a study to see what effect altering the river channel has had on the species diversity of the urban river.

 14 a List three visible differences between the two rivers.
b Suggest how the diversity of species may vary between the two rivers.

Ecological monitoring by data collection is closely linked with habitat management. If the changes in land use are shown to have a significant negative effect on the species abundance and diversity in an area, the way we use the land can be changed. Conservation programmes can be developed to keep the ecosystem stable.

Conservationists have to plan their investigations thoroughly, in order to obtain data that can be analysed to give meaningful results. The results are then used to plan the management of ecosystems, whether the habitats are to be conserved, harvested or used by humans in some other way. The demands of people on natural and semi-natural ecosystems has to be balanced against the ability of the ecosystem to adapt to change and support different species populations and communities.

Creative conservation includes any large-scale change of the landscape by human activity that presents opportunities for conservation. The opportunities can include tree planting, creation of new lakes, and provision of bird and bat boxes. Conservation is an attitude to land use that plans the use of natural resources to maintain diversity and leave the land in a fit state for the next generation.

Key ideas

- A variety of graphs can be used to illustrate data as clearly as possible.

- Statistical tests can be used to check the significance of the data analysed.

- The most appropriate sampling and analysing techniques must be chosen to provide meaningful and useful data.

- Conservation involves the planned use of natural resources based on the results of in-depth, meaningful investigations of the resources.

87

Fish food

Hundreds of British ferry passengers were stranded either side of the Channel last night as French fishermen blockaded the Dover–Calais route. Fifty trawlermen from Boulogne, protesting at imports of non-EU fish, used nine boats to barricade the entrance to Calais harbour.

Earlier, fishermen had destroyed a cargo of Scottish cod in Brittany and, in a parallel dispute over fishing rights off the Channel Islands, burned a Scottish trawler at Cherbourg. Anti-import violence first erupted at the Rugnis wholesale fish market outside Paris, where 1200 masked fishermen, wielding iron bars and baseball bats, wrecked a wide area. As police cars were overturned, 600 officers from the riot squad retaliated with baton charges and tear gas. The mob then moved to Boulogne, where they ran riot after police refused to let them into the docks. A 300-strong gang stormed three supermarkets, destroying fish products.

Source: adapted from an article by Peter Shard, *Daily Mail*, 4 February 1994

Clash between policemen and protesting trawlermen.

The British are renowned for enjoying their fish and chips. But do we understand why fish populations and the livelihood of fishermen are under threat?

More than half of the world's fishing grounds are overfished and the rest are fully exploited. Fishing wars will continue until the world's oceans are better managed. The main problem is that resources are declining rapidly. Put simply, there are too many boats chasing too few fish.

7.1 Learning objectives

After working through this chapter, you should be able to:

- **describe** the effects of underfishing and overfishing;

- **describe** the relationship between productivity and maximum sustainable yield;

- **describe** the methods that can be used to regulate fisheries, including net size restrictions, quotas, close seasons and exclusion zones;

- **evaluate** the advantages and disadvantages of the use of long lines, trawls, drift nets and purse seines for capturing fish;

- **evaluate** the success of regulation of different fisheries;

- **compare** extensive and intensive methods of fish farming;

- **evaluate** the positive and negative effects of intensive fish farms;

- **recognise** that solutions may require compromise between different interests and priorities.

7.2 Fishing dynamics

The advances in fishing technology have increased the landings of fish. Between 1980 and 1989 there was a one-third increase in world landings, to more than 100 million tonnes. Since then the figure has dropped to 97 million tonnes in 1990 and 1991. At present the size of fish catches is being maintained by catching younger, smaller fish. This ultimately threatens the survival of commercial fish stocks and wild fish populations.

 1 Suggest why taking younger, smaller fish is so dangerous to stocks.

In 1990, the United Nations Food and Agriculture Organisation (FAO) classified virtually every commercial fish species, in every ocean and sea, as being 'depleted', 'fully exploited' or 'over-exploited'. Greater efforts to catch fish are no longer producing increased landings. The over-intensive fishing could cause a collapse of fish stocks and the extinction of some species.

The **biomass** of a fish stock is the total mass of all living fish per unit volume or area, at a particular time (Fig. 1). The biomass of a population increases due to fish growth and **recruitment**. Recruitment is the addition of new individuals that are either born into the population, or join it from elsewhere. The biomass of fish stocks decreases due to natural mortality and the effects of fishing.

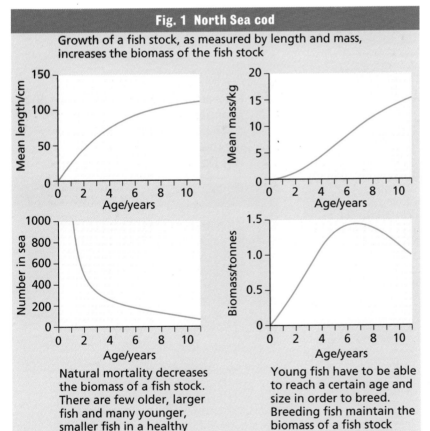

Fig. 1 North Sea cod

Growth of a fish stock, as measured by length and mass, increases the biomass of the fish stock

Natural mortality decreases the biomass of a fish stock. There are few older, larger fish and many younger, smaller fish in a healthy fish stock.

Young fish have to be able to reach a certain age and size in order to breed. Breeding fish maintain the biomass of a fish stock

In a stock of cod, it is best to let the fish reach 6 years of age before they are caught, so that they can breed for about three seasons.

Source: Macer and Easey, *The North Sea Cod and the English Fishery Laboratory Leaflet 61*, MAFF, 1988

Cod have been overfished in many areas of the world. If fewer fish are caught and sold, then the price of fish and chips has to go up.

E. S. Russell developed an equation that shows the effects of various fishing intensities on the size of fish stocks:

$$S_2 = S_1 + (A+G) - (C+M)$$

S_1 = biomass of stock at beginning of year;
S_2 = biomass of stock at the end of year;
A = biomass of young fish added to stock;
G = biomass added by growth of all fish in the stock;
C = biomass caught by fishery;
M = biomass lost through natural mortality.

If the size of the fish stock is stable then $S_2 = S_1$, i.e. there is no net increase in biomass over the year.

The **natural yield** is an increase in biomass if no fishing takes place: A + G − M. It is a measure of productivity.

If fishing occurs and the total stock biomass remains unchanged, then C + M must equal A + G. In this case fishing is removing an **equilibrium catch**, i.e. the biomass of fish that exactly equals the natural yield of the stock.

Fishing stocks can be overfished or underfished (Fig. 2). Underfishing and overfishing both push the stock biomass below the natural yield. Therefore a balance has to be struck. The ideal outcome would be to manage stocks at a level that results in a profitable catch rate for the fisherman and at the same time ensures a sustained yield. If the effort of the fishermen and the size of the catch can be kept at the right levels, a high level of productivity can be maintained. This level of productivity is called the **maximum sustainable yield** (MSY), and does not result in over- or underfishing (Fig. 3).

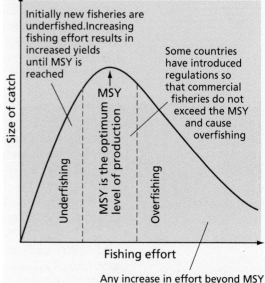

Fig. 3 The catch-effort curve

Initially new fisheries are underfished. Increasing fishing effort results in increased yields until MSY is reached

Some countries have introduced regulations so that commercial fisheries do not exceed the MSY and cause overfishing

MSY is the optimum level of production

Underfishing

Overfishing

Size of catch / Fishing effort

Any increase in effort beyond MSY will result in overfishing and productivity will fall. It is no longer economical to fish. By reducing their effort, fishermen could increase their catch

Q2 For each fishery in Fig. 4 explain the changes over time of:
(i) the total yield of the fishery;
(ii) the yield per unit effort;
(iii) the mean size of fish caught.

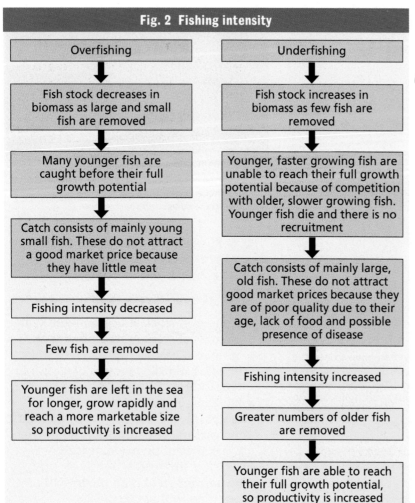

Fig. 2 Fishing intensity

Overfishing	Underfishing
Fish stock decreases in biomass as large and small fish are removed	Fish stock increases in biomass as few fish are removed
Many younger fish are caught before their full growth potential	Younger, faster growing fish are unable to reach their full growth potential because of competition with older, slower growing fish. Younger fish die and there is no recruitment
Catch consists of mainly young small fish. These do not attract a good market price because they have little meat	Catch consists of mainly large, old fish. These do not attract good market prices because they are of poor quality due to their age, lack of food and possible presence of disease
Fishing intensity decreased	Fishing intensity increased
Few fish are removed	Greater numbers of older fish are removed
Younger fish are left in the sea for longer, grow rapidly and reach a more marketable size so productivity is increased	Younger fish are able to reach their full growth potential, so productivity is increased

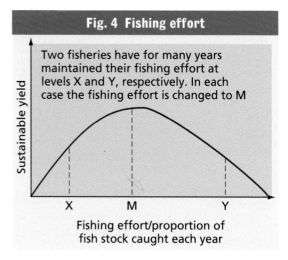

Fig. 4 Fishing effort

Two fisheries have for many years maintained their fishing effort at levels X and Y, respectively. In each case the fishing effort is changed to M

Sustainable yield

X   M   Y

Fishing effort/proportion of fish stock caught each year

New fishing technology, largely supported by European Community (EC) funding, has increased fishing effort. As a result many species are now overfished. In 1982 the Common Fisheries Policy (CFP) was agreed by the members of the EC in order to manage fish in EC waters. The policy was intended to ensure that fish stocks were healthy and that the industry remained profitable. This, it was hoped, would enable the fishing industry to match international competition, ensure a good living for its fishermen and guarantee regular fish supplies at competitive prices.

The regulations imposed are not necessarily designed to protect the fish, although conservation of fish stocks would ensure fishermen have a livelihood in the future. The main aim of regulating commercial fisheries is an economic one. Overfishing a species usually makes continued fishing unprofitable for all the companies concerned, although there is a view that overfishing while fish are available and investing the money in the bank is economically a good idea.

However, the regulations to prevent overfishing are often opposed by the people that they are designed to help. Reducing the catch in the short term, to allow recovery of stocks and provide increased catches in the future, reduces fishermen's immediate income. Reduced fish stocks may cause fishermen to fish more, so that they can get a good catch and so earn a living. This results in a further reduction in the size of the fish stock. It may also affect the reproductive capacity of the fish if they are caught before they are able to lay their eggs, called **spawn**.

There are two categories of overfishing. **Growth overfishing** is where poor catches are the result of too many fish being caught before they achieve their optimum growth. **Recruitment overfishing** is the result of too many fish being caught before they can spawn. This failure to produce enough young can lead to a rapid decline in numbers and the possibility of extinction of the species.

4 From Fig. 6, which curve represents which level of fishing? Explain your answer.

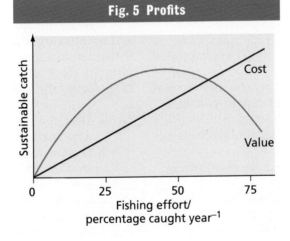

Fig. 5 Profits

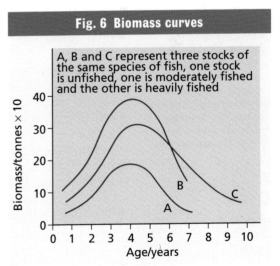

Fig. 6 Biomass curves

A, B and C represent three stocks of the same species of fish, one stock is unfished, one is moderately fished and the other is heavily fished

3 a From Fig. 5, at what level of fishing effort will the fishery show a maximum profit, and at what level will it cease to be profitable?

b If the cost of fishing was halved by a reduction in world fuel prices, but the price for the catch remained the same, at what levels of fishing effort would maximum and minimum profitability now occur?

It is not just fish species that we can bring to the point of extinction. If too many adults and juveniles are removed from a population, causing a fall in breeding rates, that population may become extinct. The extinction of one species can have far-reaching effects that are only discovered when it is too late. The humpback whale was used in Star Trek IV to make this point!

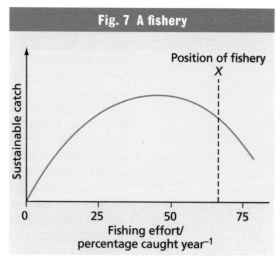

Fig. 7 A fishery

Regulations to prevent recruitment overfishing include:
- prohibiting the capture of undersized fish;
- closing spawning and/or nursery areas;
- imposing a minimum mesh or hook size.

The current method of EC management consists of a system of quotas based on the TAC. Fishermen are only able to target certain species under this system; young fish and fish caught out of season are returned to the sea. However, many of the returned fish may already be dead. The EC has no real monitoring or policing system, so fishermen can misreport their catches and virtually catch what they want, irrespective of quotas or the effects upon stocks.

The main regulations for protecting fish stocks fall into two corresponding categories.

Regulations to prevent growth overfishing include:
- total restrictions on fishing over-exploited species;
- imposing quotas limiting the total annual catch (TAC) allowed of certain species in certain areas;
- limiting the number of fishing vessels in an area;
- limiting the season and hours of fishing in an area;
- regulating the fishing equipment, for example the size of nets, used;
- imposing exclusion zones.

5 a Describe the condition of the fishery at point X in Fig. 7.
   b Outline four regulatory measures that might improve the size of the fishery's catch.
   c Describe three changes that would accompany an increase in sustainable catch.

Key ideas

- Underfishing and overfishing are both extremes that result in productivity below natural yields.
- The fishing effort should aim to give the maximum sustainable yield.

- Regulations aim to control fishing effort and so control fish stocks.
- These regulations include net size restrictions, quotas, close seasons and exclusion zones.

7.3 Fishing techniques

There are many techniques of fishing, but they can all be categorised into three main methods:
- luring fish to bite on a baited hook;
- scooping fish out of the water with a bag of netting;
- entangling fish in a net such as a drift net.

Luring fish

Long lines are the commercial equivalent of the angler's line. The length of the line may be as long as 100 km, with as many as 3000 baited hooks. The hooks are now baited by machine, but used to be baited by hand. There are demersal and pelagic long lines. **Demersal fish** live on the sea bed. Demersal long lines, with baited side lines, are anchored to the bottom of the sea bed and left for a couple of hours before hauling in.

Pelagic fish live in open water and swim in large groups called **shoals**. Pelagic long lines are buoyed up by floats at 300 m intervals. They are widely used by Japanese fishermen for catching tuna (Fig. 8).

If lines get entangled on the sea bed they can take a long time to recover and can damage marine life. More than 44 000 albatrosses are killed every year by Japanese long lines. The birds dive for the bait on the long line hooks, become hooked themselves and drown.

good condition and fetch a better price. This means it is a good technique for catching more expensive fish.

Scooping fish

Trawling involves dragging a tapering bag of netting over the sea bed to enclose fish living on the sea bottom. Trawling is the most common method of demersal fishing. There are two main types of trawl.

The **beam trawl** has been used for hundreds of years and was the main type of trawl when vessels were sail-driven (Fig. 9).

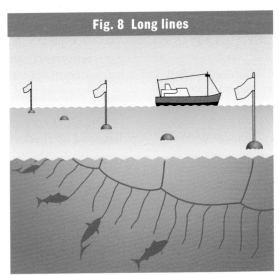

Fig. 8 Long lines

Long lines are used all over the world, and the equipment is simple and relatively inexpensive. They can be used to fish in areas where the bottom is too deep or too rocky for trawlers. Long lines can also be made selective by the choice of bait and hook size. The fish that are caught are handled individually, so they are sold in

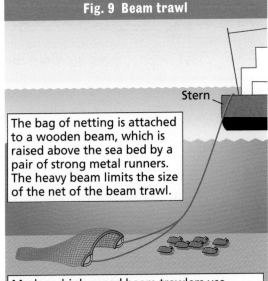

Fig. 9 Beam trawl

Stern

The bag of netting is attached to a wooden beam, which is raised above the sea bed by a pair of strong metal runners. The heavy beam limits the size of the net of the beam trawl.

Modern, high-speed beam trawlers use tickler chains to stir up the bottom-feeding flatfish. The fish swim up only to be enclosed by the net. Tickler chains and ground chains on trawls scrape up to 6 cm of sediment off the sea bed, which affects all bottom-living species. Starfish, hydroids and sea anemones can all be killed by beam trawls.

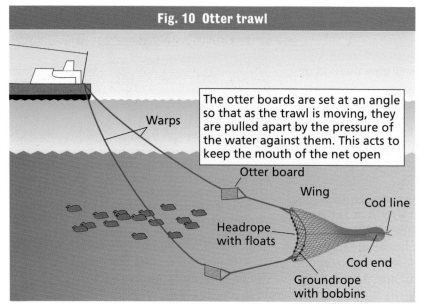

Fig. 10 Otter trawl

Warps

The otter boards are set at an angle so that as the trawl is moving, they are pulled apart by the pressure of the water against them. This acts to keep the mouth of the net open

Otter board

Wing

Cod line

Headrope with floats

Cod end

Groundrope with bobbins

Using diesel engines rather than sail means vessels can now drag bigger nets faster.

The **otter trawl** has boards called otter boards attached to the sides of the net. (Fig. 10). Otter trawls are very efficient in the capture of demersal species and much larger nets can be used than with the heavier beam trawl. But, as with all types of trawling, the trawl must not be allowed to get too full or it may split, losing the whole catch.

Some trawlers have a slipway at the stern, up which the net is hauled. This allows greater mechanisation and so greater speed than trawlers that haul in the catch from the side.

The size of the trawl has also been increased by using plastic nets. Because plastic nets are made of stronger, lighter, rot-resistant fibres, they can be much larger than the traditional nets. In water they are virtually invisible. Different parts of the net consist of different densities of plastic so, in the water, they assume the correct shape and orientation. However, these nets are non-biodegradable and if lost overboard can trap marine mammals and damage other forms of marine life.

These new nets are an example of 'better' fishing technology, which means it is easier to remove more fish, which reduces the fish stocks. This leads to limits on fishing. Also, the new, larger nets mean fewer boats are needed to fish for the same

catch of fish. So the nets may make it easier for fishermen to trawl for larger catches, but they can also be another threat to their livelihood. This is why there is so much anger and emotion over regulations restricting fishermen, and so much competition from fishermen from different countries for the same fish stocks.

6 Suggest why lost nets can be more damaging to the marine environment than lost lines.

Modern trawlers powered by a 750 kW engine can drag nets up to 100 m long over the sea bed and catch huge amounts of cod, whiting and haddock. However, trawls are not selective and non-target fish often end up in the trawl and are discarded. The **target catch** is the fish that are meant to be caught. The non-target fish are called the **by-catch**. The by-catch can include fish of the wrong species, and fish that are too young or small. The by-catch is a significant threat to the conservation of some species. In 1987, the by-catch for North Sea haddock was estimated to be 41%.

7 In the form of a table, including headings of waste, efficiency, manpower, potential damage to stock and other species, compare the advantages and disadvantages of trawling and demersal line fishing.

The EC is trying to get the traditional diamond-shaped mesh of trawls replaced by a square shape. This does not close up under the pressure of a full trawl. Younger fish are able to escape through the mesh, and survive to breed.

Landings of cod in the UK have dropped from 366 500 tonnes in 1970 to 14 800 in 1980 and 7400 in 1990. The figures for haddock have dropped from 180 000 tonnes to 52 000 over the same period. Management measures at present include:
• quotas based on TAC;
• minimum fish size (35 cm);
• minimum mesh size.

North Sea trawling for cod is not an easy job. Hauling nets up in bad weather conditions is hard and dangerous work.

The minimum mesh size is 90 mm in the EC zone, except for an area in the south-east North Sea and in the Norwegian Sea, where it is 100 mm. The mesh size controls the age at which the fish are caught. Smaller fish escape through the mesh and are able to grow to a size at which they are able to spawn. This therefore improves recruitment. Larger mesh sizes are appropriate in areas such as nursery grounds. In 1987, a minimum mesh size of 100 mm was introduced in the German Bight nursery ground, although the scientific recommendation was 120 mm.

 8 Explain the advantages and disadvantages of implementing a minimum mesh size of 100 mm rather than 120 mm.

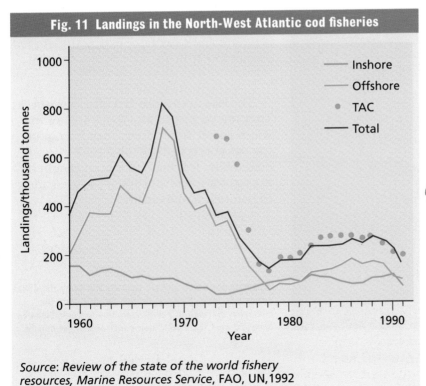

Fig. 11 Landings in the North-West Atlantic cod fisheries

Legend:
— Inshore
— Offshore
• TAC
— Total

Y-axis: Landings/thousand tonnes (0, 200, 400, 600, 800, 1000)
X-axis: Year (1960, 1970, 1980, 1990)

Source: *Review of the state of the world fishery resources, Marine Resources Service*, FAO, UN, 1992

9 Suggest why fishermen tend to resist the introduction of an increase in minimum mesh size.

Much of the North Sea supports mixed demersal fisheries, so that a boat fishing for a smaller species such as haddock will inevitably take small, young cod as well. If cod are caught below the minimum landing size, then they are thrown back into the sea. Most of these cod will be dead, but the assessment of fish stocks upon which quotas are based fails to take this into account. For this reason, TACs and quotas can never be effective in mixed fisheries.

Another strategy that could be used is closed area regulation. This would prevent fishing in areas where young or spawning fish are present. However, cod spawning areas are diffuse and distributed over very large areas.

In the 1970s, North-West Atlantic cod had been greatly overfished. Quotas were introduced for the Canadian exclusive economic zones (EEZ), where only Canadian fleets could fish (Fig. 11). But by 1992 the cod stocks were seriously low. The cod were overfished both inside the Canadian EEZ and outside it by EC fishing fleets.

The EC countries exceeded the catch limits set by the North Atlantic Fisheries Organisation, in areas just outside Canadian waters. Cod stocks collapsed and Canada closed down its cod fishery off Newfoundland, with a loss of 20 000 jobs. Canada lays the blame on overfishing by EC fleets. The EC takes the view that Canada had been taking too many cod for years and ignoring the advice of its own scientists.

10 a From Fig. 11, how effective were the TACs?
   b Suggest what could have been done to protect the fish stock from collapse.

The bass is a migratory fish found in English and Welsh inshore waters in summer. It has become a major target species for inshore commercial fisheries. Catches of bass have steadily declined since the 1950s.

Bass are able to produce large numbers of spawn in each year class. However, the young growing stock, under 5 years old and up to about 36 cm in length, appear to be overfished, because not enough survive to give a high yield for the fishery.

A useful strategy to improve the stock would be:
- to implement a minimum mesh size of 100 mm;
- close bass nursery areas.

 11 Explain how these two strategies would affect the fish stocks and yields.

Entangling fish

Drift nets are large nets suspended by floats (Fig. 12). They hang vertically like a curtain in the water and can stretch from 5 to 50 km in length. The development of light, monofilament plastic drift nets has made the nets easier to handle and allowed them to be larger. Fish that try to swim through the nets become entangled by their gill covers. Drift nets can be made selective to some extent, by altering the mesh size. If the mesh is larger, smaller fish can swim through the net.

12 Give four measures, other than mesh regulations, that can be used to control fishing effort.

Drift nets are used to catch pelagic shoaling species. The target catch in different parts of the world includes herring, mackerel, pilchard, tuna, salmon and squid. Huge oceanic drift nets attempt to catch low-density commercial species, such as albacore tuna and squid, over a wide area. They are so sheer that they can entangle entire tuna shoals. They also trap diving birds, turtles and seals who cannot see them or who may be lured by fish already caught in the nets.

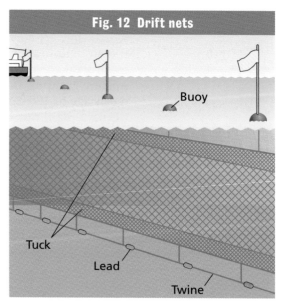

Fig. 12 Drift nets

Buoy

Tuck

Lead

Twine

The size of the nets has other drawbacks. They are very wasteful. About 40% of the South Pacific tuna fishery may fall out of the net as it is being hauled back into the boat. Many fish may have been caught in the net for hours and are net-scarred and therefore less marketable.

Drift nets can catch and kill virtually any living thing that swims into them. This has earned the drift nets the nickname the 'wall of death'. Dolphins and small whales cannot detect them with their sonar and so get caught.

Spanish trawlermen are pitted against their own government as well as British, French and Irish fishermen in a dispute about the length of nets used in drift fishing.

Declining catches of other species have led Cornish fishermen to move into drift netting for tuna. 'It is not a threatened fish stock. There's room for expansion. There's no quota on tuna', says one skipper. Cornish fishermen complain that by taking small fish the Spanish fleet, which uses old-fashioned line methods, is destroying the fish stock. But the heart of the row is over the length of drift nets used. The standard limit is 2.5 km, but many British nets are far longer, up to 6 km (3.8 miles). These large nets are allowed on the grounds that they contain long gaps between sections to allow dolphins and other sea mammals to escape. The length of actual net is still 2.5 km. With larger mesh sizes, the Cornish fishermen insist they are hauling in only large tuna.

Mr Bullens, a Cornish skipper, said 'We will have to adopt our own conservation measures. There will have to be an increase in mesh sizes and we may ignore any proposed restrictions on days at sea.'

The environmental organisation Greenpeace is backing the Spanish fishermen, and their traditional, low-tech way of life, and has sent its flagship the Rainbow Warrior to the area.

Source: adapted from articles by Adela Gooch and Owen Bowcott, *The Guardian*, 5 August, 1994

 13 Explain which technique, drift net or line, would have the most significant effect on fish stocks.

Purse seiners

Purse seiners employ ruthlessly efficient methods of modern fishing technology. They are capable of catching entire shoals of pelagic species such as herring, capelin, pollack, tuna and sardine. The curtain of netting can be up to 1.5 km long and 100m deep. With this method of capture, the fish are caught and landed in good condition (Fig. 13).

 14 Suggest why laws are needed to limit the use of purse seiners.

Fig. 13 Purse seiners

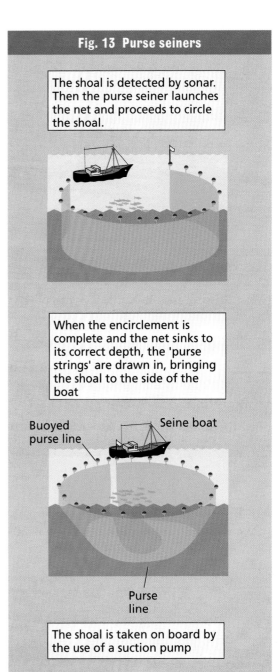

The shoal is detected by sonar. Then the purse seiner launches the net and proceeds to circle the shoal.

When the encirclement is complete and the net sinks to its correct depth, the 'purse strings' are drawn in, bringing the shoal to the side of the boat

Buoyed purse line

Seine boat

Purse line

The shoal is taken on board by the use of a suction pump

Purse seiners do have problems with by-catch, for example porpoises have been killed accidentally in the Eastern Pacific. Purse seiners are also very expensive to build. However, few fishermen are needed to operate them because of the technology used, including sonar and freezing facilities.

97

Refrigeration has meant the development of massive factory ships that are able to stay away from port for long periods and are able to process the catch on board. Fishing fleets are now able to operate far from home. Japanese, Russian and Chinese fleets roam the high seas all over the world.

15 In a table, compare the advantages and disadvantages of pelagic line, drift nets and purse seiners.

Sophisticated sonar has been developed to search out fish shoals and orientate the net into the correct position.

Key ideas

- The main demersal methods of fishing use long lines and trawls.
- The main pelagic methods of fishing are drift nets and purse seines.

- Successful regulation of fisheries depends on choosing the best methods for each fishery, and the cooperation of the fishermen.
- Advances in fishing technology, such as plastic nets and the use of sonar, have enhanced the fishing capacity of vessels.

7.4 Fish farming

There has been a remarkable increase in fish farming, called **aquaculture**, over the past 15 years.

Marine molluscs like mussels and oysters have also been cultured for many years. Mussels grown on strings suspended from rafts produce 250 tonnes of flesh per hectare per year around the Spanish coast.

These oysters are freshly harvested and boxed from an oyster farm in Oregon, USA.

Japanese raft cultures of oysters produce 50 tonnes of flesh per hectare per year.

Benefits of fish farming include:
- a controlled supply of specific fish of the required size available independent of external conditions;
- achieving an optimum growth rate, health and palatability;
- a controlled genetic selection for desired qualities such as disease resistance;
- efficient conversion of food to fish because fish are cold blooded and energy is not wasted on the maintenance of body temperature.

Fish farming has existed for many centuries, particularly in warmer parts of the world. Developments from early, primitive methods of aquaculture have given rise to various systems. These fall into two main categories:
- extensive;
- intensive.

Extensive or open systems

These employ natural production under near-natural conditions. The minimum of management is necessary. Fast growing fish such as carp are taken from a local river and placed in ponds. Animal manure is used as fertiliser to promote the growth of pondweed. The pondweed not only provides food for the herbivorous fish, but also oxygenates the water. Some effort may be made to reduce mortality by controlling competitors and predators. The extensive system described results in high productivity (Fig. 14). Along with the low food and labour costs, it ensures a highly profitable form of aquaculture.

Intensive or closed systems

These are not usually natural systems. The conditions in which fish, such as salmon and trout, are grown are strictly controlled, e.g. food, temperature, control of disease, etc. **Brood fish**, those that are to be used in reproduction, are moved to freshwater until they are ready to spawn (Fig. 15).

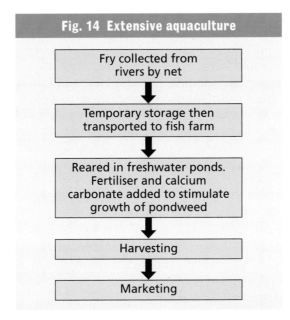

Fig. 14 Extensive aquaculture

Fry collected from rivers by net

↓

Temporary storage then transported to fish farm

↓

Reared in freshwater ponds. Fertiliser and calcium carbonate added to stimulate growth of pondweed

↓

Harvesting

↓

Marketing

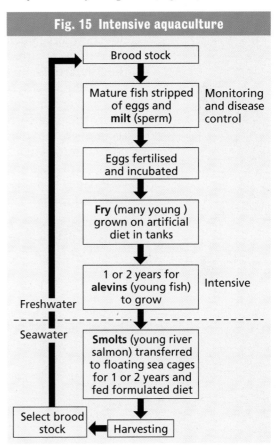

Fig. 15 Intensive aquaculture

Brood stock

↓

Mature fish stripped of eggs and **milt** (sperm) — Monitoring and disease control

↓

Eggs fertilised and incubated

↓

Fry (many young) grown on artificial diet in tanks

↓

1 or 2 years for **alevins** (young fish) to grow — Intensive

Freshwater
- - - - - - - - - - - - - - - -
Seawater

↓

Smolts (young river salmon) transferred to floating sea cages for 1 or 2 years and fed formulated diet

↓

Harvesting → Select brood stock

In the UK the main farmed fish are salmon and trout. In Scotland in particular, the rapid growth of fish farming has benefited the local communities and is regarded by many as an appropriate use of natural resources. However, the rapid increase has brought with it environmental concerns, especially as so much activity is centred in lochs and other virtually enclosed areas of seawater. Sea lochs are undergoing development in the absence of adequate long-term data on their carrying capacity. More monitoring and research needs to be done on these issues, and codes of practice need to be drawn up and enforced if these environmentally sensitive areas are to be protected.

Intensive cultivation results in large amounts of organic wastes from faeces and wasted food. The amount of suspended solids produced by one tonne of fish can be equivalent to the pollution load of 850 people. These wastes can stimulate the growth of algal blooms, producing the typical effects of eutrophication, such as depleted oxygen levels, clogging of fish gills and poisoning of fish by toxic products. In lochs, excess food and faeces builds up on the loch bottom.

Water currents within fish farms should be strong enough to remove wastes and bring in fresh, well oxygenated water. However, salinity and temperature should not show large fluctuations. Treatment of the outflow is virtually impossible when the fish farm is situated in a loch, lake or in part of the sea. Faeces and uneaten food sink and are unlikely to be carried away where the tidal current is slow. They accumulate and deoxygenate the mud and bottom waters in a similar way to sewage sludge. This can severely affect the abundance and diversity of the organisms living on the bottom of the sea or lake.

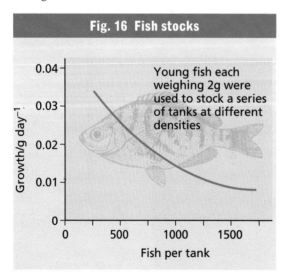

Fig. 16 Fish stocks

Young fish each weighing 2g were used to stock a series of tanks at different densities

y-axis: Growth/g day⁻¹ (0, 0.01, 0.02, 0.03, 0.04)
x-axis: Fish per tank (0, 500, 1000, 1500)

16 a From Fig. 16, assuming that there is no mortality, what will be the total mass of fish per tank after 80 days when stocked with 500 and 1500 fish? Show your calculations.
   b Comment on the difference in average mass of the fish at these two densities after 80 days.

Any organism grown in high densities is likely to suffer from disease. In the case of marine fish, this includes fish lice, viruses, fungi and bacteria. Good hygiene is practised, but the use of pesticides, applied to the water, is often necessary, for example dichlovos to control sea lice in salmon. The fish themselves can also be treated with antibiotics in their food.

Chemicals used to treat diseases and parasites in fish can be extremely toxic to other marine organisms. A code of practice needs to be drawn up and enforced to reduce the hazards of pesticide use.

Concerns also exist about the release and escape of farmed salmon. It is thought that these could adversely affect the wild salmon population by introducing diseases and parasites and interfering with homing activity, and having a genetic influence.

In order for marine aquaculture to be efficient and profitable, the stock must be in a protected area, safe from predators and competitors. Special pens are constructed that are robust enough to withstand damaging waves and high winds. The selection of stock by controlled breeding aims to develop rapid growth, improved efficiency of food conversion and disease resistance. Currently, something like 10% of the world fish yield comes from fish farming (including shellfish). True marine fish farming has yet to be shown to be profitable. In the past, hatchery-produced fry of commercial species such as plaice have been released into the North Sea. This was an unsuccessful attempt to compensate for overfishing, because its contribution was so insignificant given the vast size of the North Sea. The Ministry of Agriculture, Fisheries and Food (MAFF) does not see fish farming making up for the decreasing yields from marine fish stocks. The two operations are on a completely different scale. The possibility of marine aquaculture ever succeeding offshore is extremely unlikely.

The view in the foreseeable future appears to be that intensive marine fish farming will be a means of adding variety to our diets rather than becoming a major, economical source of protein.

Careful management of ecosystems is needed to sustain populations of organisms used as a source of food. Organisms from natural ecosystems can be harvested, but to avoid depletion their removal must be carefully controlled. Organisms can be cultivated in more artificial ecosystems, but these also have to be controlled and monitored carefully to prevent problems such as pollution.

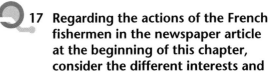 **17 Regarding the actions of the French fishermen in the newspaper article at the beginning of this chapter, consider the different interests and priorities of all the people involved, and the compromises that will have to be made to settle the dispute.**

Key ideas

- Intensive fish farming requires greater control over conditions such as food and disease than extensive methods.

- The environmental effects of intensive fish farms require thorough monitoring and research.

- Removal of organisms from ecosystems has to be controlled in order for it to be sustainable.

Pushing the limits

These farmers in Burkina Faso, in the Sahel of West Africa, are being shown how stone lines can be used to control erosion and conserve water. The low stone walls are built along level contours and soil, water and dead plant material build up behind them.

The Sahel is a huge area of Africa that is semi-desert. In Burkina Faso there has been 20 years of drought and deforestation. Bushfires, clearing of land for agriculture and uncontrolled grazing have exposed the soil. In the dry season easterly winds blow the top soil away, and in the wet season the rains wash the soil away. Many villages in the Sahel have lost up to half of their cultivable land.

Oxfam volunteers have helped villagers to build low barriers of stones to stop the water run-off. They developed the system from traditional methods. The stone lines reduce erosion and have increased crop yields by up to 50%. They are a cheap method of raising the soil level. Inside them a good crop of sorghum can be grown.

This is just one example of how developed countries can use their scientific knowledge in a simple and practical way to help developing countries increase food production. Crop scientists can help by researching which crops are the most productive in different ecosystems. But how do they compare the yields of different varieties of crops? And how can the productivity of suitable crops be increased?

8.1 Learning objectives

After working through this chapter, you should be able to:

- **use** data to give measures of crop productivity;

- **explain** how crops differ in the amount of harvestable dry matter and protein that they produce, relative growth rates, net assimilation rates, efficiency of energy conversion and leaf area index;

- **calculate** values for relative growth rate, net assimilation rate, efficiency of energy conversion and leaf area index;

- **apply** the principle of limiting factors to explain the effects of temperature, carbon dioxide concentration and light intensity on the rate of photosynthesis;

- **describe** how temperature, carbon dioxide and light intensity can be managed for crops grown in glasshouses;

- **evaluate** the economic significance of C_4 plants.

8.2 The Green Revolution

Since the 1950s, the world's grain supplies have more than doubled. Between the 1950s and 1970s, the amount of grain harvested per person rose by 40%. However, this trend is now slowing down. The grain output per person fell by 11% between 1984 and 1993 (Fig. 1).

The increase in world grain area came to a halt in the 1980s. Globally there is little new land left that can be cultivated. As the

Fig. 1 World grain production trends

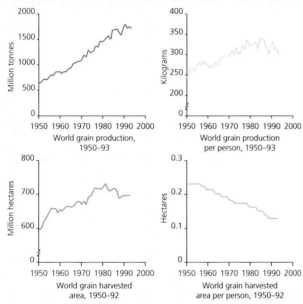

World grain production, 1950–93

World grain production per person, 1950–93

World grain harvested area, 1950–92

World grain harvested area per person, 1950–92

Source: United States Department of Agriculture, in Brown et al., 1993, 1994, adapted from WWF

This is a grain store in Burkina Faso, containing sorghum. Crop research is being carried out to try and increase crop production in desert areas.

world population is not falling, it means more has to be done to maintain food productivity and avoid famines in certain areas. There is great variation between the productivity of different crop species. Throughout the world there is also an imbalance between areas of high food productivity and areas of high population (Fig. 2).

Fig. 2 Crop production in Europe and Africa

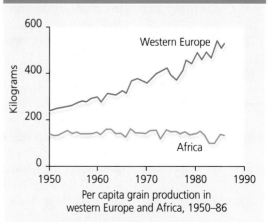

Per capita grain production in western Europe and Africa, 1950–86

Source: United States Department of Agriculture, in Brown, 1987, adapted from WWF

There are vast differences in crop productivity between different countries. Some, like the USA, have huge grain surpluses, creating 'food mountains', while elsewhere droughts and other factors have caused crop failure.

Table 1. Crop productivity		
Crop	Productivity per day of growing season/g m^{-2}	
	World average	Highest yield
Wheat	2.3	8.3
Oats	2.4	6.2
Maize	2.3	4.4
Rice	2.7	4.4
Potatoes	2.6	5.6
Sugar beet	4.3	8.2
Source: WWF		

1 a Draw a histogram of the data in Table 1.

b Suggest why there are differences between world average and the highest yields recorded.

c Suggest how world average production could be improved.

Between 1950 and 1970 the wheat harvest in India more than doubled. India became the biggest provider of food aid after the USA. In the mid-1980s it had surplus grain of 24 billion tons. But economic and distribution factors mean that India still has half of the hungry people of the Earth. People are hungry because they cannot afford to buy or afford to grow the food that they need. Their land may be used to grow crops sold to other countries.

The **Green Revolution** is a general term used to describe the ideal use of scientific knowledge from developed countries to help increase food production in other countries where people are suffering malnutrition and starvation. The knowledge can be as simple as working out the best way to build low stone walls, or involve analysing the efficiency of biochemical pathways of different crop species.

The Green Revolution began in the 1950s, when maize was one of the most widely planted crops. Maize is badly affected by drought so crop scientists began looking at ways of improving crops such as millet and sorghum. Places like Burkina Faso and areas of India need crops that can cope with a dry, hot environment and that do not need expensive fertilisers or agricultural technology. Some of the techniques used in the 1950s for increasing crop production, for example introducing new strains of crop plant or using huge quantities of fertiliser, were very successful in the short term. However, they have proved not to work in the long term, even leading to loss of soil fertility and erosion. New ideas are needed to maintain a sustainable harvest for the future.

8.3 Crop productivity

It is important to have standard, accurate methods for measuring crop productivity so that crop scientists can compare the performance of new varieties of crops. They may also need to measure the performance of a crop at various stages of its growth, or estimate the success of particular fertilisers or pesticides.

Energy enters an ecosystem through the primary producers, the green plants. This energy is then transferred by photosynthesis into organic substances, which can be used as food by humans and animals. As a result of photosynthesis there is an increase in biomass. The rate at which this happens is known as the primary productivity of the plant.

2 What is the equation for photosynthesis?

Primary productivity of crops can be measured in energy terms as the amount of energy used per area of crop leaf per unit of time: kJ m^{-2} year^{-1}. It can also be measured as the dry mass of organic substances produced in terms of g m^{-2} day^{-1}.

The rate at which photosynthetic products accumulate is **gross primary productivity** (GPP). However, plants use up some of the dry mass during respiration. The net gain of dry mass stored in the plant after respiration is known as **net primary productivity** (NPP). This represents potential food to primary consumers. NPP

With a cereal crop like barley, we are only really interested in harvesting the grain. The rest of the biomass, the stalks, roots, leaves, etc., has no economic value as a human food resource.

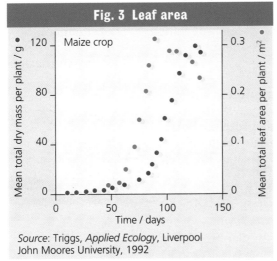

Fig. 3 Leaf area

Maize crop

(Mean total dry mass per plant / g vs Time / days, Mean total leaf area per plant / m^2)

Source: Triggs, *Applied Ecology*, Liverpool John Moores University, 1992

3 a Explain why leaf area is a measure of the photosynthetic ability of a plant.
b Why does the leaf area in (Fig. 3) reach a peak earlier in the year than dry mass?

is important to crop scientists because it gives an indication of the yield of the crop.

Data that need to be collected to measure crop productivity include:
• the total dry mass (g) per plant or per area of crop = W;
• the leaf area (m^2) per plant or per crop = LA.

Estimating dry mass is destructive because it involves drying the crop to a constant weight in an oven at 110°C. It is usual to estimate the dry mass of a whole crop from the dry mass of either a typical plant or a sample of the crop taken by quadrat.

Measuring leaf area can be done using graph paper. The leaf area is one factor that influences the photosynthetic ability of the plant.

Harvestable dry matter is the proportion of dry mass that can be harvested from a crop. In crops that are mainly grown for animal feed where everything is eaten, such as kale and forage rape, the whole of the above ground growth has an economic value. However, not all of the dry mass of other crops has an economic value, particularly as a human food resource.

The **economic yield**, for example the grain of barley, represents only a fraction of the total **biological yield**.

The ratio of the biological yield (Y biol) to the economic yield (Y econ) is known as the **harvest index** (HI).

$$HI = \frac{Y \text{ econ}}{Y \text{ biol}}$$

Successful crop management aims to maximise the HI. Applying fertilisers to a cereal crop may increase the biological yield by increasing the growth of the leaf canopy. But this can cut down light penetration to the rest of the plant, which would then lower the HI. In poorer countries, farmers may not be able to afford fertilisers, so other methods have to be researched to increase yields.

Winter wheat variety	Plant height/ cm	Grain yield/ tonnes ha^{-1}	Total biomass/ tonnes ha^{-1}	HI
Little Joss	142	6.0	16.5	0.36
Capelle Desprez	110	6.7	15.9	0.42
Norman	84	X	17.1	0.51
Holdfast	126	6.0	16.5	0.36
Maris Huntsman	106	7.5	16.3	Y

Table 2. Winter wheat

Source: OU

4 a Calculate the two missing values X and Y in Table 2.

b What is the relationship between HI and plant height?

Plant food tends to be rich in carbohydrates; animal food tends to be rich in protein. In areas of drought and desert, where it can be difficult to rear animals, estimates of **harvestable protein** have to be taken into account when researching which crops could be grown to feed humans or their livestock.

5 a Explain the role of protein in the diet.

b Why is harvestable protein a better measure of economic value for animal food crops such as kale?

When comparing crops it is useful to calculate the **relative growth rate** (RGR). This measures how quickly a crop adds new biomass, ie. the increase in plant mass per unit of total mass over time. For example, the average RGR of maize is 2.31 g g^{-1} week^{-1} and the RGR of barley is 0.92 g g^{-1} week^{-1} grown under the same conditions. RGR can be calculated using natural logarithms with a calculator (Fig. 4).

Fig. 4 Relative growth rate

$$RGR = \frac{\log_e M_2 - \log_e M_1}{T_2 - T_1} \; g\,g^{-1}\,day^{-1}$$

$\log_e M_1$ is a natural logarithm of dry mass (g) at time T_1
$\log_e M_2$ is a natural logarithm of dry mass (g) at time T_2

$M_1 = 83\,g$ $M_2 = 112\,g$ $T_2 - T_1 = 7$

$$RGR = \frac{4.718 - 4.419}{7}$$

$$= 0.043\,g\,g^{-1}\,day^{-1}$$

RGR is used to compare the growth of:
- different crop species;
- a particular crop species at different stages in its development;
- a particular crop species under different environmental conditions.

6 Explain why maize rather than barley was a good crop to use in the Green Revolution.

RGR can vary when plotted over the period of growth of the crop. This is because RGR is influenced by changes in:
- hours of daylight, temperature and water supply;
- the overall form of the plant, e.g. the proportion of leaf area to biomass;
- plant activity, e.g. flower and fruit production as opposed to leaf development;
- plant metabolism as a result of ageing.
  Net assimilation rate (NAR) is:

$$\frac{\text{increase in plant dry mass over a certain length of time}}{\text{leaf area of plant}}$$

NAR can also be calculated using natural logarithms (Fig. 5).

Fig. 5 Net assimilation rate

$$NAR = \frac{M_2 - M_1}{T_2 - T_1} \times \frac{\log_e LA_2 - \log_e LA_1}{LA_2 - LA_1}$$

$\log_e LA_1$ is a natural logarithm of leaf area (m^2) at time T_1
$\log_e LA_2$ is a natural logarithm of leaf area (m^2) at time T_2
M_1 is the dry mass (g) at time T_1
M_2 is the dry mass (g) at time T_2

$M_1 = 325\,g$ $LA_1 = 2.5\,m^2$ $T_2 - T_1 = 2$ weeks
$M_2 = 463\,g$ $LA_2 = 3.0\,m^2$

$$NAR = \frac{463 - 325}{2} \times \frac{1.099 - 0.916}{3.0 - 2.5}$$

$$= 69 \times \frac{0.183}{0.5}$$

$$= 69 \times 0.366$$

$$= 25.254\,g\,m^{-2}\,week^{-1}$$

$$= 25\,g\,m^{-2}\,week^{-1}$$

Fig. 6 Weekly NAR for four crops grown in the UK

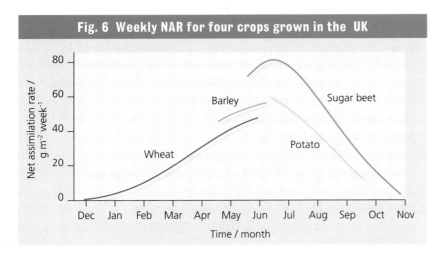

NAR relates increase in dry mass to leaf area. This indicates the efficiency of the leaves as producers of new biomass. It is a more reliable measure of plant growth than RGR because it reflects changes in efficiency, due to changes in the external environment or as a result of different treatments, more accurately than RGR.

7 a Suggest why NAR peaks in the middle of the time scale in Fig. 6.

b Would it be useful to delay an October harvest date for sugar beet until later in the year? Explain your answer.

c Would the equivalent curve for RGR in sugar beet have the same shape as for NAR?

Comparison of the **photosynthetic efficiency** between different plant species using NAR is more reliable than RGR.

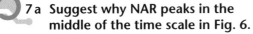

$$\text{Photosynthetic efficiency} = \frac{\text{amount of energy stored in newly formed carbohydrates}}{\text{amount of light energy that falls upon the plant}}$$

About 45% of sunlight falling on a plant is within the **photosynthetically active radiation** (PAR) waveband. Up to 85% of this is actually absorbed (see Chapter 1, Fig. 9). So the efficiency is:

$$\frac{45}{100} \times 85 = 38.25\%$$

Chloroplasts operate at about 20% efficiency so the maximum overall efficiency of photosynthesis is:

$$\frac{38.25}{100} \times 20 = 7.65\%, \text{ i.e. about 8\%}$$

Sugar cane, as in this field being harvested in south India, can produce a huge biomass in tropical ecosystems. It has a high economic value because it can be exported. But using the land for a cash crop means less land is available for growing food crops for the local people.

Table 3. Photosynthetic efficiency

Crop and location	Sugar beet (temperate crop)	Sugar cane (tropical crop)
Mean solar energy during growing season (MJ m^{-2} day^{-1})	10.9	20.9
Carbohydrate production at 8% efficiency (maximum theoretical) (g m^{-2} day^{-1})	60 (8%)	104 (8%)
Maximum recorded experimentally over a short period (g m^{-2} day^{-1})	31 (4%)	43 (3%)
Seasonal mean for commercial farming (g m^{-2} day^{-1})	9 (1.2%)	10 (0.8%)

Source: OU

The efficiency of energy conversion is usually a lot lower than 8% because of factors such as low temperature, plant dormancy and the plant's own energy needs for respiration (Table 3).

107

Table 4. Energy budget			
	Glucose/kg	Energy/10⁶kJ	% of solar energy
Solar energy		8580	100
Respiration of maize	2045	32.3	0.4
GPP of maize	8732	137.9	1.6

Measurements are of half a hectare of corn during a growing season of 100 days

Source: OU

8 a Using Table 4 calculate the value for NPP of maize.

b Calculate the efficiency of energy conversion of this crop.

The **leaf area index** (LAI) is the ratio of leaf area of a plant or the whole crop to the area of ground covered by the plant or crop. LAI can be calculated as a percentage as:

$$LAI = \frac{LA \text{ (leaf area)}}{GA \text{ (ground area)}} \times 100$$

For example, if a crop has 3 m² of leaf area above 10 m² of ground, the LAI is 30%. LAI gives an indication of the amount of light the crop can intercept. Crops with a higher LAI will absorb more light, so potentially have a higher photosynthetic rate. In a crop that has just germinated, the LAI will be less than 10% because the leaf area is insignificant compared to the ground area. As the crop grows the LAI increases. In temperate areas, the maximum possible LAI is between 20% and 100%. In tropical areas the higher solar energy means that the LAI may be greater than 200%.

With an increase in LAI, there tends to be a decrease in NAR because of the shading effects of the upper leaves. LAI gives information about the size of the photosynthetic system, whereas NAR gives information about its efficiency. The highest rate of biomass production will be when the product of LAI and NAR is at a maximum. Any factor that changes the biomass produced will be reflected in the LAI or the NAR, or both.

9 a Explain whether the following will affect NAR and LAI or both:
(i) water;
(ii) light intensity;
(iii) temperature;
(iv) carbon dioxide;
(v) fertilisers.

b Which of these factors would have the most effect on crop plants needed for dry, hot environments.

Winter wheat is sown the preceding autumn and potato is sown much later (Fig. 7)

10 Suggest why these two crops are sown at different times. Explain the changes in LAI in each case.

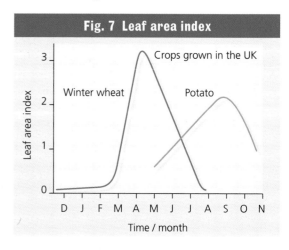

Fig. 7 Leaf area index

Key ideas

- There are large differences between the food supplies of different countries.

- The Green Revolution tries to help developing countries increase the efficiency of their food production.

- Crop growth can be measured and compared in different crops by using relative growth rate, net assimilation rate and leaf area index.

- Crops differ in their efficiency of energy conversion and the amount of harvestable dry matter and protein that they produce.

8.4 Environmental factors

The rate of photosynthesis is important in food production because it determines the crop yield. Many factors can affect the rate of photosynthesis of a crop. Environmental factors include light, temperature, carbon dioxide, water and nutrients. Good crop management involves the manipulation of these factors in order to maximise photosynthesis and achieve good yields.

If one of these environmental factors should fall below a certain level it will start to limit the rate of photosynthesis. Although temperature, carbon dioxide and light may all affect photosynthesis, only one can limit the rate at a particular moment. It is then the **limiting factor**.

The rate of photosynthesis can only be increased by increasing that one factor.

The effects of light on photosynthesis depends on the light:
• quality, i.e. the PAR;
• duration, i.e. the day length;
• intensity, i.e. how strong the light is.

Day length may be limited to 8 hours in winter in Britain, but can be double that in summer. The period of the year when day length is greatest coincides with the period when the light intensity is highest. In Britain this is midday in June. The total amount of solar energy available to a crop equals light intensity × time. In tropical countries, the amount of solar energy available can be fairly constant throughout the year.

On a winter's day in Britain, the light intensity is low.

On a bright, summer's day in Britain the light intensity is much greater. The most productive plants in temperate ecosystems have evolved to cope with the varying light intensities.

Fig. 8 Light intensity

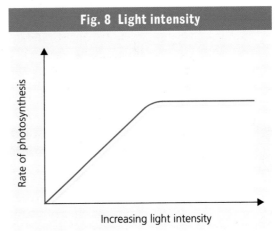

Rate of photosynthesis

Increasing light intensity

At low light intensities, an increase in the rate of photosynthesis is directly proportional to increasing light intensity (Fig. 8). But eventually the process reaches a maximum rate and fails to increase further. This could be because:
• the photosynthetic reactions are proceeding as fast as possible;
• some other factor is now limiting the rate, such as carbon dioxide concentration or temperature.

The maximum amount of light that can be used in photosynthetic reactions is estimated to be about 10 000 lux. On a clear, summer's day solar illumination may reach 100 000 lux. At this time of year, therefore, light intensity is not the limiting factor. However, at very high light intensities there may be damage to the chlorophyll molecules, resulting in a drop in the rate of photosynthesis.

When light intensity is high, increasing temperature can have an effect on the rate of photosynthesis. Between the range 10°C to about 35°C a 10°C rise in the temperature will double the rate of photosynthesis (Fig. 9).

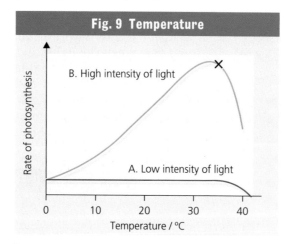

Fig. 9 Temperature

11 a **What is the limiting factor in graph A?**
   b **Suggest why the rate of photosynthesis drops at X.**

Carbon dioxide is the source of carbon atoms used to make all the organic products of photosynthesis. Carbon dioxide is needed in the light-independent reactions of photosynthesis, where it is reduced to carbohydrate and other organic compounds. Atmospheric carbon dioxide is usually about 0.03% of the volume of the air. For most plants this is lower than the optimum value for photosynthesis. So under normal conditions for crops carbon dioxide is often the limiting factor (Fig. 10).

12 **Using Fig. 11, which curve shows carbon dioxide concentration to have the greatest effect as a limiting factor?**

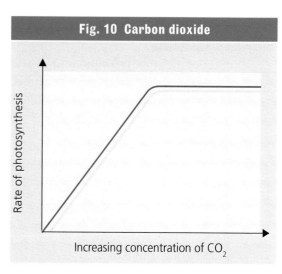

Fig. 10 Carbon dioxide

In tropical areas, temperature and light intensity are not usually the limiting factors of photosynthesis. Carbon dioxide is the limiting factor. However, in areas like the Sahel water is the overriding factor affecting crop yield. Periods of temporary wilting can lead to heavy losses in crop yield.

The rate of photosynthesis falls when plants are water-stressed. This is unlikely to be because there is not enough water for the light-dependent stage of photosynthesis. It is far more likely to be because of more indirect effects caused by water shortage. One of the first consequences of lack of water is that the stomata close. This cuts off the carbon dioxide supply to photosynthesising cells. It is impossible to measure the direct effects of water shortage on photosynthesis because it is used in so many other cell processes.

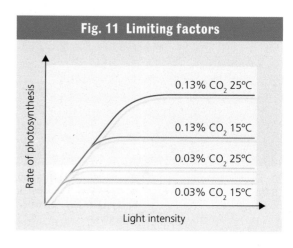

Fig. 11 Limiting factors

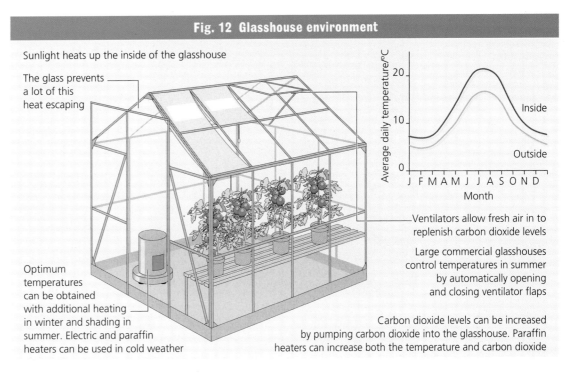

Fig. 12 Glasshouse environment

Sunlight heats up the inside of the glasshouse

The glass prevents a lot of this heat escaping

Optimum temperatures can be obtained with additional heating in winter and shading in summer. Electric and paraffin heaters can be used in cold weather

Ventilators allow fresh air in to replenish carbon dioxide levels

Large commercial glasshouses control temperatures in summer by automatically opening and closing ventilator flaps

Carbon dioxide levels can be increased by pumping carbon dioxide into the glasshouse. Paraffin heaters can increase both the temperature and carbon dioxide

Glasshouse management

In order to achieve maximum yields, possible limiting factors need to be controlled. If the physical environment can be modified the growth of crops can be regulated. This may not be possible in the case of a crop grown outside.

However, by growing crops under glass or plastic greater control of environmental conditions is possible. Glasshouse cultivation allows:
• better yields to be achieved;
• some crops to be grown out of season and so provide a better economic return;
• some plants to be grown in regions where they would not normally grow.

Over short periods, 0.5% of carbon dioxide has been found to be the optimum concentration for photosynthesis. Over longer periods, however, this concentration may cause the stomata to close, resulting in a drop in photosynthesis. For glasshouse crops like tomatoes 0.1% carbon dioxide is the optimum over long periods.

Tomatoes can be sown at a minimum daily temperature of 10°C and die off when the temperature falls below about 2°C. Temperatures above 28°C can damage tomato plants.

These glasshouses in Italy can be used to grow crops out of season or crops that could not normally be grown in that area.

13 a Using Fig. 12, how much longer is the maximum growing season for a tomato grown inside a glasshouse compared to one grown outside?
   b Suggest how you could extend the growing season inside a glasshouse even further.
   c Suggest two ways in which glasshouse temperatures could be kept below 28°C during hot days.

These sweet peppers are being grown in vast quantities in the controlled environment of glasshouses in Britain. Sweet peppers need lots of light and heat to grow well.

Artificial lighting can be used in glasshouses when natural light intensity falls too low. Shading out strong light is achieved by large mechanically operated blinds. Many glasshouses have automatic watering systems with automatic sprinklers and humidifiers. It is important to regulate humidity to control fungal diseases. Fungal diseases can increase if the humidity is too high.

All of these factors may be controlled by computers. Sensors are used to monitor the level of each factor and the feedback is processed by the computer.

14 Suggest economic and practical reasons why glasshouses would be difficult to use in areas like the Sahel.

Key ideas

- The principle of limiting factors can be applied to crop production.

- Environmental factors such as temperature, carbon dioxide concentration and light intensity can influence the rate of photosynthesis as limiting factors.

- Growth rate and crop yield can be enhanced by modifying the physical environment.

- Environmental factors can be controlled in glasshouses.

8.5 Biochemical factors

Crop plants differ in their biochemistry. Photosynthesis involves a complex series of reactions. Because these reactions follow a biochemical pathway, the rate of photosynthesis will be limited by the slowest reaction in the pathway.

The light-dependent reactions of photosynthesis use energy in light to produce ATP and NADPH. In the light-independent reactions, the ATP and NADPH provide the energy to produce carbohydrates. If light intensity is low, it limits the production of ATP and NADPH by the light-dependent reactions. Lower levels of ATP and NADPH will limit the rate of the light-independent reactions.

Most crop plants that have evolved in a temperate climate produce C_3 compounds as the first products of photosynthesis, i.e. organic compounds containing three carbon atoms. They are called C_3 **plants**.

In 1965 it was discovered that the first products of photosynthesis in sugar cane, a tropical crop, were two C_4 compounds, **oxaloacetate** and **malate**. Since then more plants, mostly tropical, have been found to have this ability. These are known as C_4 **plants**. Many of these C_4 plants are important crop plants, such as maize, millet, sorghum as well as sugar cane.

The light-independent reactions of photosynthesis consist of an intricate pathway of enzyme-controlled reactions. The series of reactions in the light-

Fig. 13 Hatch–Slack pathway

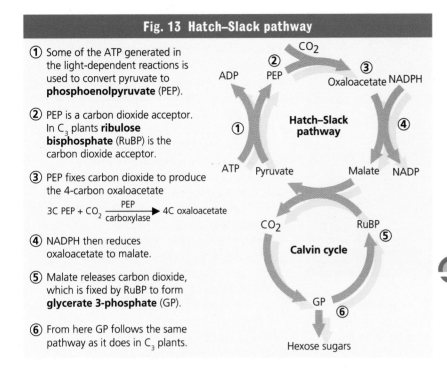

① Some of the ATP generated in the light-dependent reactions is used to convert pyruvate to **phosphoenolpyruvate** (PEP).

② PEP is a carbon dioxide acceptor. In C_3 plants **ribulose bisphosphate** (RuBP) is the carbon dioxide acceptor.

③ PEP fixes carbon dioxide to produce the 4-carbon oxaloacetate

$$3C\ PEP + CO_2 \xrightarrow[\text{carboxylase}]{\text{PEP}} 4C\ \text{oxaloacetate}$$

④ NADPH then reduces oxaloacetate to malate.

⑤ Malate releases carbon dioxide, which is fixed by RuBP to form **glycerate 3-phosphate** (GP).

⑥ From here GP follows the same pathway as it does in C_3 plants.

independent reactions of C_4 plants is called the **Hatch–Slack** pathway (Fig. 13).

The enzymes of the reaction pathways are affected by temperature. For temperate plants (C_3 plants) the optimum temperature is about 25°C, while for tropical plants (C_4 plants) the optimum rises to about 35°C.

The C_4 pathway enables plants to fix carbon dioxide with greater efficiency than C_3 plants can. This means that the stomata do not need to be open for so long to fix the same amount of carbon dioxide. In dry, hot habitats, such as the Sahel, it is an advantage to plants to be able to close stomata during periods of high temperatures. This reduces the rate of transpiration and so prevents water loss. C_4 plants also seem to be able to cope with higher light intensities.

C_4 plants have tended to evolve in drier, tropical regions of the world and exploit the higher light intensities and temperatures. The fact that they are able to use carbon dioxide more efficiently results in faster growth than C_3 plants growing in tropical environments, and they are less likely to be affected by water stress.

Sorghum is a C_4 plant and wheat is a C_3 plant.

15 a Using Fig. 14, compare the effect of increasing light intensity on the photosynthetic rate of sorghum and wheat.
   b What happens to NAR in:
   (i) C_3 plants;
   (ii) C_4 plants?
   c Which type of plant would be most suitable for growing in hot, dry areas such as the Sahel?

The potential productivity of C_4 plants in hot, dry tropical environments is greater than C_3 plants. Therefore for cash crops their economic value is higher. In temperate climates C_3 plant are more productive. Crop research scientists can discover which plants are best adapted to different environments and growing conditions. These plants can then be studied to discover how their yield can be increased.

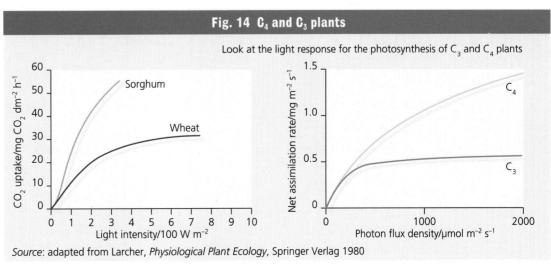

Fig. 14 C₄ and C₃ plants

Look at the light response for the photosynthesis of C_3 and C_4 plants

Source: adapted from Larcher, *Physiological Plant Ecology*, Springer Verlag 1980

These women are winnowing millet in Mali. Millet is a C_4 plant that is productive in dry, tropical environments.

Maize and sorghum are both C_4 plants, but maize is much more susceptible to water shortage. Farmers in Burkina Faso traditionally used rocks to control soil erosion. Oxfam has helped adapt the technique in order to trap water in the soil, and by planting sorghum a more sustainable crop can be grown.

The Green Revolution has not always been a success, and local people's knowledge of their own environment and farming practices need to be more highly valued and blended with green technology to produce real improvement.

Many of the plants being researched are the traditional crops of the areas concerned. Good crop management includes local knowledge as well as scientific research.

Crops that are efficient at producing biomass are needed where it is too difficult or expensive to irrigate and fertilise the land. Careful management of the ecosystem is needed to sustain harvestable yields in such environments.

However, in order to feed the growing world population, the economics and distribution of food resources has to be considered globally, as well as the productivity of particular crops.

Key ideas

- Temperature and carbon dioxide can limit the rate of light-independent photosynthetic reactions.

- C_4 plants are more efficient at fixing carbon dioxide than C_3 plants.

- C_4 plants tend to cope better with water stress and high light intensity than C_3 plants.

- C_4 plants have a greater economic value than C_3 plants in the drier, tropical regions of the world.

9

Organic farming really seems to be taking off in this country. There has been a big increase in demand for organic produce for both health and environmental reasons. A lot of people are prepared to pay more than the market rate and a number of the large supermarket chains stock organic goods. The organic food retail market is expanding all the time.

Choosing organic?

Organic food is grown without the use of artificial fertilisers, pesticides and chemical growth regulators. Crop rotations, animal manures, composting and off-farm organic wastes are used to maintain soil productivity. Instead of pesticides, mechanical methods and biological control techniques are used. The methods are labour-intensive and as a result can be more expensive. So why are people prepared to pay more? What are the advantages to the environment of organic farming? What are the drawbacks of the intensive agricultural techniques developed since the Second World War?

DIG FOR VICTORY

Since the Second World War, 1939–1945, crop productivity in the UK has shown a marked increase. The shortages of the war years fostered a belief that Britain should become self-sufficient in food. This was further encouraged by the agricultural policies of the European Community (EC), which have since resulted in large food surpluses.

9.1 Learning objectives

After working through this chapter, you should be able to:

- **describe** the various effects that plant nutrients have on crop yield;

- **explain** the importance of type, amount and time of fertiliser application;

- **calculate** the cost–benefit ratio for various fertiliser applications;

- **explain** the dangers and concerns regarding nitrates in water;

- **describe** how hydroponics can control the nutrient supply to a crop;

- **explain** the advantages and disadvantages of monocultures;

- **evaluate** the role of crop rotation in maintaining sustainable, economic crop production;

- **explain** the advantages and disadvantages of using inorganic and organic fertilisers.

9.2 Plant nutrients

Breeding new high yielding varieties, improved methods of pest control, and a massive increase in the use of **fertilisers** have been the main reasons for the huge increase in the yields of cereal crops in some countries over the last 50 years (Fig. 1). Fertilisers contain nutrients for plants.

Inorganic fertilisers, or artificial fertilisers, consist of inorganic compounds like ammonium nitrate. **Organic fertilisers**, or natural fertilisers, consist of organic materials such as animal manures, composts and sewage sludge.

Plants take up nutrients from the soil. After plant crops have been harvested, nutrients need to be put back into the soil to enable continued plant growth. Nitrogen, phosphorus and potassium (NPK) are **macronutrients**. They are needed in relatively large quantities by plants. NPK fertilisers contain nitrogen, phosphorus and potassium. Other nutrients and **essential trace elements** are only needed in small amounts and there is usually enough present continually in the soil.

Once applied to the soil, fertilisers result in increased yields. Nitrogen has the largest effect on plant growth. It is particularly important for the growth of leaves. It influences leaf expansion and the size of the leaf canopy, and so affects the yield of a crop. It is an important constituent of amino acids, proteins and nucleic acids and affects the protein content, and therefore the quality, of wheat and barley grain.

Once a certain level of fertiliser has been added, however, the crop yield begins to fall. This is an example of the **law of diminishing returns**. Beyond a certain point, any additional input results in a smaller output.

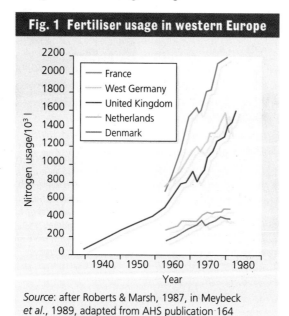

Fig. 1 Fertiliser usage in western Europe

- France
- West Germany
- United Kingdom
- Netherlands
- Denmark

Nitrogen usage/10^3 t

Source: after Roberts & Marsh, 1987, in Meybeck et al., 1989, adapted from AHS publication 164

It is now relatively easy and cheap to produce nitrogen, which has meant a fall in the price of NPK fertilisers. Atmospheric nitrogen is converted to ammonia, which is then used to produce the nitrate needed for NPK fertilisers.

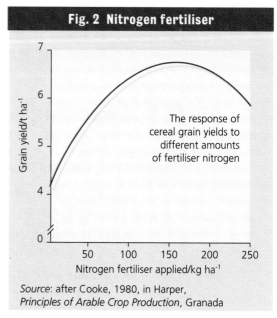

Fig. 2 Nitrogen fertiliser

Grain yield/t ha^{-1}

Nitrogen fertiliser applied/kg ha^{-1}

The response of cereal grain yields to different amounts of fertiliser nitrogen

Source: after Cooke, 1980, in Harper, *Principles of Arable Crop Production*, Granada

Q 1 Using Fig. 2, recommend the most appropriate concentration of nitrogen fertiliser. Give your reasons.

Phosphorus is important in many enzyme-catalysed reactions in plants. It is also vital for cell division and is needed in areas of rapid early growth. If it is lacking, root growth is stunted. Nitrogen and phosphorus interact to affect crop growth.

 2 Suggest the limiting factor on root yield for each curve in Fig. 3.

Fig. 3 Nitrogen and phosphorus

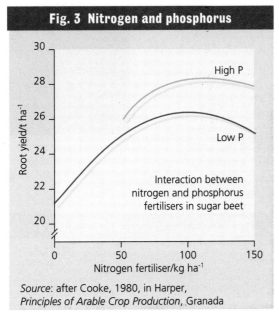

High P

Low P

Interaction between nitrogen and phosphorus fertilisers in sugar beet

Root yield/t ha^{-1}

Nitrogen fertiliser/kg ha^{-1}

Source: after Cooke, 1980, in Harper, *Principles of Arable Crop Production,* Granada

Potassium is needed to make amino acids and for protein metabolism. Efficient photosynthesis and active transport rely on an adequate supply of potassium. If it is not available, the leaves turn yellow and smaller grain forms.

Table 1. Potassium fertiliser

Fertiliser application rate/kg ha^{-1}	Grain yield/ t ha^{-1}	Thousand weight /g
0	2.24	31.8
300	2.51	32.4
600	3.84	37.9
900	4.36	38.3

3 a Plot the data from Table 1 as a graph.
b What is the percentage increase in grain yield obtained when increasing the application of potassium fertiliser:
(i) from 0 to 300;
(ii) from 300 to 600 kg ha?
c Estimate the optimum application of potassium fertiliser from your graph.
d How could you make your estimate more accurate?

9.3 Fertiliser application

Over-use of fertilisers can damage the environment. The application of fertilisers has to be a carefully controlled process. When deciding what type of fertiliser to use, important factors to take into account include:
• the amount of fertiliser needed by the crop;
• when it has to be applied;
• how it will be applied;
• how much it will cost the farmer;
• what the long-term effect will be.

Before choosing which fertiliser to use, information is obtained about the nutrient status of the soil. Such tests are carried out by advisory bodies like the Agricultural Development and Advisory Service (ADAS).

The nutrient status of the soil is affected by abiotic and biotic factors. Abiotic factors include the rock type of the area, and biotic factors include the effect of previous crops. Once a crop has been harvested, some nutrients can be left behind and others will have been used up. This will influence the amount of fertiliser that needs to be added.

Some crops use more nitrogen than others, so will leave less nitrogen in the soil after harvest. Cereals leave very little nitrogen in the soil. Oilseed rape or potatoes will leave slightly more nitrogen. Plants from the pea family, called **legumes,** can add nitrogen to the soil. Legumes have nitrogen-fixing bacteria in their roots. Residues of the legume crop left in the soil contain nitrogen in a form available for other plants to use.

Different crops require different levels of nutrients. The **NPK value** of a crop is the ratio of nitrogen : phosphorus : potassium needed. Spring barley usually requires a NPK value of 2:1:1, whereas legumes, which do not need to obtain nitrogen from the soil, require a value of 0:1:1.

 4 Looking only at levels of nitrogen, phosphorus and potassium in farmyard manure and inorganic fertiliser, as in Table 2, what would this suggest to a farmer who wanted to achieve the same yield with organic fertilisers as can be obtained with inorganic fertilisers?

Inorganic fertilisers have a high nutrient content. The amounts and ratios of plant nutrients are known, and can be matched to the needs of the crop. The nutrient content of organic fertiliser varies depending on the animal species and its diet, and it can be very difficult to match

Organic fertiliser may be messy to apply, but contains many nutrients in different forms, some which are released quickly and others that are released over time as microorganisms break down the organic matter.

Table 2. Chemical composition of fertilisers

Fertiliser	N	P	K
Inorganic NPK	12	15	20
Cattle manure	0.6	0.1	0.5
Chicken manure	1.5	0.5	0.6
Pig slurry	0.2	0.1	0.2
Sewage sludge	1.0	0.3	0.2

Values are % composition
Source: adapted from Haywood,
Applied Ecology, Nelson, 1992

Table 3. Crop yields

Crop	Control (no fertiliser)	FYM only	NPK only	FYM as % of NPK
Wheat	2.08	3.50	3.11	112
Barley	1.03	2.03	2.26	90
Sugar beet	3.80	15.60	15.60	100
Mangolds (beet for cattle)	3.80	22.30	30.90	72

The yield of crops as $t\ ha^{-1}$ is given after long-term applications of farmyard manures (FYM) and inorganic fertilisers (NPK)
Source: Haywood, *Applied Ecology*, Nelson, 1992

the nutrient needs of the crop exactly.

If soil is very low in nitrogen and a nitrogen-demanding crop is going to be grown, then the speed of release of nutrients from the fertiliser used may influence a farmer's choice. Ammonium nitrate, used in inorganic fertilisers, is very soluble and releases nitrates to the soil easily. Urea, found in organic fertiliser, gives a much slower rate of release.

However, some nutrients in organic fertilisers are present in a soluble, readily available form, and more nutrients are released over a longer time by the decomposition of organic matter by microorganisms. One application of organic fertiliser can have a much longer-lasting effect than inorganic fertiliser (Table 3).

Fertilisers need to be added to the soil ready for when the plant's demand for nutrients is at its greatest. Nitrates and ammonium ions are highly soluble and during periods of rainfall there is a risk of nutrient loss due to **leaching**. Leaching is the drainage of nutrients through the soil dissolved in water. Nitrogen is rarely applied during autumn because of the danger of leaching over the wet winter months. For autumn-sown crops, it is added in two stages. An early application of nitrogen, in late February to early March, to autumn-sown cereal crops stimulates the growth of side shoots. A second application in late April to early May avoids the problems of nutrient loss by leaching due to spring rains. With spring-sown crops such as spring barley, potatoes and sugar beet, the nitrogen is either applied just before sowing, or at the same time as the seed.

Potassium and phosphorus are not very soluble, so losses from the soil by leaching are small. These nutrients are usually ploughed into the soil just before sowing.

Inorganic fertilisers are expensive and farmers do not want to use more than they must. The value of the increased yield is known as the **yield return**. This must be greater than the cost of applying the fertiliser. The value of the increased yield minus the cost of the fertiliser application is called the **maximum net yield**.

The **cost–benefit ratio** is the value of the yield return divided by the cost of applying the fertiliser chosen.

The value of the crop in Table 4 is £100 per tonne and the fertiliser costs 50p per kg.

Once a farmer has the right machinery, free-flowing fertiliser pellets are easy to apply evenly over a field.

Table 4. Yield return of a cereal crop					
N applied/kg ha^{-1}	0	50	100	150	200
Yield/t ha^{-1}	2.9	3.4	4.3	4.7	4.8

Source: Harper, *Principles of Arable Crop Production*, Granada

5 a Draw a graph of the data in Table 4.
  b Describe any relationship that you can observe.
  c Calculate the cost–benefit ratio for each fertiliser application.
  d Does the yield return exceed the cost at all fertiliser applications?
  e Which fertiliser application would you think is most economical? Explain your answer.

Eventually there is a point at which the application of extra nitrogen fertiliser is not covered by the value of the increased yield. This is an example of the law of diminishing returns. There is less return from the crop from increased fertiliser applications.

Prevailing weather conditions is another factor to take into account when considering the economics of applying inorganic fertiliser. With an application of nitrogen of 60 kg ha^{-1}, the winter wheat yield in the drought of 1976 was 3.02 t ha^{-1} compared with 4.5 t ha^{-1} in years of normal rainfall.

Farmers also have to consider the costs of machinery and labour. Many inorganic fertilisers come in granules or pellets and specialised machinery is needed for spreading them over the land. However, the machinery is light, and the fertiliser is easy to store and to handle. If kept in moisture-proof conditions the fertiliser can be stored for long periods of time.

Organic fertilisers like farmyard manure are bulky and difficult to store. There may be insufficient organic material available on site and it may have to be transported from livestock areas into **arable** areas. Arable land is land used for crop production. Heavy machinery is needed to handle the fertiliser, and it can be difficult to apply evenly over a field. Weed seeds and fungal spores that cause plant diseases may be present in animal manures. Sewage sludge may contain heavy metals such as lead, zinc and nickel, which can be toxic to plants.

However, recycling of organic wastes makes good environmental sense. The nutrients in the organic material are added to soil where they will be used up by the crops sown. If organic material is just left, for example in land fill sites, then there can be problems of uncontrolled leaching.

9.4 Nitrate run-off

Adding nitrate fertilisers to soil stimulates the growth of microorganisms. This results in the release of nitrogen that is normally held in the soil in organic form and not usually subject to leaching (Fig. 4). The nitrate enters the ground water systems from which we extract our drinking water. Because of the increased use of inorganic nitrogen fertilisers, there has been an increased problem with nitrate run-off from leaching since the 1940s.

The European Community (EC) limit on nitrate in water is 50 mg dm^{-3}. Medical opinion is that 80 mg dm^{-3} poses no threat to human health. However, water from

rivers in lowland England often has in excess of 100 mg dm^{-3} and has to be diluted down with low nitrate water before it is drinkable.

High nitrates in drinking water are known to be a cause of 'blue-baby syndrome'. Bacteria in the gut of a baby reduce the nitrate to nitrite. Haemoglobin in the blood of the baby takes the nitrite in preference to oxygen, leading to respiratory failure. The lips and body of the baby go blue. Only a handful of cases have ever occurred in Britain, but even so in agricultural areas of south-east England nursing mothers have been supplied with

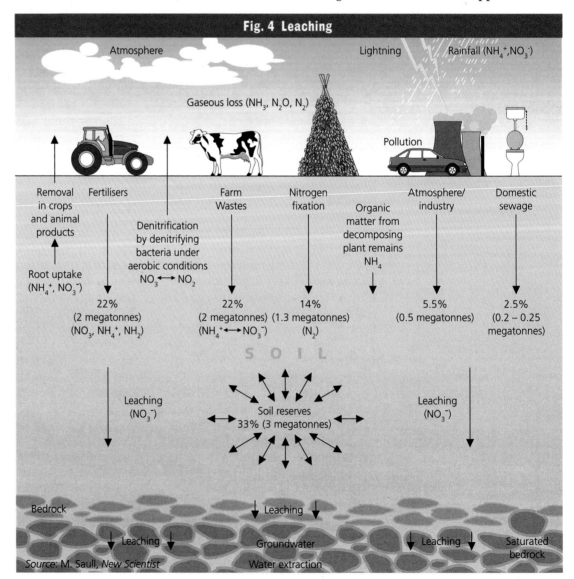

Fig. 4 Leaching

Source: M. Saull, *New Scientist*

Incorrect application of inorganic fertilisers can result in both loss of fertiliser and environmental hazard due to leaching and run-off. Excess nutrients in ditches and streams causes non-crop plants to grow in abundance.

Fig. 5 Nitrate levels

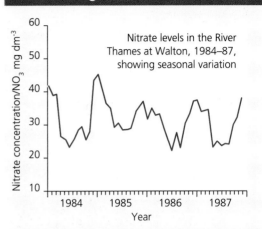

Nitrate levels in the River Thames at Walton, 1984–87, showing seasonal variation

Source: *Journal of Biological Education*, Vol.22, p.4, 1988

bottled water because their drinking water exceeds the EC nitrate maximum.

It has also been suggested that there is a link between high nitrate water and stomach cancer. N-nitroso compounds can cause cancer in laboratory animals. It may be that nitrates can be converted, via nitrites, to N-nitroso compounds in the human gut.

A number of changes in farming strategy could result in reducing the current loss of nitrates into rivers and streams. At the same time, these would not significantly reduce crop productivity. The changes include:

- avoiding the overuse of nitrate fertiliser by matching the fertiliser applications accurately to the needs of the crop;
- avoiding winter applications, when soils are wet and fertiliser is more likely to be leached;
- not applying nitrate fertiliser too early in the spring or before forecast heavy rains;
- splitting fertiliser applications;
- growing autumn-sown crops in preference to spring-sown crops, and sowing them as early as possible so that they use up nitrate left from the previous crop;
- using slow-release fertilisers, which give up their nitrogen gradually;
- not ploughing up grassland, as this releases large amounts of nitrate.

6 a What trends can you observe in the data in Fig. 5?
  b Apart from nitrate fertiliser, suggest four other possible sources of the nitrate.
  c How might the nitrate level be reduced by natural biological processes?

Key ideas

- Crops need nitrogen, phosphorus and potassium if they are to grow well.

- Fertilisers replace the nutrients that the harvested crop has removed.

- The correct amount of NPK fertiliser will allow crops to achieve their full growth potential if no other factor is limiting.

- Inorganic fertilisers are expensive, but they are easy to apply and store and are rich in easily released nutrients.

- Organic fertilisers are difficult to store and apply but have a long-lasting effect and are cheaper.

- A farmer has to consider the economics of applying fertiliser to maintain high, sustainable yields.

- The possible sources of high nitrate levels in water need to be investigated so that the levels can be reduced.

9.5 New techniques

Advances in modern technology, greater understanding of plant nutrition and the availability of fertilisers has led to changes in crop production both in fields and in glasshouses.

Hydroponics means growing plants without soil. Instead of soil, the plants are grown in another medium, for example peat, rockwool or sand, and fed by a chemical nutrient solution. In the UK the majority of the tomatoes, cucumbers and sweet peppers sold have been grown in a soil-less culture.

The most familiar soil-less technique is **peat culture**. Grow bags, for example, are popular with amateur gardeners, but seldom used by commercial growers because they are so expensive. Peat contains very few plant nutrients, and is very acidic. Calcium and magnesium carbonate are added to peat composts to raise the pH and add nutrients. Other plant nutrients have to be added, but are often lost due to leaching.

Rockwool slabs is a soil-less culture technique used by commercial growers. The fibres are light, sterile and retain more air and water than sand or gravel. Rockwool fibres are also used by builders for insulation in cavity walls and roof spaces.

The demand for peat from UK gardeners has meant the digging up of peat bogs in environmentally sensitive areas. Although it is popular as a plant growing medium, it is naturally very low in nutrients and added nutrients are easily lost from it by leaching. Plant nutrients have to be added regularly.

Nutrient film technique involves a flowing water culture that means the plant roots get a good supply of oxygen and nutrients (Fig. 6).

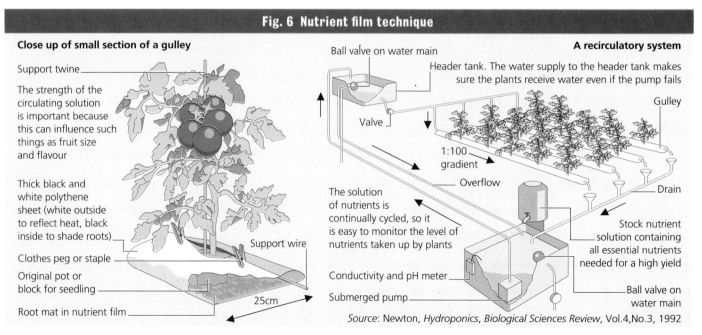

Fig. 6 Nutrient film technique

Close up of small section of a gulley

Support twine

The strength of the circulating solution is important because this can influence such things as fruit size and flavour

Thick black and white polythene sheet (white outside to reflect heat, black inside to shade roots)

Clothes peg or staple

Original pot or block for seedling

Root mat in nutrient film

Support wire

25cm

A recirculatory system

Ball valve on water main

Header tank. The water supply to the header tank makes sure the plants receive water even if the pump fails

Gulley

Valve

1:100 gradient

Overflow

Drain

The solution of nutrients is continually cycled, so it is easy to monitor the level of nutrients taken up by plants

Conductivity and pH meter

Submerged pump

Stock nutrient solution containing all essential nutrients needed for a high yield

Ball valve on water main

Source: Newton, *Hydroponics, Biological Sciences Review*, Vol.4, No.3, 1992

These aubergines are being grown by nutrient film technique in a glasshouse in England.

With increased understanding of plant nutrition, advances in agricultural technology and economic pressures, monoculture systems have been developed since the Second World War.

Fig. 7 Tomato yields

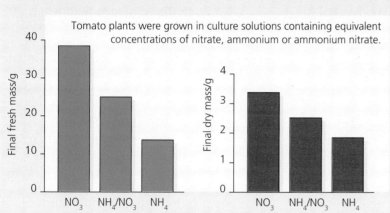

Tomato plants were grown in culture solutions containing equivalent concentrations of nitrate, ammonium or ammonium nitrate.

7 a From Fig. 7, which source of nitrogen gives the highest yield of tomato plants? Suggest why.
 b Explain why the results are shown as dry mass as well as fresh mass.
 c How could you monitor:
   (i) nutrient medium concentration;
   (ii) pH of the culture solutions?

A **monoculture** involves growing the same crop on the same land, year after year. The main benefit of monocultures is an economic one. The increase in mechanisation and reduction of labour means that continuous cropping of one crop brings a greater economic return per unit area of land. However, the system demands high inputs of inorganic fertilisers and pesticides to maintain the high yields.

Table 5. Sustained yield

Annual treatment since 1844 /kg ha^{-1}			1980–1982 yields/t ha^{-1}	
N	P	K	Wheat	Potatoes
0	0	0	1.69	8.47
96	0	0	3.68	8.30
0	77	107	2.04	16.83
96	77	107	6.60	38.57

Source: Rothamsted Experimental Station, FMA publication

Yields of wheat and potatoes can be kept high year after year, so long as fertiliser input is high enough (Table 5). Continuous application of inorganic fertilisers means there does not have to be a period when the monoculture crop is not sown.

Expensive inorganic fertilisers have to be applied regularly, otherwise there is a decline in the fertility of the soil. Monocultures also provide large areas that can become infested with pests and diseases associated with the crop. These have to be controlled with expensive pesticides. An increase in weeds such as couch grass and wild oats can be difficult and costly to control over large areas.

Disposal of the vast areas of straw left by cereal monocultures is a problem because ploughing in is expensive and burning causes environmental hazards.

9.6 Crop rotations

The use of inorganic fertilisers has led to crop specialisation and the loss of traditional crop rotations. Reliance on inorganic fertilisers can result in lower organic matter in the soil, which then supports fewer soil organisms and has a poorer soil structure. Organic farming means growing crops without the use of inorganic fertilisers, pesticides or plant growth regulators. Instead of soluble inorganic fertilisers, the organic farmer relies on organic manures and composts, crop residues and off-farm organic wastes like spent mushroom compost.

Organic fertilisers return high levels of organic matter to the soil, which binds the soil particles together. This improves the overall soil structure by aiding aeration and drainage in clay soils, and water retention in light, sandy soils. Organic material acts as a food resource for soil organisms, and the activity of animals such as earthworms also improves soil aeration and drainage. Organic matter releases nutrients over a longer period of time as a result of the action of microorganisms.

Crop rotation influences the amounts of nutrients that need to be added for different crops. Winter wheat grown after another cereal needs far more of each nutrient than it does if grown after root crops. This is because a root crop like potatoes takes up far less nutrients than a cereal crop.

Table 6. Fertiliser recommendations

Crop	Fertiliser recommendations/kg ha^{-1}		
	N	P	K
Winter wheat after cereals	150–200	50–100	50–100
Winter wheat after roots	50–100	40–60	0–60
Spring barley after cereals	125–150	50–100	50–100
Spring barley after roots	40–75	40–60	0–60
Sugar beet	125–150	65–125	150–200
Potatoes	120–200	150–220	150–250
Oilseed rape	120–200	60–80	60–80
Maize	100–150	60–90	60–90
Mown grass	200–400	80–100	60–200
Grazed grass	150–350	50–60	60–100

Source: Haywood, *Applied Ecology*, Nelson, 1992

8 a From Table 6, compare the difference in recommended levels after cereals and after roots for spring barley.
   b How do the nutrient demands of winter wheat (after cereals) compare with those of sugar beet.
   c What might happen if these recommended levels of fertilisers were:
   (i) exceeded:
   (ii) not met?

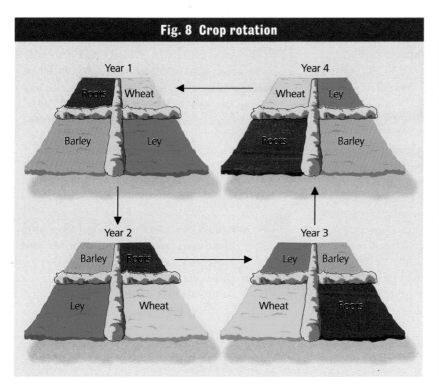

Fig. 8 Crop rotation

Year 1

Roots | Wheat
Barley | Ley

Year 2

Barley | Roots
Ley | Wheat

Year 3

Ley | Barley
Wheat | Roots

Year 4

Wheat | Ley
Roots | Barley

A mixture of different crops rather than one huge monoculture is better for the environment and can still be economical for the farmer.

The practice of growing a planned sequence of crops has been used for many years. Towards the end of the nineteenth century fixed crop rotations, like the Norfolk four-course rotation, were used (Fig. 8). A **ley** is a grass/legume mix that can be grazed by livestock. Soil nitrogen is increased by the inclusion of legumes in crop rotations.

Different crops need different methods of cultivation, which leads to an improved soil texture, and growing different crops breaks the life-cycles of crop pests and disease-causing organisms. There is less chance of pests and diseases associated with one crop becoming established than with monocultures. Keeping the soil covered by growing crops all the year round helps keep the soil healthy. Growing an early crop, like winter wheat, in the rotation, means that it is more difficult for certain weeds to germinate and become established. Growing a crop in the rotation that will be grazed by livestock over the winter means that nutrients in the soil are used over the winter. As a result there is less likelihood of nutrient loss by leaching, and organic matter is returned in the faeces from the animals.

Over the last 50 years, farmers have been encouraged to use nitrate fertilisers to increase their yields. Intensive arable agriculture is dependent on them. The increased use of inorganic fertilisers has enabled improved varieties of crops to reach their full growth potential. This is especially true of cereal production. When Britain first joined the EC in 1973, the drive for increased food production was encouraged by its Common Agricultural Policy (CAP). This guaranteed the farmer an agreed price on cereals. But there is increasing criticism that high-yield, intensive farming based on nitrate fertilisers has led to economic problems caused by overproduction. There are huge butter and grain mountains in developed countries that have to be stored until they can be sold, often at a loss. Food surpluses are low in some countries such as the UK because farmers are encouraged to set land aside, and not use it for growing crops.

Other consequences of the overuse of nitrate fertiliser in high production agriculture are:
- economic loss to the farmer due to the wastage of expensive fertiliser;
- nitrate run-off finds its way into rivers and streams, leading to eutrophication;
- high nitrate levels can damage human health.

A return to traditional methods may be more labour intensive, but it is less damaging to the environment. Yields of crops may not be as high, but they are easier to sustain and do not cause problems of over-production. Organic farming including crop rotation maintains the soil in a healthier condition and helps control pests and weed without the need for expensive chemicals. Using organic fertiliser uses an available natural resource.

By controlling its use within a crop rotation system, the nutrients are recycled and used by the growing crops. However, if the ever-increasing world population is to be fed, the issue of continued inorganic farming cannot be ignored. High yields need to be sustained, and organic methods alone may not be sufficient on a global scale. The needs of different countries vary depending on the population size and availability of cultivable land, and local and global needs may clash.

 9 a **Draw up a table of advantages and disadvantages of using organic and inorganic fertilisers.**
  b **Draw up a table of differences between inorganic and organic farming systems.**

Key ideas

- Hydroponics is crop production without soil. It requires the controlled addition of nutrients.

- Monocultures are a product of intensive agricultural practice. Large areas of land can be devoted to one crop because of the use of inorganic fertilisers.

- Crop rotations have many advantages, especially the inclusion of a legume to increase the nitrogen content of the soil for the next crop.

What a pest!

Agrochemical companies are keen to promote the benefits of pesticide use. They say these include improving food quantity and quality; reducing food prices; helping animal welfare and habitat management; helping gardeners by controlling weeds; and making food production more profitable. Often these organisations use dramatic language to market pesticides: 'Today 41 000 children will die from starvation'; 'Today in the world, there will be 200 000 more mouths to feed than yesterday'.

The world's population is growing daily, putting increasing demands on the world's resources, especially its food supply. If we were to stop using modern pesticides, this could lead to a catastrophic shortage of food in some parts of the world. But do these agrochemicals have effects on the environment and ecosystem that we need to take into consideration? Will the chemicals always be as effective? Are there any alternative methods for pest control that do not depend on chemicals?

The potato is the staple diet of many people around the world. The use of pesticides can increase the yield of a crop, so that there is more, cheaper food on the market.

Fresh fruit and vegetables are essential for a healthy diet. Pesticides can prevent disease affecting a crop. But residues of the chemicals used can be left on the food and enter the food chain.

10.1 Learning objectives

After working through this chapter, you should be able to:

- **describe** the problems caused by pests, weeds and diseases of crop plants;

- **explain** the principles of the use of herbicides and fungicides;

- **evaluate** the advantages and disadvantages of the use of insecticides;

- **outline** the principles of cultural methods of control of pests, weeds and diseases;

- **explain** the principles of biological control of pests;

- **describe** the benefits of integrated pest management.

10.2 Pests, weeds and diseases

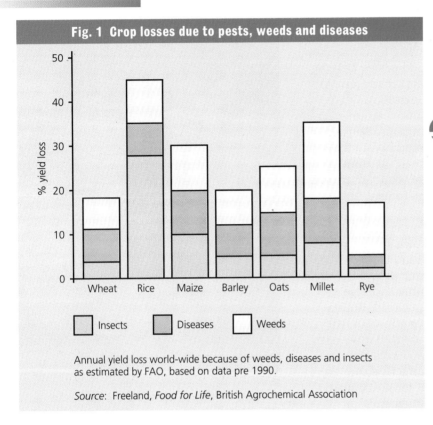

Fig. 1 Crop losses due to pests, weeds and diseases

% yield loss

Wheat Rice Maize Barley Oats Millet Rye

☐ Insects ☐ Diseases ☐ Weeds

Annual yield loss world-wide because of weeds, diseases and insects as estimated by FAO, based on data pre 1990.

Source: Freeland, *Food for Life*, British Agrochemical Association

A crop species remaining from the previous year, for example these potatoes growing among a wheat crop, is a weed known as a volunteer.

Crop productivity can be limited by:
- organisms eating the plants;
- competition from other plants for essential nutrients and space;
- diseases that affect the plant's growth.

All of these factors reduce the crop yield and the commercial value of the crop (Fig. 1). On a global scale, efforts have to be made to get the best possible yields of crops from suitable land in order to feed the growing population. However, farmers need to make a profit from the sale of their crops, and agrochemical companies want to make a profit from the sale of the chemicals.

A **pest** is an organism that reduces the yield of a crop. If a large area of the green leaves of a crop is eaten by a pest, the plant's rate of photosynthesis is reduced. Most crop pests are **arthropods**, which include insects, mites, millipedes and woodlice. There are 20 000 insect pest species world-wide. Other pests are molluscs, birds and rodents.

A **weed** is a plant growing in the wrong place at the wrong time, competing with the crop plant and so reducing crop yield.

Weeds can also be hosts for pests and disease-causing organisms. For example, fungi can survive in many grass species and then infect cereal crops. Seeds from weeds can get mixed up in harvested seed, so are sown along with the crop seed.

1 Suggest how weeds affect crop productivity.

There are two kinds of weed:
- **annuals**, which complete their life cycle in less than a year;
- **perennials**, which can grow and reproduce for many years.

A successful annual weed produces a lot of seeds so that new populations can grow quickly. The greater plantain may produce more than 13 000 seeds per plant. The seeds of annual weeds can lie in the soil for a long time before conditions are right for them to germinate. Even after being in the soil for 16 years, 47% of Shepherds purse seeds can still germinate. Most fields have an average of 2.5×10^8 weed seeds that could germinate per hectare. Successful weeds also often have well developed seed dispersal mechanisms, so that they can colonise new habitats.

Perennial weeds produce smaller numbers of seeds than annuals. Instead, some have large roots and some have **rhizomes**. Rhizomes are underground stems that can produce roots and shoots. These act as food stores so that the weed can survive unfavourable conditions. Examples include docks and dandelions.

Disease in crops can be caused by organisms such as fungi, viruses and bacteria, or from lack of essential nutrients and other abiotic factors (Fig. 2). Disease-causing organisms lower the growth rate of plants. Lack of essential nutrients can change the appearance of a crop, for example the leaves may go yellow as a result of lack of iron or magnesium, needed for the synthesis of chlorophyll.

In the UK, plant diseases reduce the potential production of a crop by 10–15%. A further 5% is lost after harvesting because of disease caused by fungi.

Fig. 2 Factors causing disease

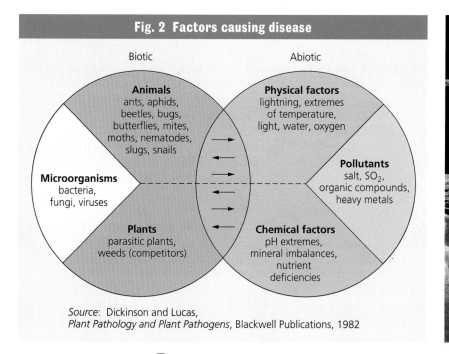

Source: Dickinson and Lucas,
Plant Pathology and Plant Pathogens, Blackwell Publications, 1982

Viruses cause many plant diseases. Viruses cannot move about on their own. Aphids feed by inserting their mouthparts into plant cells and sucking up sap. If the plant is infected, the aphid may suck up viral particles. When the aphid feeds on another plant, that plant will become infected.

2 a From Table 1 calculate the percentage of combined losses for each crop and put them in order starting with the highest.

b What was the actual percentage production for sugar?

c Which of the three types of loss had the greatest impact on reducing crop productivity?

Table 1. World losses/tonnes x 10^6				
Crop	Potential production	Losses due to disease	Losses due to insect pests	Losses due to weeds	Actual production
Wheat	356.8	33.8	18.1	35.1	269.8
Rice	445.7	40.0	122.6	47.4	235.7
Maize	344.9	33.2	44.7	45.0	222.0
Potatoes	406.4	90.3	24.2	16.8	275.1
Sugar (beet and cane)	1351.7	236.0	232.1	177.9	705.7
Vegetables	284.4	31.6	23.8	24.1	204.9
Fruit	200.4	33.1	11.5	11.8	144.0

Source: adapted from Cramer, Plant protection and world crop production,
Pflanzenschutz Nachrichten, Bayer, 20, 1967, based on data pre 1967

10.3 Chemical control

Many farmers use chemicals to encourage healthy crop growth, prevent weed growth and prevent damage by pests and disease. This boosts the commercial value of the crop but may mean the crops are not as healthy to consumers because traces of the chemicals are left in the plants.

Pesticides are chemicals that destroy pests, weeds and diseases. The yield of crops may be dramatically increased when pesticides are used. Pesticides can be split into categories that are specific to the type of organism they are used to control:

- **insecticides**, for the control of insects;
- **herbicides**, for the control of weeds;
- **fungicides**, for the control of fungi.

Broad-spectrum insecticides kill a wide range of insect pests, including the insects' natural enemies. **Narrow-spectrum** insecticides only kill specific insect species.

There are many ways of applying insecticides to crops (Fig. 3). Ideally they need to be applied to a crop in such a way that they stick to the surface of the plant or pest and remain active for several days or even weeks.

Insecticides that coat the leaves with poison are most useful for treating a crop that has been infected by a pest. They are usually cheaper than other types of insecticide but are only effective for a short time and have to be reapplied. Insecticides that are absorbed into the tissues of the plant can provide long-term protection because they are not affected by environmental factors such as light and rain.

 3 **How could applying an aphid-specific insecticide control plant diseases caused by viruses?**

Some herbicides are **non-selective**. This means they will kill any plant, including crop plants. Therefore they have to be used before a crop has germinated or been sown. They can be used to clear areas before cultivation. Other herbicides are **selective**. They have been developed to affect only certain types of plant. They can be applied after a crop has germinated, and will only kill the weeds.

Contact herbicides affect only the area of the plant they are applied to. They kill

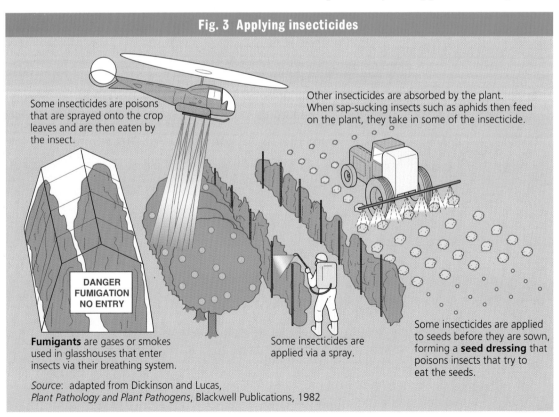

Fig. 3 Applying insecticides

Some insecticides are poisons that are sprayed onto the crop leaves and are then eaten by the insect.

Other insecticides are absorbed by the plant. When sap-sucking insects such as aphids then feed on the plant, they take in some of the insecticide.

DANGER FUMIGATION NO ENTRY

Fumigants are gases or smokes used in glasshouses that enter insects via their breathing system.

Some insecticides are applied via a spray.

Some insecticides are applied to seeds before they are sown, forming a **seed dressing** that poisons insects that try to eat the seeds.

Source: adapted from Dickinson and Lucas, *Plant Pathology and Plant Pathogens*, Blackwell Publications, 1982

all the above-ground parts of the weed they have been applied to. **Systemic herbicides** are absorbed by plants, and can kill all the plant tissues. Once inside the plant, systemic herbicides are not affected by light, which can break down some contact herbicides, or rain, which can wash off contact herbicides.

 4 a Explain the disadvantage of applying contact herbicides to perennial weeds with large, underground roots.
  b If weeds are growing among a crop that is nearly ready to harvest, explain the problems a farmer has to consider before applying a herbicide.

Fungi spread by spores that are carried by wind. Spores can also be present in the soil. When the environmental conditions, for example air temperature and humidity, are right the spores in the air or in the soil can infect a plant, causing disease.

Some fungicides are **protectants**. They remain on the surface of the plant and prevent the fungus from attacking the plant. Other fungicides are absorbed by the plant. They spread throughout the plant tissue, so can reach all the diseased parts and kill the fungus.

There are many factors that affect the successful use of fungicides, for example the weather, rate of application, method of application, etc. Some farmers apply sprays frequently regardless of whether the disease is present, in order to prevent the disease occurring.

 5 Suggest economic and environmental reasons why it is much better to apply fungicides only at times of high risk of disease.

If the cause of a disease is known, the risk of contracting the disease can be reduced. For example, if the air temperature is greater than $10°C$ for 48 hours, and the relative humidity is greater than 89% for 11 hours or more in each day, farmers are warned by the Agricultural Development and Advisory Service (ADAS) to spray potato crops. This is because these conditions are ideal for the fungus that causes late potato blight to develop.

Asulam is a selective systemic herbicide that was originally developed for use against docks but has been found to be very effective against bracken in upland areas. It is selective so does not harm other plants or animals and can be sprayed from helicopters in remote areas such as the North York Moors.

Key ideas

- Pests are animals (often insects) that reduce the yield of a crop.

- Weeds are plants growing in the wrong place at the wrong time.

- Diseases of crops can be caused by fungi, viruses and bacteria.

- Pesticides are chemicals that destroy weeds, pests and diseases.

- Insecticides can be broad spectrum or narrow spectrum.

- Herbicides can be selective or non-selective and contact or systemic.

- Fungicides can be applied when the environmental conditions are known to cause an outbreak of fungus.

10.4 Environmental impact

The use of chemicals to protect crops is not a new idea. Three thousand years ago sulphur was used by the Greeks to kill pests, and the Chinese used arsenic in AD 900. More recently, naturally occurring chemicals such as nicotine from ground-up tobacco leaves and pyrethrum from certain Kenyan daisies have been used. Since 1950 more than 500 chemical substances have been registered for use as pesticides in the UK alone. Some of these do not occur naturally but have been made in laboratories. These are **synthetic** pesticides.

The increased use of pesticides is one of the factors that have led to the increase in yield of crops. Farmers can protect their crops. Some crops can now be grown in areas or at times of year when before they could not be grown because of the presence of a successful pest, weed or disease.

However, some insecticides are not broken down completely or very quickly once they have been applied. They remain in the environment for a long time. This is known as **persistence**. Many natural insecticides are quickly decomposed in the environment. Synthetic insecticides may not be decomposed as quickly (Fig. 4).

6 Suggest one advantage and one disadvantage of an insecticide that takes a long time to be broken down by decomposers.

When insecticides are not broken down they may persist in food chains. As the chemicals pass from one trophic level to another, they become concentrated, particularly in fat deposits of top carnivores such as birds of prey. This is called **bioaccumulation**. The effect may be quite dramatic, as with DDT which is now found in virtually all animal tissue, in every food chain, and even the Antarctic snow.

Aquatic ecosystems can be affected by insecticides when excess insecticide is washed off the land into rivers and streams. If insecticides in the food chains affect soil microorganisms and invertebrates, the rate of decomposition will be affected (Fig. 5).

In the late 1950s sparrowhawk and peregrine population levels fell dramatically following the introduction of insecticides such as dieldrin and DDT (Fig. 6). These insecticides and a fungicide containing toxic compounds of mercury were used to treat the cereal seeds before they were sown. When these compounds were first used on cereal seeds they caused the death of many wildlife species, including long-

Fig. 4 Breakdown rate

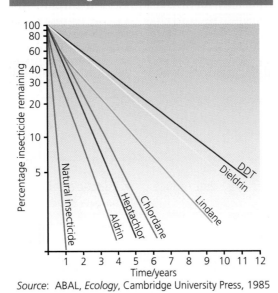

Source: ABAL, *Ecology*, Cambridge University Press, 1985

Fig. 5 Rate of decomposition

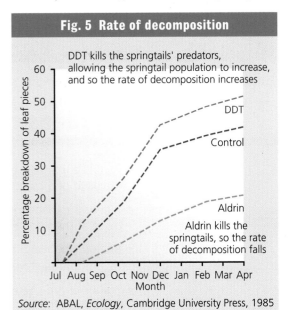

Source: ABAL, *Ecology*, Cambridge University Press, 1985

Fig. 6 Peregrine populations

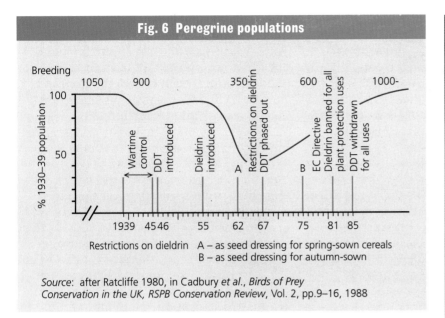

Breeding
1050   900   350dieldrin   600   1000-

Restrictions on dieldrin   A – as seed dressing for spring-sown cereals
B – as seed dressing for autumn-sown

Source: after Ratcliffe 1980, in Cadbury *et al.*, *Birds of Prey Conservation in the UK*, RSPB Conservation Review, Vol. 2, pp.9–16, 1988

tailed field mice, which are prey for sparrowhawks and peregrines (Table 2).

Ecologists trapped field mice and determined the concentrations of dieldrin and mercury in body residues. Two traps were used for four days before seeds treated with the chemicals were sown, and four traps for six days after the seeds had been sown.

7 a From Table 2, what effect did sowing a field with wheat seed treated with dieldrin have on long-tailed field mice?

b Suggest the effect this would have on the peregrines feeding on the mice.

Professor Ian Newton, an ecologist with the Institute of Terrestrial Ecology, spent many years proving that the declines in the shell thickness, breeding success and population of sparrowhawks are due to the use of pesticides such as DDT. He compared recent shells with historical ones housed in museums and private collections.

Table 2. Long-tailed field mice

Period	Trap	Number of mice caught	Number of mice analysed	Mean concentration of dieldrin/parts per million (ppm) (wet mass)	Mean concentration of mercury compounds/ppm (wet weight)
Before application	1	11	9	0.15	0.05
	2	15	4	0.23	0.03
After application	1	18	2	6.49	0.28
	2	18	7	10.96	0.41
	3	9	5	8.70	0.39
	4	12	5	12.06	0.42

Source: Jefferies *et al.*, *Journal of Zoology*, vol. 171, pp. 513–539, 1973

133

When Professor Newton was investigating the decline in sparrowhawk populations, he produced circumstantial evidence showing that shell thinning in wild populations of sparrowhawks in the UK began immediately after DDT started to be used in agriculture. If the eggs fall below a certain mass they break during laying. In general, the egg shells were thinner in the intensively farmed south east compared with the north and west where DDT was less widely used. Experimental evidence on captive birds of prey confirmed that DDT causes shell thinning in various species.

The use of chemicals such as DDT has been restricted. Sparrowhawk and peregrine populations have risen and birds are returning to areas where they had disappeared. The amount of insecticide residues in their bodies has fallen, shell thickness has improved, the reproductive rate has increased, and survival has increased. Ecological evidence like this has resulted in the ban of some pesticides and the development of better testing and improved methods of pest control by agrochemical companies. Humans as well as birds of prey can be affected by pesticides used on crops. We may be poisoned directly by eating treated food products or we may just breathe in the pesticides.

Pesticides are chemicals that are manufactured specifically to be toxic. When they are released into the environment, for example by spraying,

they can cause accidental death of humans, pets and domestic animals. This is called **direct killing**. There are approximately 150 deaths a year in the USA from insecticides, and thousands each year in developing countries due to warnings on labels not being read or interpreted properly.

Careless spraying may allow the pesticide to drift to other areas. For example, in the 1950s in the USA large doses of dieldrin were applied to kill a grassland pest, the Japanese beetle. The chemical also killed several birds as well as most farm cats. All new pesticides are rigorously tested for their effects on **non-target** species. The **target** species is the species that needs to be killed or controlled. The non-target species are all the other species in the habitat that should not be affected by the pesticide.

 8 Will the effect of drifting be more severe with broad-spectrum or narrow-spectrum insecticides? Explain your answer.

All members of a pest species are not equally likely to be affected by a particular insecticide. Some individuals are genetically less susceptible and may survive to pass on their resistance to the next generation. This could lead to the development of significant **pest resistance**. Most insects have rapid reproductive rates, so the evolution of resistance can be quite quick (Fig. 7). With female aphids, capable of breeding two weeks after birth, large numbers of resistant individuals have the potential to appear in the population in a single growing season. The more frequently an insecticide is used, the more likely resistance in the pest insect species is to evolve.

9 a Approximately how much insecticide achieved a 50% kill in:
(i) 1968;
(ii) 1970?
b If the volume or concentration of insecticide has to be increased, what could be the effects on other species in the habitat?

The number of resistant species increases every year. By 1987 there were over 500 insect species, 150 plant disease-causing

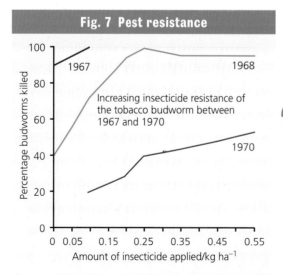

Fig. 7 Pest resistance

Percentage budworms killed

1967   1968

Increasing insecticide resistance of the tobacco budworm between 1967 and 1970

1970

Amount of insecticide applied/kg ha⁻¹

Source: ABAL, *Ecology*, Cambridge University Press, 1985

Fig. 8 Pest replacement

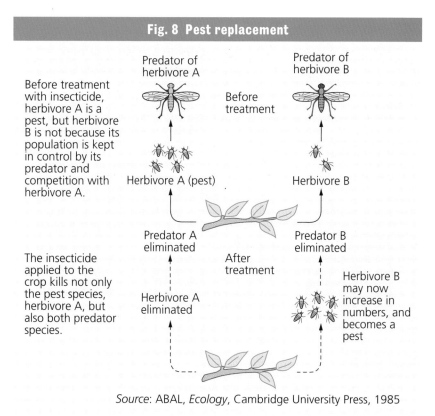

Before treatment with insecticide, herbivore A is a pest, but herbivore B is not because its population is kept in control by its predator and competition with herbivore A.

The insecticide applied to the crop kills not only the pest species, herbivore A, but also both predator species.

Predator of herbivore A

Predator of herbivore B

Before treatment

Herbivore A (pest)

Herbivore B

Predator A eliminated

After treatment

Predator B eliminated

Herbivore A eliminated

Herbivore B may now increase in numbers, and becomes a pest

Source: ABAL, *Ecology*, Cambridge University Press, 1985

Fig. 9 Pest resurgence

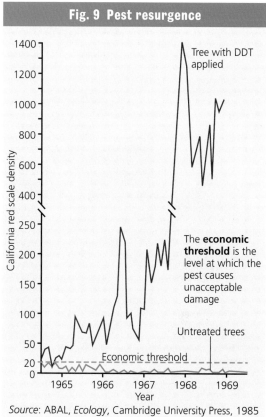

Tree with DDT applied

The **economic threshold** is the level at which the pest causes unacceptable damage

Untreated trees

Economic threshold

Source: ABAL, *Ecology*, Cambridge University Press, 1985

organisms and 50 weed species all resistant to the chemicals developed to kill them. Some species have developed resistance to more than one type of pesticide. Different insecticides have to be used for the same insect pest to delay resistance development.

Agrochemical companies are constantly trying to produce new and better pesticide products that are safe and effective. It takes at least 8–10 years of research and development at a cost of £20–60 million to produce a new product. Only a small number of products ever makes it to the market out of all of those initially tested.

Pest replacement, or secondary pest outbreak, occurs where crops become affected by another pest species. Once one pest species is killed, another species that is not affected by the insecticide may become a pest (Fig. 8).

Pest resurgence is when non-selective insecticides kill not only the pest species but its natural predators. If a small pest population survives but its predators do not, it can multiply unchecked to a level much worse than before the insecticide was applied. This situation occurred in the late 1960s in California with red scale insects on citrus trees (Fig. 9).

Information about a possible new pesticide may come from biologists who have observed the effects one organism has on another, or from chemists who have observed the effects of certain substances on biochemical pathways. The chemical substance is then either extracted from a natural source or made in a laboratory. Tests are carried out on the target species and non-target species to work out what levels are needed to kill the pest, weed or

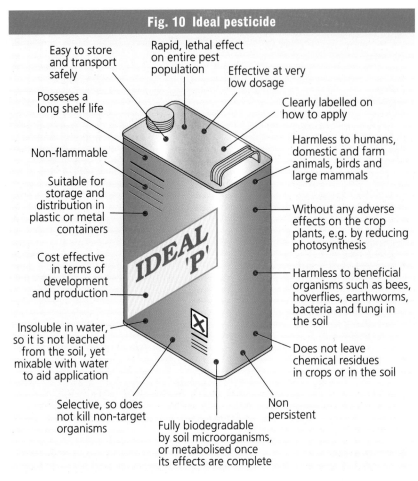

Fig. 10 Ideal pesticide

Easy to store and transport safely

Rapid, lethal effect on entire pest population

Effective at very low dosage

Posseses a long shelf life

Clearly labelled on how to apply

Non-flammable

Harmless to humans, domestic and farm animals, birds and large mammals

Suitable for storage and distribution in plastic or metal containers

Without any adverse effects on the crop plants, e.g. by reducing photosynthesis

Cost effective in terms of development and production

Harmless to beneficial organisms such as bees, hoverflies, earthworms, bacteria and fungi in the soil

Insoluble in water, so it is not leached from the soil, yet mixable with water to aid application

IDEAL 'P'

Does not leave chemical residues in crops or in the soil

Selective, so does not kill non-target organisms

Non persistent

Fully biodegradable by soil microorganisms, or metabolised once its effects are complete

disease, and what levels are safe for all other species in the habitat. The tests are first carried out in glasshouses with strictly controlled environmental conditions, and later under normal farming conditions.

10 Suggest why it is safer to try new pesticides in glasshouses first, before using them in the field.

In the UK, the law on the sale and use of pesticides was made stricter by the Food and Environment Act 1985 and the Control of Pesticide Regulations 1986. Agrochemical companies have a legal duty to ensure their products are properly used. There is a wide range of information and advice to make sure this happens. Monitoring has to be carried out to prevent too much of one pesticide being used.

The most important benefit of pesticide is an increase in crop productivity. The use of pesticides has saved millions of people from starvation in developing countries. The problem with early pesticides is that they were often introduced with little knowledge of their effects on harmless or helpful organisms within the ecosystem. This was the problem with non-selective or broad-spectrum insecticides such as DDT. The development, manufacture and application of pesticides is now strictly regulated, and certain ideal characteristics are aimed for (Fig. 10). However, the environmental and long-lasting impact of pesticides must not be overlooked. They can cause harm to humans, and other beneficial animals and plants.

Key ideas

- The early use of pesticides concentrated on their effectiveness in killing the target species and their immediate benefits such as an increase in crop yield.

- Harmful effects have gradually been recognised. Extreme toxicity can cause fatal accidents.

- Lack of specificity can kill non-target species such as natural predators.

- Persistence of pesticides in the environment leads to bioaccumulation.

- Frequent use of pesticides leads to genetic resistance.

10.5 Cultural control

These men are hoeing sugar beet before the Second World War. Hoeing used to be done by hand, which was very labour-intensive, but today can be done by machines.

Tillage involves working the soil to improve its physical condition in relation to the growth of crops. Primary tillage involves deep ploughing and uproots weeds, turning them into the soil. Animal pests such as wireworms are exposed on the soil surface, where predators such as birds can easily feed off them.

Cultural control methods for pest, weed and disease management date back to the earliest days of agriculture. Some people believe cultural control methods provide the best long-term management system for food production because they encourage good crop growth and aim to prevent crop damage and infection. If the crop is healthy, chemicals do not need to be added to kill pests, weeds and disease-causing organisms.

Looking after the crop by making sure the plants are kept in good conditions, for example by irrigating the land and applying fertiliser, plays a major role in the control of pests and diseases. Healthy plants are less likely to suffer from attacks by pests and diseases. If the crop plants are growing vigorously, they have a better chance in competing for space and other resources with weed plants.

Waste material, for example weed rhizomes and crop waste left after harvesting, can provide habitats for pests, weeds and disease-causing organisms. All plant rubbish and diseased plants should be reduced or removed. Stubble left after harvesting wheat crops used to be burned. This kills weeds and their seeds, and fungus spores and pests. However, it produces its own form of pollution. The resulting smoke releases large quantities of carbon dioxide, so stubble burning was banned in the UK in 1992.

As herbicides have become cheaper, a practice called **direct sowing** has become common. Crop seeds are planted into the soil through the remains of the previous crop once it has been harvested.

11 Suggest advantages and disadvantages of direct sowing for pest and weed control.

Crop rotation is very important. A break in the growing of a particular crop reduces the amount of material left capable of transmitting disease. However, if the pest, weed seed or disease-causing organism is capable of surviving long periods of time without its host crop plant, rotation will have only a temporary effect on pest numbers.

Varying the sowing and harvesting times of the crop disrupts the life cycle of the pest. It may be possible to avoid the egg-laying period of certain pests, for example aphids, by sowing cereals in autumn. Early harvesting of potatoes as 'new potatoes' reduces losses caused by the potato tuber nematode.

Secondary tillage, such as **harrowing**, destroys weed seedlings and uproots

137

vegetative growths such as rhizomes. These actions may need to be repeated together with hand weeding or **hoeing**. If the young shoots of weeds are continually disturbed by hoeing, their growth rate is severely reduced and they will not flower and produce seed. Young shoots that are killed can be left to provide organic matter that can be broken down by microorganisms. This releases nutrients used by the weeds back into the soil.

Q 12 Hoeing has more of an effect on annual weeds than perennial weeds. Explain why.

Mulching involves covering the soil with organic material such as manure, or non-organic material such as plastic sheeting. This prevents light from reaching the weeds; these plants cannot photosynthesise and so growth is reduced.

Some traditional, cultural methods do use chemicals. These include liming and sterilisation. Lime increases the soil pH and is added to avoid nutrient deficiencies and promote growth. It also reduces the effect of club root, a fungus that attacks the roots of cabbages.

Soil sterilisation is an expensive procedure and requires an enclosed environment. For these reasons its use is restricted to glasshouse crops such as tomatoes, which are infected by the potato cyst nematode.

There are two main methods of sterilisation. Steam sterilisation is the most effective and expensive method. The steam is injected directly into the soil or via perforated steel pipes under a plastic sheet. This method heats the soil to 82°C to a depth of 15–38 cm. Pests, weeds and disease-causing organisms cannot survive this heat.

Chemical sterilisation is cheaper. However, it cannot kill 100% of potato cyst nematodes. It can be applied by injection, drenching, granular application or as a gas under plastic sheeting.

10.6 Biological control methods

Biological control is another method of pest control that does not use chemicals which may contaminate the crop. It involves introducing another species to control the population of a pest species.

The introduced species could be:
- a predator, for example predatory mites;
- a parasitoid, for example wasps which lay their eggs on or in other insects;
- a parasite, for example nematode worms that live in slugs;
- a disease-causing organism, for example a bacterium that affects beetles.

Biological control is an old idea. In the thirteenth century, Chinese farmers used to put ants on citrus trees to protect the trees from pests like aphids.

Introducing a predator to the pest reduces the pest's population to a new lower level by increasing the death rate. It does not get rid of the pest completely. Some pests must survive or else the predator's population would also die out.

This insect breeder is preparing food cages on leaf circles for use in shipping predators to commercial growers and gardeners.

13 Why do you think the numbers of pests fluctuate in Fig. 11, both before and after the introduction of control measures?

A biological control programme consists of the following stages:
- finding where the pest species comes from originally;
- finding enemies of the pest, to become the control species;
- testing the control species to make sure no unwanted diseases are introduced and that only the target species is attacked;
- finding out whether the control is likely to work on a large scale;
- breeding or mass culture of the control species;
- releasing the control species;
- monitoring and evaluating the success of the programme.

If properly chosen, biological control agents will usually attack only one pest, with few if any adverse effects on other organisms. Biological control can be a cheaper method than chemical insecticides if the control species can reproduce in the habitat where it is needed. A successful biological control method would replace the use of insecticides. The levels of insecticides in food chains and ecosystems would then fall.

14 Why is a high degree of specificity necessary with a biological control agent?

Although many biological control products are being developed, they still

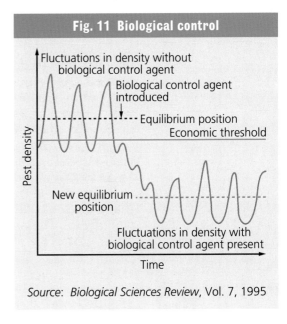

Fig. 11 Biological control

Fluctuations in density without biological control agent

Biological control agent introduced

Equilibrium position

Economic threshold

Pest density

New equilibrium position

Fluctuations in density with biological control agent present

Time

Source: Biological Sciences Review, Vol. 7, 1995

continue to account for less than 1% of the total crop protection market. Biological control is unlikely to be the only control measure used. It often takes some time for the control species' population to increase to such a level that it has an impact on the pest's population level. In the meantime, a lot of crop damage may have occurred.

Bracken is a problem in areas such as the North York Moors. Traditionally, cattle grazing used to keep it in check, because their frequent trampling prevented growth. Populations of natural insect herbivores feeding on bracken are kept in check by predators such as sawfly larvae and parasites. However, these herbivores rarely cause any significant damage and so cannot be used for bracken control. More recently, the selective herbicide asulam has been sprayed on a large scale.

If an insect could be found that fed on bracken but had no predators in that habitat to prevent its population from growing, then a more permanent solution would be found. A search for such an insect was started. From laboratory tests the most promising insect was a South African moth whose caterpillars feed on the fronds of the bracken. They come from a region in South Africa where the weather is very similar to that in Britain. Trials involving caged caterpillars revealed that the caterpillars were plant-specific.

However, areas where bracken is wanted

A species of nematode worm can be used to control slugs. The worm is a natural parasite found in the soil. It burrows into the slugs via a tiny pore on the back of the slug. Inside the slug it reproduces, eventually killing the slug. The nematode offspring then look for their own hosts. Trails show them to be effective against most slug pest species. The nematodes are suitable for commercial production because they can be cultured on a large scale.

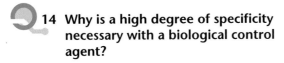

could also be affected. A lot of monitoring and aftercare would be necessary to ensure successful control. This could probably only be achieved in association with herbicide application. This is why biological control often cannot be seen as the only way to control pests, but it can mean that far less agrochemicals have to be used.

Some biological control species have been very successful. The prickly pear was an accidental introduction into Australia from America. It grew to be such a problem that it made 12 000 000 hectares of grazing land useless. The situation was brought under control by introducing the moth *Cactoblastis*. Its larvae bore holes into the prickly pear, allowing fungi to invade the weed. It took only five years for the biological control to be successful. Cottony cushion scale is an insect pest of citrus fruits in California and was controlled by the introduction of its native Australian predator, the ladybird.

The predatory mite has been used commercially for control of red spider mites in glasshouses for years.

 15 Why do you think biological control is most successful in enclosed areas such as glasshouses?

10.7 Integrated pest management

There are three major methods of pest control:
- chemical;
- cultural;
- biological.

Fig. 12 Integrated pest management

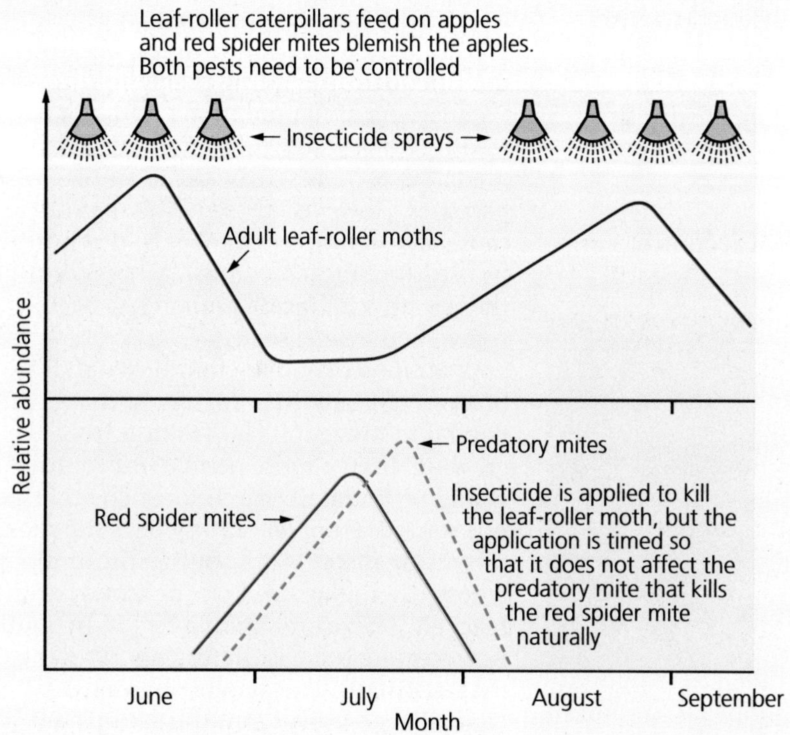

Leaf-roller caterpillars feed on apples and red spider mites blemish the apples. Both pests need to be controlled

Insecticide sprays

Adult leaf-roller moths

Red spider mites

Predatory mites

Insecticide is applied to kill the leaf-roller moth, but the application is timed so that it does not affect the predatory mite that kills the red spider mite naturally

Relative abundance

June   July   August   September
Month
Source: *Biological Sciences Review*, Vol. 7, 1995

These control methods are often combined through the practice of **integrated pest management**. This uses all suitable control techniques, methods and knowledge of a pest's population dynamics and habitat in order to reduce and maintain pest levels so that they do not cause too much damage. Integrated pest management can also be used to try and minimise the amount of agrochemicals used, and so reduce the impact of chemicals on the environment and on the food produced.

An understanding of the population dynamics of a pest species is very important for pest control. The aim is to keep the size of the pest population below the level where it causes severe crop loss. This level is called the economic threshold.

Population size is governed by four processes:
- increasing the death rate;
- decreasing the birth rate;
- increasing the emigration rate;
- decreasing the immigration rate.

In different habitats different insecticides can have more long-lasting or severe effects on the environment. In developing countries, insecticides may be too expensive for the local farmers to buy. In countries that have used insecticides a lot over the last few decades, many species are resistant to the chemicals, and the chemicals have entered the food chain.

Natural control factors such as predators, parasites and diseases should be used wherever possible. This means limiting broad-spectrum insecticides to a minimum to allow non-target species to survive. Insecticides still play an important role but their use is restricted to times when they will be most effective (Fig. 12).

In addition to cultural, chemical and biological control methods, the resistance of the crop species forms part of an integrated pest control programme. Crop plants can be bred that are resistant to particular pests. However, new crop varieties have to be produced every year to adapt to changes in pest populations.

Genetic engineering can introduce genes from insects into plants so the plants produce toxins against those insects. Again, the situation can change. Pests exposed to genetically manipulated plants may develop resistance themselves.

Legislation can also help control pests. The aim is to prevent pests being introduced into countries where they do not yet exist.

Successful integrated management involves the collection of a great deal of background information, including:
- crop growth characteristics;
- type, number and life cycle of the pest species;
- pest population dynamics and its relationship to crop damage;
- pest–host plant relationships;

A good example of effective pest control by legislation is the Colorado beetle. This pest can cause a great deal of damage to potatoes. In the UK, anybody who finds a Colorado beetle has to report it. There was a poster campaign so that everyone knew what it looked like. This insect has not established a population in the UK.

- pest–predator relationships and their effect on pest population dynamics;
- effects of insecticides on crops, pests and non-target species.

The level of success and the cost will decide whether farmers and producers adopt integrated pest management on a wider scale. Because they are commercial organisations, agrochemical companies produce products for a market with the intention of making a profit. This profit can be used to research and develop new products. So long as the world population continues to increase there will always be a demand for pesticides. The challenge for agrochemical companies is to produce safer, more effective pesticides that cannot cause direct killing of non-target organisms and do not leave harmful residues in the food that we eat. Chemical control should be combined with other non-chemical methods to reduce any unwanted effects on the environment and our food produce.

Key ideas

- Cultural methods keep the soil healthy and help the crop plants grow quickly and healthily.

- Biological control involves introducing an enemy species to control the population of a pest species.

- Integrated pest management involves the use of a variety of appropriate control methods. It emphasises the use of natural factors such as predators, parasites and disease-causing organisms while restricting pesticide use to a minimum.

Switching on growth

I am a lowland dairy farmer with a herd of 120 Friesian cows. I milk them twice a day. In 1988 I was approached by an agrochemical company to trial a new drug that increased the production of high yielding milk cows by up to 5 kg a day. I was very enthusiastic. This drug is called bovine somatotrophin (BST) and is a genetically engineered version of a growth hormone that occurs naturally in cows. Using this hormone would be a great benefit to me because it would increase milk production per cow. I would get more milk from fewer cows, saving me money on the cost of feed.

Before 1984 there was so much overproduction of milk in the European Community (EC) that much of the surplus was literally poured down the drain! Since then milk quotas have been imposed to control the supply and price of milk. So why do some people think we need to use hormones like BST to increase production? Animal welfare groups, environmentalists and some scientists say that the use of the hormone is unnatural and unhealthy for the cows. We need to know if artificially produced hormones are safe, and to work out if they have a role in agriculture. Are the hormones and plant growth substances added to crops and livestock still present in the food we eat? Can they affect us?

11.1 Learning objectives

After working through this chapter, you should be able to:

- **explain** the principles underlying the use of animal hormones in food production;

- **explain** how auxins cause cell enlargement;

- **describe** the use of auxins as rooting powders, selective weedkillers and in the storage of crops;

- **outline** the suggested mechanism for the action of gibberellins during cell differentiation;

- **describe** the use of gibberellins for inducing parthenocarpy;

- **explain** the role of cytokinins in RNA synthesis and their use in the delay of senescence;

- **explain** the role of abscisic acid as an antagonist to other plant promoters and its use in regulating fruit drop;

- **outline** the use of ethene in the induction of flowering and fruit ripening;

- **evaluate** the advantages and disadvantages associated with the use of plant and animal hormones.

11.2 The use of animal hormones

Farmers are always looking for ways of growing their product more quickly, more efficiently and more cheaply. They aim to increase their profits, but efficient food production will obviously also help meet the rising global need for food.

Animal farmers can increase meat production in two ways:
• by making individual animals grow faster;
• by rearing more animals.

Animals that grow faster have a higher **protein conversion efficiency** (PCE) value. In other words more of the food fed to the livestock is converted into meat.

$$PCE = \frac{\text{mass of protein produced}}{\text{mass of protein consumed}}$$

Traditionally, to rear more animals meant selecting breeds that had multiple offspring or a short **gestation**. Gestation is the time from when an egg is fertilised to when the fetus is born.

Current technology uses **hormones** to increase the growth rate and reproduction rate and reduce the gestation of livestock. Hormones are chemicals secreted by glands that control processes in the body.

Another essential for fast growth is a high nutrient input. Cattle and sheep have a relatively low PCE. Their diet consists of plant materials such as grass that are high in carbohydrates such as cellulose. The plant carbohydrates have to be converted to protein by the animal. Microorganisms in the gut of sheep and cattle synthesise amino acids from nitrogen sources in the gut. Pigs and poultry have a higher PCE. They can be fed diets containing more protein. Pigs are fed bonemeal, fishmeal, soya and offal. These are all rich in protein.

In intensive rearing of pigs, the feeding programme makes sure that a high proportion of the diet is protein from early on in a pig's life. Pigs are **weaned** early at three weeks so that the sows can become pregnant again. Weaning is when piglets are gradually given less of their mother's milk, and more of other foods. Milk powder supplements are given to the piglets. They are allowed unlimited feeding up to the age of 16 weeks. Muscle grows faster than fat when the pigs are young, so they are killed at 25 weeks, when they have reached maturity but still have relatively little fat.

Pigs are also fed antibiotics to reduce risk of infection and colouring agents to improve the colour of the meat. Pigs produce a natural growth hormone called **porcine somatotrophin** (PST), which can be made in a laboratory and is implanted as a pellet in the animal's body to promote growth. Its use is banned in European Community (EC) countries.

The growth rates of pigs and other livestock can be greatly increased by intensive feeding and breeding. Their surroundings are closely monitored to ensure even ventilation, correct temperature and reduced risk of infection by removal of faeces. But the movement of the pigs is restricted.

In many ways, outdoor production provides a better environment for the animals. Feeding is carried out by scattering large pellets of food over a wide area, which encourages the pigs to forage. Disadvantages included fighting between animals and potential injuries.

 1 From the photographs, list the advantages and disadvantages of the different ways of rearing pigs.

Fig. 1 Embryo transplantation

A cow with the desired characteristics is treated with **follicle-stimulating hormone** (FSH). This hormone increases the growth of follicles and so more eggs are released

Valuable donor cow

FSH treatment

Releases more eggs

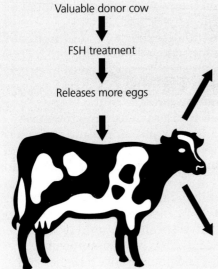

Embryo transfer
1. Artificial insemination using sperm from a bull with the desired characteristics
2. Embryos are taken out of the donor cow after 6–8 days
3. The embryos are transferred to the uterus of recipient cows under anaesthetic or are frozen for later use

In vitro fertilisation
1. Eggs are collected and cultured in the laboratory for 5 days
2. The eggs are fertilised with sperm from a bull with the desired characteristics, cultured for 5–6 days and frozen until required
3. The eggs are transferred to the uterus of recipient cows under anaesthetic

Source: adapted from Larkcom and Miller, *Food Production, Biology Advanced Studies*, Nelson, 1994

Until recently, it was common practice in intensive livestock rearing to use steroid hormone growth promoters, more commonly known as **anabolic steroids**. These are synthetic **androgens**, male sex hormones, or **oestrogens**, female sex hormones. Anabolic steroids increase the body's ability to retain nitrogen and build up protein levels. Androgens act directly on muscle cells, increasing protein synthesis and decreasing the rate of protein turnover. Oestrogens exert a less direct effect, by acting on other hormones.

An implant containing the hormone is placed under the skin of the ear of the animal, for example 3–4 months before slaughter. The best results are obtained when female animals are given androgens and male animals are given oestrogens.

Castrated animals are male animals that have had their testicles removed. Testicles produce natural growth hormones so these animals tend to have a slower growth rate. However, castration reduces aggression and makes animals easier to handle. More than 50% of all beef cattle are castrated bulls. In their case they are often given a mixture of both types of anabolic steroids to increase growth.

Anabolic steroids are used by humans as performance-enhancing drugs in sport. The use of anabolic steroids in meat production is now banned in EC countries because of fears of hormone residues in the meat being eaten by humans. However, there is evidence that meat from untreated animals has higher concentrations of anabolic steroids than treated meat.

2 Explain why it is impossible to have meat that contains no anabolic steroids.

The development of **embryo transplantation** techniques has increased the potential productivity from rearing livestock (Fig. 1).

Artificial insemination is when sperm are taken from male animals and injected into the females by the farmer or veterinarian. Mating does not take place. The semen from one male can be used to produce thousands of offspring. Embryo transplantation may become more widely used as more offspring can be reared from desirable cows. The sex of the sperm, i.e. whether they carry a X or Y chromosome, can also be chosen before the eggs are fertilised. If the sex of the embryos is known, farmers will be able to choose whether they want males for rearing as beef cattle or females for dairy cows.

To increase production, farmers can select breeds that give birth to multiple offspring. Productivity can be further increased by selecting animals that have frequent periods of **oestrus** and short gestation. Oestrus is the time when a female can become pregnant. Frequent oestrus and short gestation in pigs allows several litters to be produced in one year.

With bigger livestock such as cattle, it may not be possible to select for all these characteristics. With cattle, usually only one calf is born, although cows can be mated again as soon as they stop producing milk. Sheep have a short gestation time and can have multiple offspring, but they only

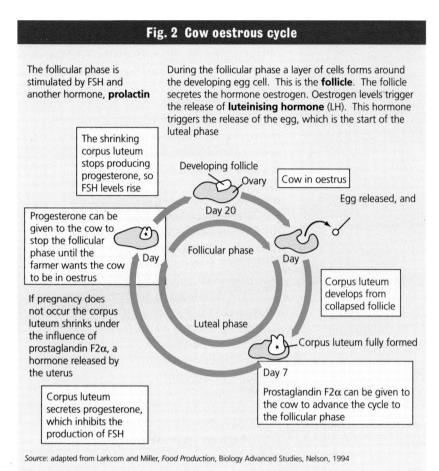

Fig. 2 Cow oestrous cycle

The follicular phase is stimulated by FSH and another hormone, **prolactin**

During the follicular phase a layer of cells forms around the developing egg cell. This is the **follicle**. The follicle secretes the hormone oestrogen. Oestrogen levels trigger the release of **luteinising hormone** (LH). This hormone triggers the release of the egg, which is the start of the luteal phase

The shrinking corpus luteum stops producing progesterone, so FSH levels rise

Progesterone can be given to the cow to stop the follicular phase until the farmer wants the cow to be in oestrus

If pregnancy does not occur the corpus luteum shrinks under the influence of prostaglandin F2α, a hormone released by the uterus

Corpus luteum secretes progesterone, which inhibits the production of FSH

Developing follicle
Ovary
Cow in oestrus
Egg released, and
Day 20
Follicular phase
Day
Day
Corpus luteum develops from collapsed follicle
Luteal phase
Corpus luteum fully formed
Day 7
Prostaglandin F2α can be given to the cow to advance the cycle to the follicular phase

Source: adapted from Larkcom and Miller, *Food Production*, Biology Advanced Studies, Nelson, 1994

come into oestrus once a year.

Artificially produced hormones can be used to control the oestrous cycle of livestock. A farmer can then control when and how many of the livestock become pregnant. If a number of cows are mated at the same time, they can be looked after together during their gestation. This makes it easier to give them the same feeding programme. The farmer and veterinarian can be ready for the calves, which will all be born at about the same time.

In cows, two methods of controlling the oestrous cycle are used. The first maintains a high level of **progesterone** in the blood. Progesterone prolongs the life of the **corpus luteum**. The corpus luteum is a group of cells in the ovary that secretes hormones after the release of an egg and during pregnancy. When progesterone levels drop, there is a shorter follicular phase (Fig. 2) which leads to ovulation. A coil containing progesterone can be inserted in the cows' vagina. The effect of the coil is to mimic

days 7–18 of the oestrous cycle. Or coil is removed, the drop in prog levels leads to the developmer follicle. By adjusting the ar progesterone administered t(herd, the farmer can make th oestrous cycles coincide.

The second method involve **prostaglandin F2α**. F2α is a h(secreted by the uterus, which n corpus luteum get smaller. If r occurs, the corpus luteum nat in size and disappears. By injec oestrous cycle can be advanced ovulation occurs within 3 days.

Lactation is the period during which a cow gives milk. Several hormones control the length of this time and the amount of milk produced per day (Fig. 3).

Bovine somatotrophin (BST) is a synthetic version of a naturally occurring bovine growth hormone called **somatotrophin**. This hormone is secreted from part of the brain called the **pituitary gland** and causes

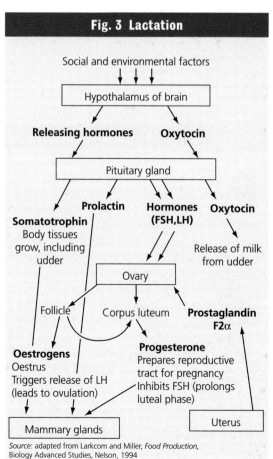

Fig. 3 Lactation

Social and environmental factors

Hypothalamus of brain

Releasing hormones   **Oxytocin**

Pituitary gland

Somatotrophin   **Prolactin**   **Hormones (FSH,LH)**   **Oxytocin**
Body tissues grow, including udder   Release of milk from udder

Ovary

Follicle   Corpus luteum   **Prostaglandin F2α**

Oestrogens
Oestrus
Triggers release of LH (leads to ovulation)

Progesterone
Prepares reproductive tract for pregnancy
Inhibits FSH (prolongs luteal phase)

Mammary glands   Uterus

Source: adapted from Larkcom and Miller, *Food Production*, Biology Advanced Studies, Nelson, 1994

145

Cows naturally only produce milk when they have had a calf, and will stop producing milk after a while, before they have another calf. By using hormones such as BST, milk could be produced continuously. This is useful for cheese makers as it cuts down on storage costs by allowing them to stagger their production throughout the year, instead of concentrating production when milk is available from their cows.

a general increase in body size. In early trials pituitary extracts from slaughtered animals were injected into cows and increased milk yields.

Somatotrophin causes cells to divide, and so growth occurs. Increased growth can lead to larger udders, which can therefore produce greater quantities of milk. The milk production increases because the animal eats more and a larger proportion of the cow's food is used for milk production by diverting body fats, glucose and fatty acids to the mammary glands. Cows injected with synthetic BST can have a 21% increase in milk yield.

Long-term studies have not detected any major effects on the health of animals. However, milking needs to be carried out more often to avoid discomfort to the cow from the larger than normal udder. There is disagreement as to whether the hormone will affect humans drinking the milk. In the EC, where there is an overproduction of milk, there seems little point in using the hormone. However, in other parts of the world the synthetic hormone could play a role in preventing starvation.

In developing countries the dairy cattle often yield very low quantities of milk compared to dairy cattle in developed countries. Some people believe BST should be used in developing countries to improve the milk production.

 3 Do you support the use of BST, in developed and developing countries? Explain your answer.

" No tests for risks in 'hormone' milk "

Pregnant women and babies were not tested for possible hazards before they drank milk from cows injected with the genetically engineered hormone BST. The Ministry of Agriculture has refused to identify the experimental herds or quarantine their milk, despite protests from supermarkets and consumer groups. The Milk Marketing Board wants BST banned.

There have been warnings that genetic developments such as BST could harm not only livestock, but also people who consume their milk and meat. The milk-boosting hormone weakens a cow's immune system. All the drugs that must be administered to the animal to protect it from disease, may also end up in the meat and milk.

Source: adapted from an article by James Erlichman, in the *Guardian*, 8 October 1988

" Chemicals in cows "

The manufacturers point out that BST is a natural hormone likely to be present in milk already. Even if it does get into milk, the digestive juices in our stomachs would break it down into safe chemicals. So drinking milk with traces of BST should not do us harm.

But the question remains as to whether we really need BST at all. The drug is there to help farmers to manage their herds more successfully. These days the dairy farmer is allowed to produce so much milk and no more. But it is difficult for a farmer to judge exactly how much milk the herd will produce over a year. If too much milk is produced, the farmer will lose money. If too little milk is produced, the farmer will lose money. BST would help the farmer to produce the right amount. Some say that it is the quota system that needs to be changed, then BST would not be needed.

Source: Farmer's Weekly

Key ideas

- Animal hormones are used in agriculture to increase meat and milk production.

- Some animal hormones can be used to increase ovulation, providing eggs for fertilisation and embryo transplantation.

- Some animal hormones can be used to control the timing of the oestrous cycle.

- The use of some animal hormones in food production has been banned because of concerns of scientists, animal welfare groups and consumer groups.

11.3 The use of plant hormones

In contrast to animal hormones, **plant growth substances** (PGS), the plant equivalents to hormones, have been used for many years by horticulturists to improve crops. However, the same degree of controversy does not seem to surround the use of plant 'hormones', even though levels in food produce can be high.

PGS are naturally occurring compounds that control the growth and responses of plants. Usually only very low levels are found naturally in plants. They differ from animal hormones in the following ways.

- PGS are produced in certain areas by unspecialised cells.
- PGS are not always transported widely in the plant, and some are formed at the site of activity.
- PGS are not specific and the same substance can influence different tissues and organs in contrasting ways.

Many people are unaware that most of the fruit and vegetables they buy from the supermarket will have been treated in some way with plant growth substances to promote growth or ripening.

Q 4 List the similarities and differences between PGS and animal hormones in a table.

Plant growth regulators (PGR) are synthetic versions of PGS. PGR have more of an effect on a plant because they are less easily broken down by the plant. This is why they have been developed by plant growers.

PGS can be divided into five groups according to their chemical nature. This is easier than grouping them by the effect they have. Although each of the five groups of compounds has individual effects, many processes are brought about by an interaction of two or more of them. When PGS interact to increase each other's effects they are said to be **synergistic**. Where PGS decrease each other's effects they are said to be **antagonistic**.

Auxin

The first PGS to be isolated was an auxin. Auxins are growth-promoting substances found in very small quantities in plants.

Charles Darwin, in 1880, saw that grass **coleoptiles** responded to the direction of a light source. A coleoptile covers the embryo leaves and young stem. Coleoptiles respond to light, a response known as **phototropism**. It involves the growth of plants either towards light, positive phototropism, or away from light, negative phototropism. Shoots are positively phototropic and roots are negatively phototropic.

Darwin's observations were extended by other workers during the early part of the twentieth century. However, it was some

Fig. 4 Cell elongation

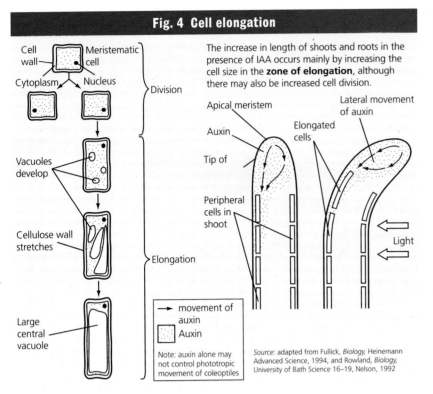

Cell wall — Meristematic cell
Cytoplasm — Nucleus

Division

Vacuoles develop

Cellulose wall stretches

Elongation

Large central vacuole

The increase in length of shoots and roots in the presence of IAA occurs mainly by increasing the cell size in the **zone of elongation**, although there may also be increased cell division.

Apical meristem
Auxin
Tip of
Peripheral cells in shoot

Elongated cells
Lateral movement of auxin

Light

→ movement of auxin
☐ Auxin

Note: auxin alone may not control phototropic movement of coleoptiles

Source: adapted from Fullick, *Biology*, Heinemann Advanced Science, 1994, and Rowland, *Biology*, University of Bath Science 16–19, Nelson, 1992

Fig. 5 Shoot and root growth

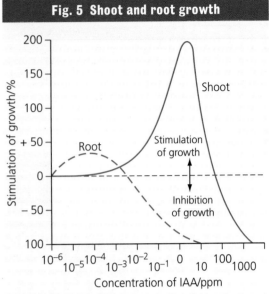

Source: Rowland, *Biology*, University of Bath Science 16–19, Nelson, 1992

IAA is made in the regions of actively dividing cells, called **meristems**, of a plant, and is transported to regions of growth in the plant. **Apical meristems** are found at the tips of shoots and roots. Therefore, the highest concentrations of IAA are found in the tips of the stems and roots and in young growing leaves, flowers and fruits. There is less IAA in the roots than there is in the tips of the stem.

With phototropism most shoots grow towards the light (Fig. 4). The Cholodny-Went hypothesis suggests that the source of light is detected by a receptor within the coleoptiles. This results in the movement of IAA to the shaded side of the coleoptile, by a mechanism that is as yet unknown. Cell elongation is stimulated by a relatively high concentration of IAA. So an increase of IAA on the shaded side of a coleoptile will cause the cells on that side to grow longer, and the coleoptile will bend towards the light.

5 What do the effects of differing concentrations of IAA (Fig. 5) on root and shoot growth suggest about the production and distribution of IAA by the seedling?

time before the chemical nature of auxin was identified. This was mainly because the **active substance** occurs in such small amounts. The active substance is the chemical that causes the effect. In 1934 a substance was isolated from human urine that was found to have the same effect on oat coleoptiles as an auxin! This substance was the organic acid indoleacetic acid (IAA).

Taking a 'cutting' is probably the most commonly used method of producing many plants in horticulture. Treating roots with high levels of IAA inhibits root elongation, but stimulates the growth of side roots.

Substances that alter the rate of plant growth or the pattern of plant development can help to control weed populations, and so improve crop productivity. After the chemical structure of IAA was determined, synthetic versions were made. There are many compounds similar to IAA that have similar effects upon growth and development, and some have stronger effects than IAA.

Research into hormone weedkillers or herbicides started during the Second World War. Early experiments showed that two substances were very effective, 2,4-D and MCPA. At very low concentrations their effects are similar to IAA. At slightly higher concentrations they are toxic to **dicotyledonous** or broad-leaved plants. Many weeds are dicots. Cultivated grasses such as wheat, which are **monocotyledonous**, are unaffected. This makes these substances excellent weedkillers. They are systemic herbicides, which means they are taken up and transported within the plant. They affect the growth of meristems, causing death from excessive growth. Because they are systemic they also kill the roots.

Artificial auxins are normally used as rooting powders because they are easy and cheap to make, and are not broken down by the plant's enzymes. This means synthetic auxins persist in the plant for longer.

At higher concentrations, IAA prevents the growth of lateral shoots. Lateral shoots grow off the main stem. Harvested potatoes can be treated with IAA so that they do not form lateral shoots off the tuber. Treated potatoes can then be stored for longer than natural ones.

Gibberellins

Gibberellins were first discovered by Japanese scientists investigating a fungal disease of plants. Active substances were successfully isolated from the fungus *Gibberella fujikuroi* in 1935, and called gibberellins after the fungus.

It is now known that there are more than 50 naturally occurring gibberellins. Sometimes they are referred to as **gibberellic acid** (GA) because they contain a carboxyl group that makes them weakly acidic.

Gibberellins are produced in seeds, young leaves and young apical tissues, particularly the roots. Gibberellins appear to be transported in the xylem and phloem to other plant organs. The mode of action of gibberellins is still unclear. There is evidence that it stimulates synthesis of an enzyme, α-amylase, in cereal grains. The concentration needed to stimulate this protein is so small that it is thought they must affect molecules rather than cells. It has been suggested that gibberellins can 'switch' genes on or off during cell differentiation. Genes control the production of proteins, including enzymes.

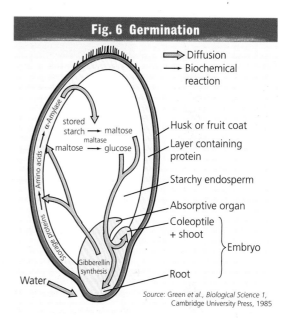

Fig. 6 Germination

⇒ Diffusion
→ Biochemical reaction

Husk or fruit coat
Layer containing protein
Starchy endosperm
Absorptive organ
Coleoptile + shoot
Embryo
Root

α-Amylase
stored starch → maltose
maltose → maltose → glucose
maltase
Amino acids
Storage proteins
Gibberellin synthesis
Water

Source: Green et al., Biological Science 1, Cambridge University Press, 1985

When water is absorbed by the seed, **dormancy** is broken and germination begins. Dormancy is a period of low metabolic activity. Gibberellins play a part in breaking dormancy in cereal seeds. After water has been absorbed by the seeds, gibberellins diffuse from the embryo of the seed to a layer where the enzyme α-amylase is made (Fig. 6). This enzyme breaks down stored food which then diffuses into the embryo, causing growth to occur.

Gibberellins also affect stem elongation. In dwarf plants, normal growth is prevented by the absence of the gene for the production of gibberellins. When gibberellins are sprayed onto the surface of the dwarf plants, growth to normal heights is possible. This suggests that gibberellins are needed for stem growth in all plants.

Reducing the stem length of cereal crops such as wheat to reduce lodging increases the ratio of harvestable to non-harvestable material, because the same amount of grain is produced on much shorter stems.

Lodging is when wheat crops are blown over because the stems are so long they become weak and cannot stand up to high winds. Lodging makes it very difficult to harvest the crop. Substances are applied to the crop that block the synthesis of gibberellins. The stems then do not grow as long, and are stiffer than untreated varieties. The action of this substance is not species-specific and it is used with a variety of crops.

Gibberellins are probably the most widely used PGS. They are produced on a commercial scale from fungal cultures. One major use is to induce **parthenocarpy** in fruit. Parthenocarpy is fruit development without fertilisation. Fruits that develop in this way do not need pollination to form fruits and seeds. Some plants do show parthenocarpy naturally, for example dandelions. Horticulturists have developed the process in other plants, to produce seedless fruit including grapes, bananas, pineapples and cucumbers. High levels of gibberellins, acting synergistically with auxin, promote parthenocarpy.

Cytokinins

The first cytokinin was isolated from a non-plant source: herring sperm! In the 1950s a substance was found in coconut milk, which is the liquid food store that surrounds the embryo coconut plant. This substance was called kinetin because it promoted growth. It was then discovered that it controlled cell division, so the substance was eventually termed cytokinin after the process of cell division, cytokinesis. The substance isolated was very similar in structure to adenine found in deoxyribonucleic acid (DNA) and ribonucleic acid (RNA) molecules.

Cytokinins are found in parts of the plant where rapid cell division occurs, such as in fruits and seeds. They are produced in the root tip and are transported upwards in either the xylem or phloem towards the stem and the leaves, where they accumulate. Some molecules from transfer RNA (tRNA) have been shown to have a similar function to cytokinins. Because they are similar in structure to adenine, cytokinins may play a part in RNA synthesis.

Cytokinins often act synergistically or antagonistically with other PGS. They promote cell division in the presence of auxins.

Q 6 Is the effect of cytokinins on cell division in the presence of auxin synergistic or antagonistic?

Cytokinins have many uses commercially. They are used to promote growth of tissue cultures, and are included in mineral solutions used by florists to keep cut flowers fresh. Their widest use, however, is in the delay of **senescence**. Senescence is the natural process of ageing that occurs in plant tissues, such as leaves before they fall from the trees in autumn. High levels of cytokinin prevent senescence.

Fruit ripening is the start of the senescence process. As fruit ripen, the plant respiration rate increases. The production of cytokinin is reduced, growth stops and senescence begins (Fig. 7). There is evidence that, at the same time as fruit ripening, cytokinins are transported from older leaves to younger leaves via the phloem.

In commercial crops cytokinins are often added before and after harvesting by spraying, to delay senescence. This means the shelf-life is longer, and so the quality of the fruits and vegetables is better for longer. Fresh leaf crops such as lettuce and cabbages are treated in this way.

Cytokinins and fungicides are mixed

Proteins, DNA, RNA and chlorophyll are broken down in senescence. This can lead to spectacular changes in colour.

with waxes, which are used to cover the surface of apples. The wax also reduces water loss and decreases the diffusion rates of oxygen and carbon dioxide. Together, the wax, cytokinins and fungicides increase the life of the stored apple. The wax also allows the apple to be polished, making it look better on the shelf. Consumer groups are worried about the health and safety of this practice, because we end up eating the wax.

Abscisic acid

Abscisic acid is a growth inhibitor. It is an antagonist to the other groups of PGS, which all promote growth. High concentrations of abscisic acid can stop plant growth altogether. It was discovered during investigations in the early 1960s into seed dormancy and leaf fall. In 1967 the active compound was found to be abscisic acid (ABA). ABA has a complex structure.

ABA is made in leaves, stems, fruits and seeds. The exact mode of action for ABA is unknown. It is involved in breaking bud dormancy and in starting flowering. Levels of ABA drop as levels of other PGS rise. It also has a role in wilting. Wilting tomatoes have 50 times the normal concentration of ABA in their leaves. Its effect may be to cause the stomata to close. If a synthetic version of ABA could be made, it could possibly be used to prevent water loss from transpiration.

ABA levels are high in fruits before they fall. **Abscission** is when a plant lets its leaves, fruit or unfertilised flowers fall. The fall of leaves can be to stop water loss by transpiration. Fruits drop from the plant so that they can be dispersed and germinate. Unripe seeds produce auxins. During ripening of fruit, auxin production falls and ABA production can rise.

Fig. 7 Senescence

Changes in respiration rate and growth rate in an apple from early development to senescence

(Graph: y-axis left "Relative rate of respiration" from 50 to 100; y-axis right "Relative growth rate" from 50 to 100; x-axis "Time". Curves labelled "Growth" and "Respiration". Stages marked below: Cell enlargement, Ripening, Cell division, Maturation, Senescence)

Source: Larkcom and Miller, *Food Production, Biology Advanced Studies*, Nelson, 1994

The most important commercial use of ABA is its effect on fruit drop. ABA is applied as a spray on tree crops such as apples and oranges to regulate fruit drop. If the fruit are all ready to drop at the same time, harvesting is easier. The length of time spent harvesting the fruit is shorter than if the fruit trees were left to ripen and drop in their own time. Time and money are saved.

During germination of barley seeds, the enzyme α-amylase is produced. This process is influenced by gibberellins. The effect of different concentrations of gibberellins was determined in the presence and absence of ABA (Fig. 8).

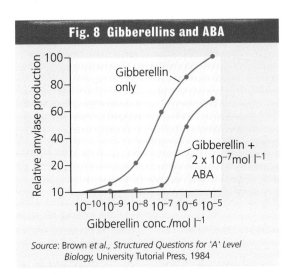

Fig. 8 Gibberellins and ABA

Gibberellin only

Gibberellin + 2×10^{-7} mol l^{-1} ABA

Source: Brown et al., *Structured Questions for 'A' Level Biology,* University Tutorial Press, 1984

Fig. 9 Fruit ripening

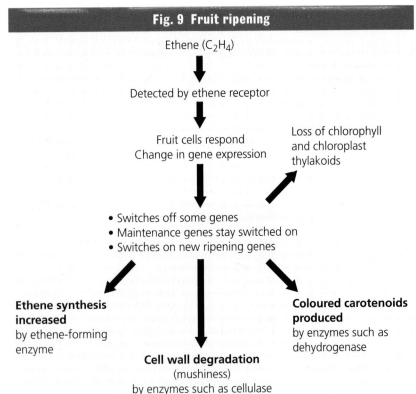

Ethene (C_2H_4)

↓

Detected by ethene receptor

↓

Fruit cells respond
Change in gene expression

Loss of chlorophyll and chloroplast thylakoids

- Switches off some genes
- Maintenance genes stay switched on
- Switches on new ripening genes

Ethene synthesis increased
by ethene-forming enzyme

Cell wall degradation
(mushiness)
by enzymes such as cellulase

Coloured carotenoids produced
by enzymes such as dehydrogenase

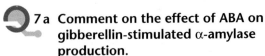

7 a Comment on the effect of ABA on gibberellin-stimulated α-amylase production.

b Suggest and explain what might happen during germination to the levels of ABA found naturally in the plant.

Ethene

The fact that ethene affected plant growth and development was observed long before it was known that plants actually produced ethene from their own tissues. Bananas held in the hold of ships from Jamaica to Europe used to ripen more quickly than if they were kept in the open air. It was found that ethene was being made from fungi covering the surface of oranges held in the same hold. Since then ethene has been shown to be generated by a wide range of fruits, including bananas themselves.

Ethene is a simple hydrocarbon compound. It is made in the meristem and young growing tissues of plants. It is not transported easily through the plant. As it is a gas, it normally leaves a plant by diffusing through the plant's surface. It has been shown to have a role in 'switching' on and off genes involved in the ripening process (Fig. 9).

Ethene usually exerts its effect in the presence of auxin, and sometimes has similar effects on the growth of tissues as those shown by adding IAA. Artificially high levels of auxin can promote ethene production, and this causes problems when trying to interpret results of experiments where auxin is applied externally. Ethene may require the presence of auxin, or it may sensitise the tissue to the auxin already present. Ethene can act as an inhibitor in certain cases, such as the elongation of roots and stems in plants. It can also promote abscission synergistically with ABA.

Ethene is made as a result of the breakdown of substances in and between cell walls by specific enzymes. This results in a change in texture. This is the mushiness that develops in ripening in fruit such as tomatoes.

Ethene can be used to make a crop ripen at the same time, making harvesting and selling the crop easier.

of tissues that produce them and the complexity of the interactions between them and effects that they have (Fig. 11).

We know even less about the effect of artificially raised levels of PGS that may be in our food because of treatments the plants have received. As PGS are presumably plant-specific, the potential effect on humans has to be less than animal hormones. Consumers are far more concerned about hormone treatment of animal food products, because both the animals and ourselves could be affected. All mammals produce growth hormones, for example, so a synthetic form may affect humans as well as the pig or cow it was injected into. People in favour of the use of BST argue that it is not a way of producing more milk per farm, but a way of producing more milk from fewer cows, i.e. it is a way of producing milk more efficiently. What may seem an appropriate use of hormone technology in one situation may not be in another, so it has to be used with caution and careful monitoring.

Ethene can be used to make all the plants in a batch flower at the same time. Pineapples can be made to flower at the same time by covering them in polyethylene after they have been harvested, or by the traditional method of lighting fires around the pineapple crop. The smoke contains ethene.

Commercial growers maintain high levels of ethene in their greenhouses to increase yield of cucumber plants. Cucumber plants have separate male and female flowers. Only the female flowers produce the cucumber fruit. Ethene promotes female flower production in cucumber plants, so the grower can control how many male and female flowers are produced.

8 a Explain the relationship between the level of ethene and the degree of firmness in Fig. 10.
   b Suggest disadvantages of ethene for the shelf-life of harvested produce.

We still do not fully understand the cause and effect of PGS due to the low levels found naturally in plants, the variety

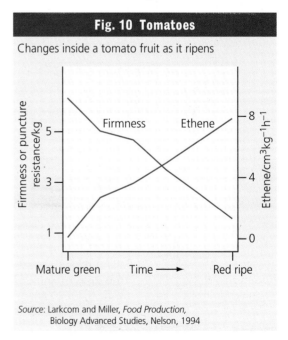

Fig. 10 Tomatoes

Changes inside a tomato fruit as it ripens

Source: Larkcom and Miller, *Food Production, Biology Advanced Studies*, Nelson, 1994

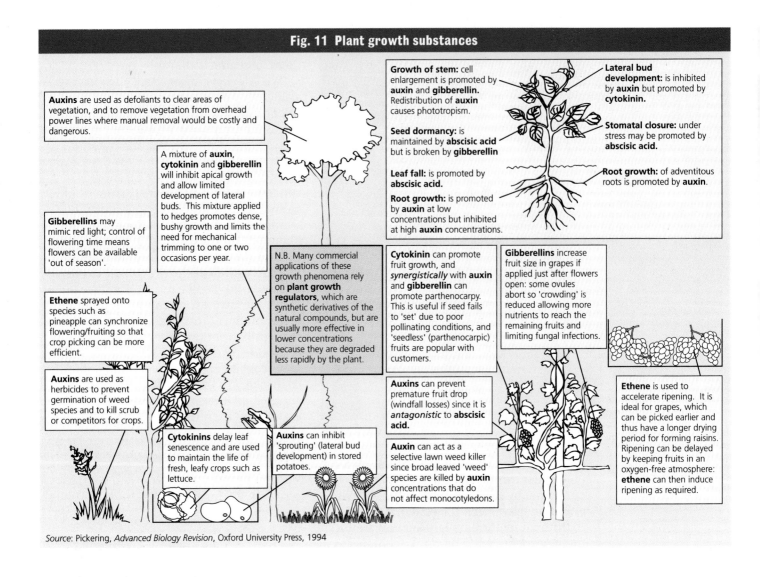

Fig. 11 Plant growth substances

Auxins are used as defoliants to clear areas of vegetation, and to remove vegetation from overhead power lines where manual removal would be costly and dangerous.

A mixture of **auxin**, **cytokinin** and **gibberellin** will inhibit apical growth and allow limited development of lateral buds. This mixture applied to hedges promotes dense, bushy growth and limits the need for mechanical trimming to one or two occasions per year.

Gibberellins may mimic red light; control of flowering time means flowers can be available 'out of season'.

Ethene sprayed onto species such as pineapple can synchronize flowering/fruiting so that crop picking can be more efficient.

Auxins are used as herbicides to prevent germination of weed species and to kill scrub or competitors for crops.

Cytokinins delay leaf senescence and are used to maintain the life of fresh, leafy crops such as lettuce.

Auxins can inhibit 'sprouting' (lateral bud development) in stored potatoes.

Growth of stem: cell enlargement is promoted by **auxin** and **gibberellin**. Redistribution of **auxin** causes phototropism.

Seed dormancy: is maintained by **abscisic acid** but is broken by **gibberellin**

Leaf fall: is promoted by **abscisic acid**.

Root growth: is promoted by **auxin** at low concentrations but inhibited at high **auxin** concentrations.

N.B. Many commercial applications of these growth phenomena rely on **plant growth regulators**, which are synthetic derivatives of the natural compounds, but are usually more effective in lower concentrations because they are degraded less rapidly by the plant.

Cytokinin can promote fruit growth, and *synergistically* with **auxin** and **gibberellin** can promote parthenocarpy. This is useful if seed fails to 'set' due to poor pollinating conditions, and 'seedless' (parthenocarpic) fruits are popular with customers.

Auxins can prevent premature fruit drop (windfall losses) since it is *antagonistic* to **abscisic acid**.

Auxin can act as a selective lawn weed killer since broad leaved 'weed' species are killed by **auxin** concentrations that do not affect monocotyledons.

Lateral bud development: is inhibited by **auxin** but promoted by **cytokinin**.

Stomatal closure: under stress may be promoted by **abscisic acid**.

Root growth: of adventitous roots is promoted by **auxin**.

Gibberellins increase fruit size in grapes if applied just after flowers open: some ovules abort so 'crowding' is reduced allowing more nutrients to reach the remaining fruits and limiting fungal infections.

Ethene is used to accelerate ripening. It is ideal for grapes, which can be picked earlier and thus have a longer drying period for forming raisins. Ripening can be delayed by keeping fruits in an oxygen-free atmosphere: **ethene** can then induce ripening as required.

Source: Pickering, *Advanced Biology Revision*, Oxford University Press, 1994

Key ideas

- There are five classes of plant growth substances.

- Plant growth substances are similar in function to animal hormones but the way they have an effect is different.

- Plant growth substances and regulators are used a great deal in horticulture and agriculture to improve crop yield and crop quality, and control and increase the efficiency of harvesting.

- Auxins promote cell enlargement.

- Gibberellins promote the synthesis of enzymes in the seed by 'switching' on and off the appropriate genes.

- Cytokinins are very similar in structure to adenine and possibly play a part in the synthesis of RNA.

- Abscisic acid is involved in fruit drop.

- Ethene is involved in the ripening process, which alters the colour, texture and flavour of a crop.

Breeding the best

It may soon be possible to transfer genes into cells of crop plants such as rice or wheat that will mean these crops can be their own source of fertiliser, saving money and increasing yields. This will have an enormous impact on the ability of developing countries to grow their own food.

Not everyone is enthusiastic about the release of genetically modified organisms, claiming they are unnatural and that they may upset the natural ecological balance. As a result many regulations control the use and release of such organisms.

However, food production has always involved altering the genetics of plant and animal species, by selective breeding. Some crop plants have been mass produced from identical clones for many years. Commercial plant breeders maintain a range of genetic types to provide genes for work with crop species. This is so that strains of plants can be developed to resist disease and produce high yields. Where do we draw the line with the manipulation of plant and animal genetics? What is the effect, if any, of altering the genetic make-up of the plants and animals we eat?

Here genetically engineered seeds of potatoes are being given a white protective coating. Plant biotechnology includes research into the cultivation of disease-free potatoes from seed. The aim is to be able to plant an acre of land with no more than one pound in weight of seed, instead of tons of potato tubers. Seeds instead of tubers are less likely to rot in storage, so will reduce waste and save growers' costs.

12.1 Learning objectives

After working through this chapter, you should be able to:

- **explain** the principles involved in selective breeding;

- **illustrate** selective breeding by referring to examples;

- **explain** the principles underlying F_1 and F_2 hybrids;

- **outline** the advantages and disadvantages of producing crops by vegetative propagation;

- **explain** the principles involved in the cloning of animals;

- **explain** the principles involved in micropropagation;

- **describe** how genetic engineering is being applied to plant breeding;

- **evaluate** the economic, ethical and social issues concerning the development of genetically engineered plants and animals.

12.2 Genetic methods

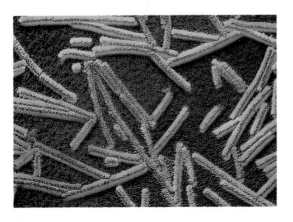

One way farmers increase productivity of a crop or animal species is to choose or select a variety better suited for a specific habitat. Different varieties of a crop species or breeds of an animal species have different **genotypes**. The genotype is the composition of the genes of an individual organism. Some genotypes are better adapted for a particular habitat than others.

Farmers also regularly improve the productivity or quality of a crop by altering its environment, for example by irrigation, adding fertilisers or using pesticides. Some features of the **phenotype** of a crop or animal species may be improved by adding plant growth substances or hormones. The phenotype of an organism is how it appears. It is the result of the environmental characteristics of the organism's habitat affecting the organism's genetic make-up.

Commercial production of new crop and animal varieties to suit different or changing habitats involves a combination of old and new technologies. Some are based on the genetic variety that results from **sexual reproduction**. Sexual reproduction is when cells from two individual organisms are combined. Other techniques use the advantages of **asexual reproduction**. Asexual reproduction is when a single parent organism produces many offspring that are genetically identical.

 1 **What do you think are the commercial advantages of asexual reproduction in crop plants?**

12.3 Selective breeding

Today's crop plants are the result of thousands of years of selection by people keeping the seed from the best plants for planting the next crop. About 10 000 years ago Neolithic farmers harvested wheat by cutting the stalks with flint-bladed sickles. As a result a lot of grain was lost from 'loose' ears. The grain that was collected was therefore from 'tighter' ears. It was this seed that was used to provide the seed for

These different cereal ears are all variations that have been cultivated from the same ancestral species thousands of years ago. Different varieties have specific qualities that are useful to humans. When a crop has more than one use, different selections take place by different breeders. Wheat used for making bread has been selected for high levels of the protein gluten, whereas wheat used for making biscuits has been selected for low gluten content.

the following year's crop. This is a form of **artificial selection**, even though the selection of tighter ears had not been planned.

Since the start of the twentieth century selective breeding has been made more powerful by our increased knowledge of genetics. Within the nucleus of the cells of plants and animals are chromosomes. These are made from **deoxyribonucleic acid** (DNA) and protein. Chromosomes exist in pairs. The number of chromosomes in a body cell is known as the diploid number (2n). For sexual reproduction, the pairs of chromosomes are halved during cell division to form **gametes**. Gametes are sex cells. They contain a haploid (n) number of chromosomes. When two gametes fuse in fertilisation, the chromosomes are paired again, and the cells have the diploid number of chromosomes.

Chromosomes contain **genes**. Genes are sections of the DNA. Each gene controls some aspect of the growth, development and functioning of an organism. Many genes can exist in more than one form, called **alleles**. These exist at the same position on a chromosome. It is the alleles that contribute to the genotype of the plant and are eventually expressed as the phenotype or appearance of the plant. For example, the gene for plant height may exist as two alleles, tall or short.

The **gene pool** is the total of all the alleles that exist in a breeding population. Selecting a particular characteristic of a species alters the frequency of alleles in the gene pool. Alleles for desired characteristics gradually increase in frequency while alleles for undesirable characteristics decline in frequency.

 2a If 'loose ear' and 'tight ear' were inherited characteristics of wheat, what would selection for 'tight ear' do to the frequencies of the alleles for these two characteristics?

b What would happen to the phenotype of the crop over many generations?

The development of short-strawed wheat is an example of artificial selection.

Originally cereals had very long stalks. During the last century the number and size of the grains produced by a plant has been increased by using fertiliser and selective breeding. This has led to an increase in lodging or fallen wheat, which makes mechanical harvesting difficult. So shorter stalks were selected for. Dwarf Japanese wheat varieties were first released in 1935 and later crossed with American short-stalked varieties to produce semi-dwarf hybrids that have been widely used since.

3 Suggest advantages that dwarf wheats may have compared to tall ones when grown in the British climate.

Plant breeders can alter the gene pools in different ways, depending on the intended use of the plants (Fig. 1).

Crop breeders are interested in any characteristics that contribute to an improvement in yield or in quality. These include:
- rapid early growth;
- good response to fertilisers;
- high leaf surface area;
- tolerance of varying climatic conditions, especially drought;
- pest and disease resistance;
- amino acid balance.

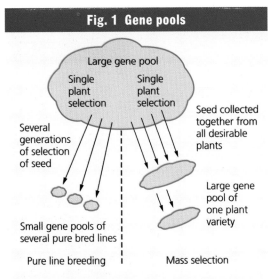

Fig. 1 Gene pools

Source: Hayward, *Applied Genetics, University of Bath: Science 16 – 19*. Nelson, 1992

4 Explain why a high leaf surface area is a good characteristic for a crop plant.

Some of these characteristics are controlled by a single pair of alleles. An individual plant contains two genes for each characteristic, one on each chromosome. There can only be one allele per gene. Individuals with only one sort of allele are **homozygous**, i.e. they have two identical alleles. A plant that has different alleles for a particular gene in the pair is **heterozygous** for that characteristic. One aim of artificial selection is to produce strains homozygous for the desired characteristics. The next generation will then always have the desired alleles.

It is important to keep detailed records of the history of each experimental line. Pure bred varieties will not contain all the original gene pool's alleles. To increase variety again, plant breeders can combine favourable characteristics by crossing one line with another. For example, a variety of wheat that is high yielding but is badly affected by frost can be crossed with another variety that is low yielding but is tolerant of frost. This is an example of **hybridisation** (Fig. 2).

To sell these F_1 hybrids commercially, all the seed must be the same to give guaranteed results. This can only happen if the parent plants are homozygous for the desired characteristic. F_1 plants are heterozygous.

The type of breeding programme used

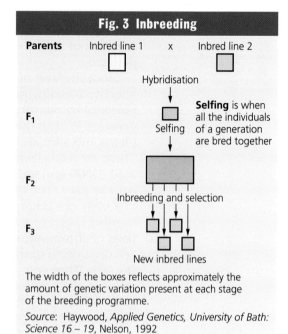

Fig. 3 Inbreeding

The width of the boxes reflects approximately the amount of genetic variation present at each stage of the breeding programme.

Source: Haywood, *Applied Genetics, University of Bath: Science 16 – 19*, Nelson, 1992

depends on whether the plant is an **inbreeder** or an **outbreeder**. Inbreeding plants are self fertilising. The male and female gametes on one plant can fertilise each other. The offspring of these plants can easily have the same alleles as each other and so have very similar phenotypes (Fig. 3). Wheat and tomatoes are inbreeding plants.

5 In the example given in Fig. 2, if the F_1 plants were used to provide seed for the next crop, what proportion of that crop would have the same phenotype as the F_1s assuming that the F_1 plants all pollinate each other?

Outbreeding plants are fertilised by **cross-pollination**. Gametes from unrelated plants fuse. A particular plant produces male and female gametes at different times, so that they cannot fertilise themselves. The offspring have a variety of alleles and display a variety of phenotypes. Maize, oil seed rape and fruit trees are examples.

Maize, or sweetcorn, is usually sold as F_1 seed. However, it is naturally an outbreeder. Producing homozygous parents requires inbreeding (Fig. 4). Inbreeding naturally outbreeding plants can lead to **inbreeding depression**. This is a drop in yield or growth because the plants are not adapted for high levels of homozygous alleles in the

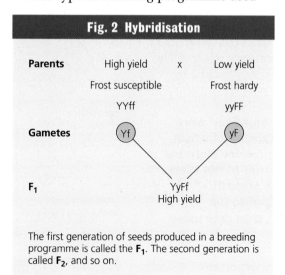

Fig. 2 Hybridisation

Parents	High yield	x	Low yield
	Frost susceptible		Frost hardy
	YYff		yyFF
Gametes	Yf		yF
F_1		YyFf	
		High yield	

The first generation of seeds produced in a breeding programme is called the F_1. The second generation is called F_2, and so on.

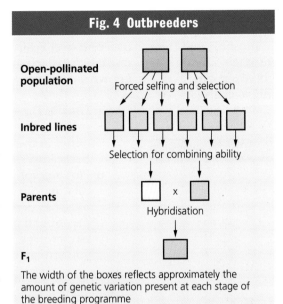

Fig. 4 Outbreeders

Open-pollinated population

Forced selfing and selection

Inbred lines

Selection for combining ability

Parents □ x ■

Hybridisation

F₁

The width of the boxes reflects approximately the amount of genetic variation present at each stage of the breeding programme

Source: Haywood, *Applied Genetics, University of Bath: Science 16 – 19*, Nelson, 1992

F_1 plants are often more vigorous than the homozygous parents, and exhibit the desired characteristics to a greater extent than either parents. This is why so many F_1 hybrid varieties of crops, including vegetables, have been developed. Many of the seeds bought from garden centres to be grown in gardens and allotments are F_1 seeds.

gene pool. This problem can only be overcome with many years of selective breeding to produce varieties that can withstand a high level of homozygosity.

Maize has to be self fertilised by hand to allow inbreeding. It has both male and female wind-pollinated flowers on the same plant. To produce F_1 seed on a commercial scale, lines of plants are sown. To prevent cross-pollination between lines, the male flowers or tassels are removed from the plants that are going to grow the F_1 seed.

The final problem with F_1 hybrids is that the next generation, the F_2 generation, will not breed true. The F_1 seed is heterozygous so the F_2 seed will display a variety of phenotypes. This means the farmer cannot simply collect seed at the end of the season to produce the next year's crop. Fresh batches of F_1 seeds must be bought from the seed merchant each year. This makes money for the seed merchant but is an expensive process for the farmer.

When a good crop variety lacks a desirable character, such as disease resistance, it can be crossed with an otherwise less good variety that does have disease resistance. This variety can even be from a different species. The F_1 generation is then **interspecific**. For example, genes for resistance to the fungus disease eyespot were transferred from goat grass to a French wheat variety to produce an interspecific F_1 hybrid variety named 'Rendezvous'. This hybrid has qualities of both disease resistance and raised yield.

Interspecific hybrids are usually infertile because the set of chromosomes they inherit from one species will not pair exactly with the set of chromosomes from the other species. However, mutations can occur, for example in cereal plants and potatoes, that double the number of chromosomes. Every chromosome will then have a pair. This chromosome doubling can occur naturally or plant breeders can induce it by using a chemical called **colchicine** (Fig. 5).

Hybrids that are disease resistant can be bred with the original good yield variety over and over again, and selection made for resistance in each generation. This is known as **backcross** breeding (Fig. 6).

6 a Look at Fig. 6. Calculate the proportions of wild and cultivated genes in the offspring after 3 and 4 backcrosses.

   b Plot a graph to show the relationship between the proportion of genes derived from the wild parent and the number of backcrosses. Comment on the trend you obtain.

Fig. 5 Interspecific hybrids

Parents Species X   Species Y

2n = 6   2n = 8

Gametes

n = 3   n = 4

F₁

2n = 7

Sterile – cannot go through meiosis since chromosomes cannot pair

Mutation or treatment with the chemical colchicine can double chromosome number

2n = 14

Can now go through meiosis because each chromosome has a partner, so offspring now fertile

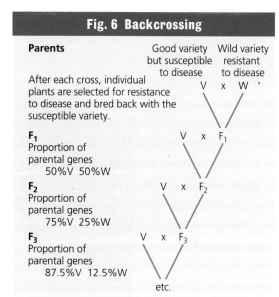

Fig. 6 Backcrossing

Parents   Good variety   Wild variety
                       but susceptible   resistant
                       to disease   to disease

After each cross, individual plants are selected for resistance to disease and bred back with the susceptible variety.

V   x   W

F₁
Proportion of parental genes
50%V 50%W

V   x   F₁

F₂
Proportion of parental genes
75%V 25%W

V   x   F₂

F₃
Proportion of parental genes
87.5%V 12.5%W

V   x   F₃

etc.

Key ideas

- Sexual reproduction produces genetic variety.

- Artificial selection is used to breed varieties homozygous for a desired characteristic.

- F₁ hybrids are produced as seed to grow plants with combined, desired characteristics.

- F₁ hybrids are heterozygous and may be infertile.

- F₂ hybrids can be homozygous or heterozygous for the desired characteristics, so their phenotypes will be varied.

12.4 Vegetative propagation

One of the drawbacks with selective breeding programmes is the length of time it takes to develop the ideal variety. If only one single plant existed with all the desired characteristics, few of the F_1 generation would have the desired characteristics. If the plant belonged to an outbreeding species it may be pollinated by less desirable plants, resulting in a more varied F_1 set with few plants with the desired combination of characteristics. This would be disastrous on a commercial basis, where all the offspring must be the same.

Q 7 Can you suggest a combination of genotype and breeding system that would produce seed all with the same genotype and phenotype as the 'ideal' parent plant?

Asexual or **vegetative propagation** is widely used in commercial plant production. Many flowering plants reproduce asexually by producing vegetative structures, such as bulbs in daffodils, corms in crocuses, runners in strawberries, tubers in potatoes and rhizomes in irises. One potato plant can produce many potato tubers that will all be genetically identical. At the moment this is quicker and cheaper than producing potato seed. Large areas can then be planted with a type of potato that is known to be a good performer.

Some vegetative structures, such as roots and stems, can be cut into separate pieces and planted. The pieces all grow into new plants. This is **artificial propagation**. There are three traditional methods of artificial propagation: leaf cuttings, stem cuttings and grafts. All the plants resulting from leaf or stem cuttings are genetically identical to the original plant. They are called **clones**.

Commercial plant growers rely on leaf cuttings as a method of propagating plants such as African violets and begonias. All that is necessary is for the leaf to be rooted in compost. In some cases the whole leaf does not need to be rooted as long as a fragment of the leaf has part of the mid-rib.

The common household geranium is

The Bramley is a very successful variety of apple because it is naturally disease resistant. This means it is often used as a rootstock for other varieties. The process of grafting is very difficult and is usually performed by commercial growers.

easy to propagate from stem cuttings. The stem produces roots at the lower end and continues shoot growth at the upper end. This is possible because the cells dividing at the cut ends of the stem can develop into specialised root and stem cells.

In many plants such as apples it is difficult to get cuttings to root. In these cases it is necessary to graft the cutting onto part of another plant, called the rootstock, so that they grow as one plant. This is how varieties such as the eating apple Cox's Orange Pippin and the cooking apple Bramley's have been propagated since their discovery in a hedgerow and a back garden, respectively, more than a hundred years ago! Grafting also has the advantage of combining the best characteristics of both the rootstock and cutting. It is common practice to grow apple varieties on dwarf plants to save space. More trees can be planted in the same area, so increasing the yield.

12.5 Micropropagation

For commercial plant growing, there are some species of plant that cannot be easily produced by either a breeding programme or vegetative propagation. During the last 30 years or so, simple asexual vegetative propagation techniques such as stem cuttings have been developed as high technology tissue cultures. This is called **micropropagation**.

Micropropagation involves the growth of **plantlets** from single cells, pieces of tissue or organs, using sterile laboratory techniques (Fig. 7). Plantlets are very small plants produced asexually. Plantlets grown by micropropagation are virus-free clones.

All plant cells have the ability to give rise to an identical genetic copy of the parent plant. This is another way to produce clones. In the case of the oil palm the clones are derived from pieces of leaf tissue.

Plants can be cultured from haploid male gametes. From these diploid, fully

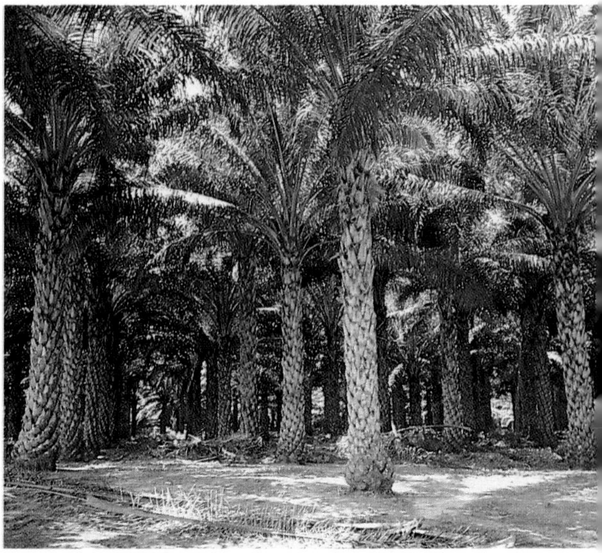

The oil palm is an important tropical crop. This plantation is 15 years old. A traditional breeding programme would take many years because useful phenotypic characteristics take several years to appear. Vegetative propagation is limited because each oil plant can only give rise to one plant if a cutting is taken, which is hardly an improvement if the aim is to produce a large number of plants in a short period of time! Oil palms have been successfully bred by micropropagation and grown in plantations in Malaysia since 1977.

Fig. 7 Micropropagation

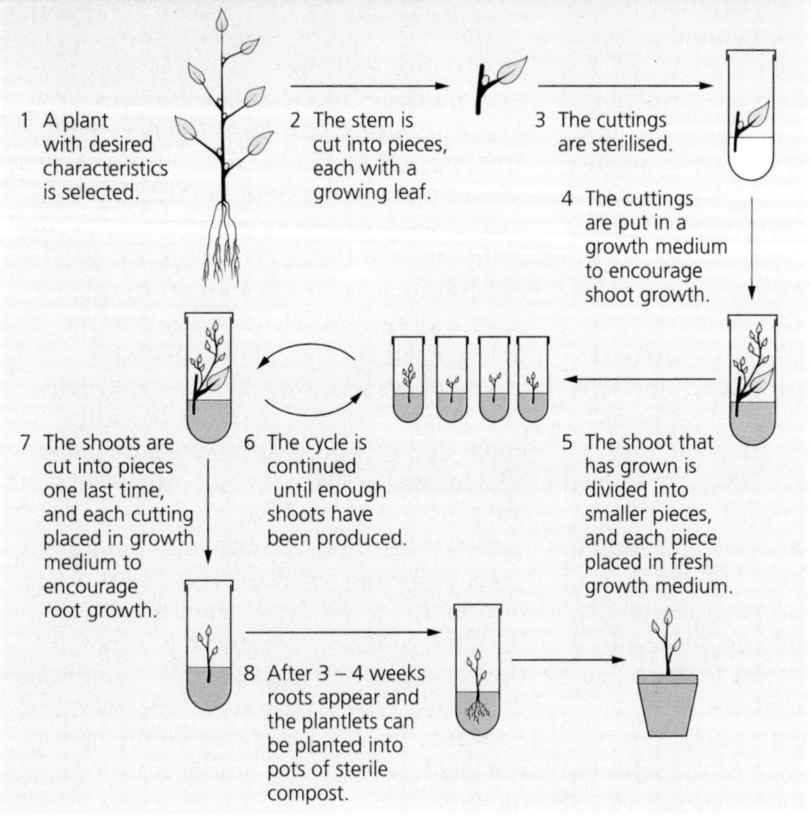
1 A plant with desired characteristics is selected.
2 The stem is cut into pieces, each with a growing leaf.
3 The cuttings are sterilised.
4 The cuttings are put in a growth medium to encourage shoot growth.
5 The shoot that has grown is divided into smaller pieces, and each piece placed in fresh growth medium.
6 The cycle is continued until enough shoots have been produced.
7 The shoots are cut into pieces one last time, and each cutting placed in growth medium to encourage root growth.
8 After 3 – 4 weeks roots appear and the plantlets can be planted into pots of sterile compost.

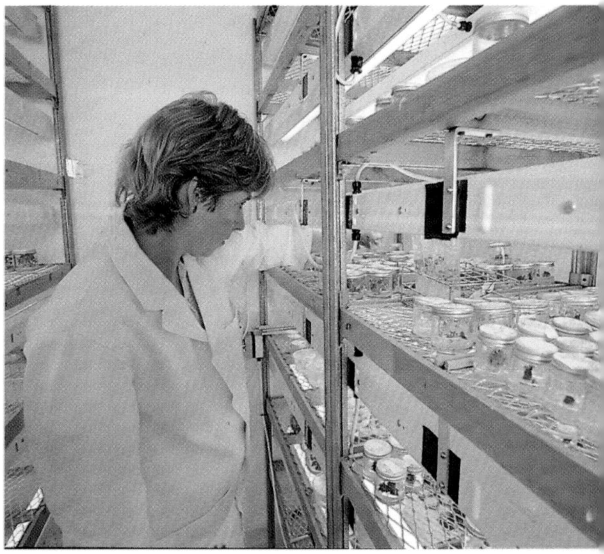

Constant environment growth rooms are used for raising cultured plant material such as oil palm plantlets. The conditions are kept sterile, which means the plantlets are kept free from disease. Environmental conditions, e.g. temperature, are kept at the best levels for healthy growth.

If a single cell or part of a plant, such as a cauliflower floret, is provided with a complex nutrient medium that contains various plant growth regulators and a source of nitrogen and carbon, the cells divide to form an undifferentiated tissue called a callus. From this mass of actively dividing cells, roots and shoots develop to form a complete plant.

homozygous plants can be obtained by inducing chromosome doubling with the chemical colchicine. This technique is used with Brussels sprouts to obtain homozygous F_1 hybrids in two years rather than the usual 5–10 years. These plants can then be used to produce pure breeding lines.

Widespread use of crop plants reared from one set of clones will, however, reduce the number of alleles in the gene pool.

Table 1. Advantages of micropropagation	
Advantage	**Use**
High rates of production of clones can be achieved	Useful in producing large numbers of plants from new varieties to meet market demands
	Useful for increasing stocks of plants that are otherwise difficult to propagate
	Useful in enabling the reproduction of plants that are otherwise sterile, e.g. interspecific F_1 hybrids
Large numbers of plants can be raised in a relatively small space	Cultures from calluses give rise initially to small shoots and plantlets
	Individual commercial units may produce millions of plantlets per year
Sterile propagation produces plants free from disease	Virus-free stock may be produced
Culture conditions can be programmed and carefully controlled	Plants of consistently high quality can be produced and marketed
	All year-round production is possible

 8 How will this reduced number of alleles in the gene pool affect selective breeding programmes?

The cells in callus growths tend to become genetically unstable as the culture ages. The rate of mutation increases, leading to genotypic and phenotypic variability in the plants grown from the cells. If the breeder is looking for some variation in the plant breeding programme, then this may be useful. If the plant breeder wants identical plants, the variation is a disadvantage.

Usually, the best varieties of a crop species are used in cell culture. The regenerated plants can then be used in breeding programmes to improve characteristics. Substances can also be added into the culture medium to select for desired characteristics such as resistance to herbicides.

9 Compare genetic instability in micropropagation with true selective breeding techniques. In what ways are they similar?

Plants grown by vegetative propagation can easily be infected with viral particles. Potato tubers saved from the previous year's crop for planting can contain viruses that will greatly reduce the yield. The viruses are usually spread by aphids feeding on the sap of the adult plants. Potatoes to be sold commercially as seed potatoes can only be grown in aphid-free areas such as Scotland.

The rapidly dividing cells of the growing points of roots and shoots of plants infected with a disease often lack viral particles. Cultures using these growing cells will therefore be virus-free. **Meristem micropropagation** involves culturing the growing point of a plant together with a few young leaves. The structure is very small in size, 0.1mm in diameter and 0.2–1.4mm in length.

Meristem culturing can be a very time-consuming and technically demanding method of tissue culture, particularly for commercial scale production. It is more common to use whole shoot tips and buds, which are easier to handle and can rapidly produce clones of plants. Sugarbeet and cauliflower are regularly produced by this method.

Since the early 1970s the impact globally of micropropagation techniques has been immense. There are many advantages (Table 1). However, there are disadvantages too. They require skilled staff and specialised production facilities. Many experiments have to be carried out to identify the best propagation conditions for each species. This means unit costs can be high compared with other, simpler techniques.

If it is so easy to clone plants, can animal cells be cloned? The cloning of humans from single, highly differentiated adult cells is still in the realms of science fiction.

However, very young embryo animal cells can give rise to a genetically identical copy. An embryo can be split after it has more than 2 cells but fewer than 8. The fragments from the original can be grown by tissue culture techniques to produce embryos. These embryos can be inserted into surrogate mothers. This technique is regularly used to produce cow clones.

10 **What advantage could this have in breeding programmes to select cows that produce more milk?**

Key ideas

- Vegetative propagation means many, identical plants can be grown quickly from one plant showing desirable characteristics.

- Vegetative propagation can reduce the variation in the gene pool of a crop species.

- Vegetative propagation can pass disease on from one plant to the many clones.

- Micropropagation can be used to select desirable features in slow-growing species.

- Micropropagation can be used to produce virus-free plantlets.

- Animal embryos can be cloned by splitting cells apart early in development.

12.6 Genetic engineering

These tomatoes are all the same variety, same age and grown in the same way. The squashy, infected ones are the usual variety. The healthy-looking ones have been genetically modified to produce low levels of ethene. This slows down the ageing process. The modification was done with natural tomato genes. There was no physical or chemical treatment of the tomatoes. All of the genetic changes are inherited. These modifications could be made to other fruits, vegetables and flowers.

Traditional plant and animal breeding methods form new genotypes by combining genes from different parents. The parents come from the same or closely related species. Genetic engineering can speed up this process. If the gene for the desired characteristic can be isolated, it can be added to the crop plant or animal without waiting for fertilisation between the selected individuals. Different techniques are used to copy the desired DNA. This DNA is then combined with the host organism, again in different ways. The host then has a new combination of desirable genes.

Research is continuing to improve the efficiency and reliability of genetic engineering. The effects of factors such as the genotype and age of material, the composition of the growth medium and the time for which the material is cultured have to be investigated. What is different to

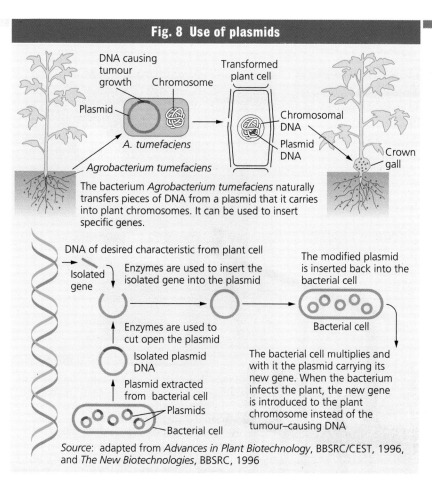

Fig. 8 Use of plasmids

DNA causing tumour growth

Chromosome

Plasmid

Transformed plant cell

A. tumefaciens

Agrobacterium tumefaciens

Chromosomal DNA

Plasmid DNA

Crown gall

The bacterium *Agrobacterium tumefaciens* naturally transfers pieces of DNA from a plasmid that it carries into plant chromosomes. It can be used to insert specific genes.

DNA of desired characteristic from plant cell

Isolated gene

Enzymes are used to insert the isolated gene into the plasmid

The modified plasmid is inserted back into the bacterial cell

Enzymes are used to cut open the plasmid

Bacterial cell

Isolated plasmid DNA

Plasmid extracted from bacterial cell

Plasmids

Bacterial cell

The bacterial cell multiplies and with it the plasmid carrying its new gene. When the bacterium infects the plant, the new gene is introduced to the plant chromosome instead of the tumour-causing DNA

Source: adapted from *Advances in Plant Biotechnology*, BBSRC/CEST, 1996, and *The New Biotechnologies*, BBSRC, 1996

In potatoes, resistance to three major virus diseases has been transferred into the domestic potato from the naturally resistant, but sexually incompatible wild species found in South America. In countries such as Peru, where potato is an important local crop, this could have a great impact on the crop yields. The wild potatoes need to be kept to provide genetic variety that can be used to increase the gene pool.

traditional selective breeding is that genetic engineering is able to transfer genes between species. The organisms produced by this technique are called **transgenic**.

Protoplasts are plant cells from which the cell wall has been removed by treatment with enzymes. Cultured plant protoplasts may eventually regrow a cell wall and divide to produce callus tissue, which can in turn yield many plants. Protoplasts from different species can be fused to produce hybrids that contain two complete sets of chromosomes.

Before protoplasts can be used to produce new crops regularly, the methods used to grow whole plants from them must be improved. Embryo cells in culture are not able to grow for long, although growth of a complete plant has been achieved from protoplasts after as little as 12 weeks. Some protoplast-derived plants of grass species have recently been successfully established in soil for the first time. Previous attempts to regenerate grass protoplasts had resulted in plants that lacked chlorophyll, hardly an improvement!

Foreign genes can transfer into plant cells naturally. The soil bacterium *Agrobacterium tumefaciens* causes 'crown gall' infection. It attacks wounds in plants and causes the cells to multiply, creating a tumour. The *Agrobacterium* does this by inserting genes into the plant chromosome from a **plasmid**, a small loop of DNA. The plasmid contains genes which enable it to link with the plant DNA, and other genes which can trigger the growth of the tumour.

It is now possible to remove the genes causing the tumours and replace them with useful genes. This modification of a naturally occurring genetic engineering system has been used to transfer desirable genes into plants (Fig. 8). The genes are then passed on to the offspring.

Agrobacterium has been used to introduce various genes that help potato plants resist diseases. Potato leaf roll virus

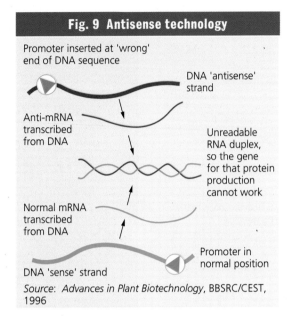

Fig. 9 Antisense technology

Promoter inserted at 'wrong' end of DNA sequence

DNA 'antisense' strand

Anti-mRNA transcribed from DNA

Unreadable RNA duplex, so the gene for that protein production cannot work

Normal mRNA transcribed from DNA

DNA 'sense' strand

Promoter in normal position

Source: Advances in Plant Biotechnology, BBSRC/CEST, 1996

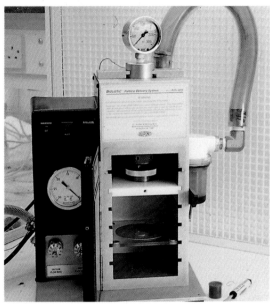

Some plants, e.g. wheat, cannot be easily modified using *Agrobacterium*, and their protoplasts do not regenerate well. So other techniques are needed. This Biolistics particle accelerator shoots tungsten or gold particles coated with the selected DNA directly into plant cells. The particles are about 1 micrometre in diameter. The DNA-coated particles travel through the walls of plant cells placed in their path and lodge within them. The DNA introduced in this way, e.g. to wheat embryos, is expressed and incorporated into the genetic information of the cell. Plants produced by this technique are being assessed for use in breeding programmes.

(PLRV) has a severe economic impact on potato yields. A gene has been introduced that affects the viral coat proteins. Two normally susceptible potato varieties now have improved resistance. The transgenic plants produced can be infected with the virus but show no disease symptoms.

For cells to produce protein, copies of the genetic code held in the DNA are made by RNA. This is called transcription. The strand of copied DNA is called messenger RNA (mRNA). Normally, only one strand of mRNA is made from one strand of DNA, called the sense strand. The complimentary DNA strand that is not normally copied is the antisense strand. Antisense technology uses plant genes in the antisense orientation, transferred to the plant by *Agrobacterium* plasmids (Fig. 9).

A length of DNA known as a promoter is found at the start of a gene sequence. By inserting a promoter at the wrong end of the DNA sequence on the antisense strand, RNA transcription can be forced from the antisense strand. If this modified gene is added to a plant cell, the anti-mRNA joins to the normal mRNA to form a RNA double helix. This stops the normal mRNA strand from carrying its message, so the protein is not made. Genes are therefore 'turned off'.

The Flavr-Savr tomato produced by a company called Calgene went on sale in the USA in 1994. An antisense gene was used to 'turn-off' an enzyme that breaks down cell walls. As a result, the modified tomatoes can develop in colour and flavour without becoming over-ripe. The antisense genes were introduced in *Agrobacterium* plasmids.

In February 1996 a genetically modified tomato purée produced by a company called Zeneca went on sale in the UK. A different technique again was used. The genetic improvement in the tomatoes makes them easier to make good purée, so that less waste is produced, less energy is used and the product is thicker and cheaper for the consumer.

Viruses could also be very useful in transferring genetic information into plants, by introducing genes when they are injected into the subject. Since viruses have high replication rates, viral vectors may allow more copies of the gene product to be made.

Legume plants such as peas and clover form associations with nitrogen-fixing bacteria called *Rhizobium*. The bacteria obtain nutrients from the host plant, while the host plant obtains a source of nitrogen from the bacteria. Soon it may be possible to introduce this ability to form associations with nitrogen-fixing bacteria into non-leguminous plants such as rice, by transferring the nitrogen-fixing genes directly into other plants. This will improve yield because the plants will have constant source of nitrogen.

11 a Why do plants need nitrogen, and in what form is it taken up in non-nitrogen fixing plants?
  b What would be the advantages of introducing nitrogen-fixing genes to crop plants in developing countries?

For nitrogen fixation to happen, **nodulation** has to occur. This is the production of nodules on the host root by infection with *Rhizobium* bacteria. Nodulation is controlled by specific genes. Different strains of *Rhizobium* nodulate different legumes. The complete DNA sequence of the nodulation gene of one strain of *Rhizobium* that nodulates peas has been worked out. Rhizobia also differ in their ability to compete for nodule sites. The genetic basis of nodulation needs to be understood so that the best characteristics can be selected in order to modify other host crop plants. Different strains of *Rhizobium* are being tested in the field for their competitiveness.

Another group of genes controls the

expression of nitrogen-fixing genes in response to the level of oxygen. Nitrogen-fixing genes, or nif genes, are expressed only in an environment which is low in oxygen. Plant root nodules exist in a low-oxygen environment.

The process of nitrogen fixation involves the conversion of nitrogen into ammonia. This requires large amounts of energy and the bacterial enzyme **nitrogenase**. Another nitrogen-fixing soil bacterium, *Azotobacter*, has genes to produce three types of nitrogenase. Each type needs a different metal ion in order to work. This variety could allow the bacteria to survive in different soil conditions. If these genes could be transferred to other plants, they too could fix nitrogen.

Although a lot is now known about the genetic and molecular basis of nitrogen fixation, and nif genes have been successfully isolated, sequenced and cloned in bacteria, researchers are still looking for ways of placing them into the cells of crop plants such as wheat and rice.

Nitrogen fixation requires a lot of energy, in the form of ATP from respiration. Glucose is the usual respiratory substrate.

12 Can you suggest why nitrogen-fixing cereals might produce more protein but less carbohydrate and overall yield less, than normal cereals?

All new discoveries and procedures, especially those involving the manipulation of an organism's genotype and its subsequent environmental impact, are subject to a degree of risk. The question is whether the risk is large or small, and whether the potential benefits outweigh the possible costs. Opinions vary between the two extreme views, that genetic engineering will eventually solve the problems of global food production, and that genetic engineering will cause

These experimental plots show the effect of low nitrogen input (right) on growth of wheat. If crops could be genetically modified so that they could form symbiotic relationships with nitrogen-fixing bacteria, or to produce nitrogen-fixation even in high concentrations of oxygen, yields would be increased without the need for fertiliser.

permanent harm to the world environment.

Humans have been altering the genetic make-up of plant and animal species for many hundreds of years, simply by breeding and selecting animals and plants with the qualities that are most useful to us. Genetic manipulation also occurs naturally, for example by bacteria causing the growth of galls. As we learn more, we may be able to alter safely plants and animals so that there is less global food shortage, and less energy wasted in the food processing business. These are important facts to consider. However, the potential damage that could be done to other organisms and the environment must not be overlooked.

Fertiliser use can have an adverse effect on the environment. If legume genes could be used so that non-leguminous plants can fix nitrogen, crop plants should be able to grow healthily without the need to add fertilisers. The effect of genetically modifying the plants may reduce the environmental impact of crop production because fewer chemicals need to be used as pesticides and fertilisers. This may be acceptable to many people, but genetic engineering of animals is often more difficult to accept.

 13 Where would you draw the line? Are you happy for farmers to use genetically modified plants and animals? Would you be happy to eat genetically modified foodstuffs? Explain your thoughts on this issue and give evidence to support your ideas.

Key ideas

- Genetic engineering is a process that can be used to speed up the results of selective breeding.

- Transgenic organisms are produced by adding genes from one species into the DNA of another.

- Plasmids can be used to introduce genes from one species into another.

- Antisense technology is one way of genetically altering an organism.

Appendix 1

Random sampling numbers

20	17	42	28	23	17	59	66	38	61	02	10	86	10	51	55	92	52
74	49	04	49	03	04	10	33	53	70	11	54	48	63	94	60	94	49
94	70	49	31	38	67	23	42	29	65	40	88	78	71	37	18	48	64
22	15	78	15	69	84	32	52	32	54	15	12	54	02	01	37	38	37
93	29	12	18	27	30	30	55	91	87	50	57	58	51	49	36	12	53
45	04	77	97	36	14	99	45	52	95	69	85	03	83	51	87	85	56
44	91	99	49	89	39	94	60	48	49	06	77	64	72	59	26	08	51
16	23	91	02	19	96	47	59	89	65	27	84	30	92	63	37	26	24
04	50	65	04	65	65	82	42	70	51	55	04	61	47	88	83	99	34
32	70	17	72	03	61	66	26	24	71	22	77	88	33	17	78	08	92
03	64	59	07	42	95	81	39	06	41	20	81	92	34	51	90	39	08
62	49	00	90	67	86	83	48	31	83	19	07	67	68	49	03	27	47
61	00	95	86	98	36	14	03	48	88	51	07	33	40	06	86	33	76
89	03	90	49	28	74	21	04	09	96	60	45	22	03	52	80	01	79
01	72	33	85	52	40	60	07	06	71	89	27	14	29	55	24	85	79
27	56	49	79	34	34	32	22	60	53	91	17	33	26	44	70	93	14
49	05	74	48	10	55	35	25	24	28	20	22	35	66	66	34	26	35
49	74	37	25	97	26	33	94	42	23	01	28	59	58	92	69	03	66
20	26	22	43	88	08	19	85	08	12	47	65	65	63	56	07	97	85
48	87	77	96	43	39	76	93	08	79	22	18	54	55	93	75	97	26
08	72	87	46	75	73	00	11	27	07	05	20	30	85	22	21	04	67
95	97	98	62	17	27	31	42	64	71	46	22	32	75	19	32	20	99
37	99	57	31	70	40	46	55	46	12	24	32	36	74	69	20	72	10
05	79	58	37	85	33	75	18	88	71	23	44	54	28	00	48	96	23
55	85	63	42	00	79	91	22	29	01	41	39	51	50	36	65	26	11
67	28	96	25	68	36	24	72	03	85	49	24	05	69	64	86	08	19
85	86	94	78	32	59	51	82	86	43	73	84	45	60	89	57	06	87
40	10	60	09	05	88	78	44	63	13	58	25	37	11	18	47	75	62
94	55	89	48	90	80	77	80	26	89	87	44	23	74	66	20	20	19
11	63	77	77	23	20	33	62	62	19	29	03	94	15	56	37	14	09
64	00	26	04	54	55	38	57	94	62	68	40	26	04	24	25	03	61
50	94	13	23	78	41	60	58	10	60	88	46	30	21	45	98	70	96
66	98	37	96	44	13	45	05	34	59	75	85	48	97	27	19	17	85
66	91	42	83	60	77	90	91	60	90	79	62	57	66	72	28	08	70
33	58	12	18	02	07	19	40	21	29	39	45	90	42	58	84	85	43
52	49	70	16	72	40	73	05	50	90	02	04	98	24	05	30	27	25
74	98	93	99	78	30	79	47	96	62	45	58	40	37	89	76	84	41
50	26	54	30	01	88	69	57	54	45	69	88	23	21	05	69	93	44
49	46	61	89	33	79	96	84	28	34	19	35	28	73	39	59	56	34
19	64	13	44	78	39	73	88	62	03	36	00	25	96	86	76	67	90
64	17	47	67	87	59	81	40	72	61	14	00	28	28	55	86	23	38
18	43	97	37	68	97	56	56	57	95	01	88	11	89	48	07	42	07
65	58	60	87	51	09	96	61	15	53	66	81	66	88	44	75	37	01
79	90	31	00	91	14	85	65	31	75	43	15	45	93	64	78	34	53
07	23	00	15	59	05	16	09	94	42	20	40	63	76	65	67	34	11
90	98	14	24	01	51	95	46	30	32	33	19	00	14	19	28	40	51
53	82	62	02	21	82	34	13	41	03	12	85	65	30	00	97	56	30
98	17	26	15	04	50	76	25	20	33	54	84	39	31	23	33	59	64
08	91	12	44	82	40	30	62	45	50	64	54	65	17	89	25	59	44
37	21	46	77	84	87	67	39	85	54	97	37	33	41	11	74	90	50

Source: after Lindley and Miller (1953)

Appendix 2

Critical values of chi-squared

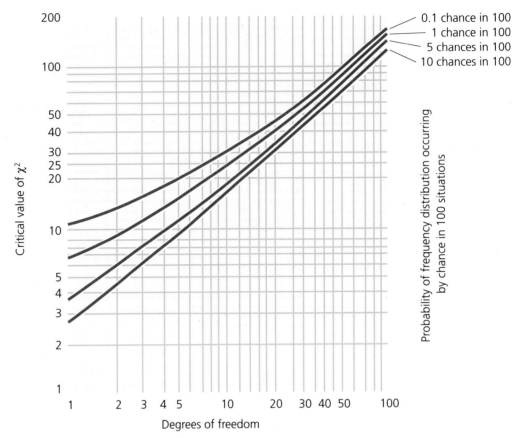

Source: based on McCullagh, *Data Use and Interpretation*

Answers to questions

Chapter 1

1. (i) An ecosystem is made up of two parts: a biotic (living) part called the community and an abiotic (non-living) part called the habitat. The habitat provides the conditions needed for a plant or animal to exist. It is the place where a particular organism lives.
   (ii) A community is made up of all the plants and animals that live in a particular habitat. Each community is made up of different populations of plants and animals. A population is a group of individuals of the same species living in the same habitat.

2. (i) Autotrophs are able to make their own organic food by using inorganic nutrients and a source of energy, e.g. green plants use solar energy to make food from carbon dioxide and water during photosynthesis. Heterotrophs cannot make their own food. They have to take food into their bodies ready made.
   (ii) Decomposers are microorganisms, e.g. bacteria and fungi, that break down dead plants and animals and waste materials. Detritivores are small animals, e.g. woodlice and earthworms, that feed on detritus. Detritus is made up of fragments of dead and decaying materials.

3. **a** Primary consumers: limpets, mussels and flat periwinkles. Secondary consumers: barnacles (assuming the zooplankton is herbivorous), dogwhelks (when feeding on mussels), turnstones (when feeding on limpets and periwinkles), crabs (when feeding on mussels). Tertiary consumers: dogwhelks (when feeding on barnacles), turnstones (when feeding on dogwhelks), gulls. Both crabs and gulls are detritivores, since they are feeding on dead organisms.
   b Mussels→dogwhelks→turnstones
   Diatoms (on seaweeds)→flat periwinkles →turnstones
   Diatoms (on rocks)→limpets→ turnstones
   c There are several food chains present in this ecosystem. A food web is the better description since some organisms, e.g.

diatoms and turnstones, appear in more than one food chain.

4. **a** 29 more (30 could be supported on a diet of frogs compared with 1 on a diet of trout).
   b 900 – 30 = 870 more.

5. In June the oak tree will have all its leaves and flowers out. By December these will have been shed.

6. (i) Pyramids of number give us information about the numbers of individuals at each trophic level. However, they do not take into account the size (biomass) of individuals, so for instance an oak tree and a grass plant both count as one individual.
   (ii) Pyramids of biomass overcome the problem of size of each individual. However, estimating dry mass can be impracticable and undesirable. Biomass pyramids also do not take into account how fast an organism grows, i.e. its productivity, since they only give measurements of a standing crop.
   (iii) Pyramids of energy are able to reflect productivity since they show the amount of energy transferred from one trophic level to the next in kJ m^{-2} year^{-1}. However, collection of data for energy pyramids is difficult since it involves burning samples of organisms from each trophic level in a calorimeter in order to estimate energy content.

7. **a** Photosynthetic efficiency = amount of energy incorporated into newly formed carbohydrate ÷ amount of light energy falling on the plant:
   $$\frac{92}{1000} = 0.092$$
   b Energy absorbed by chloroplasts = 400. Energy 'lost' during photosynthetic reactions = 308. Percentage loss:
   $$\frac{308}{400} \times 100 = 77\%$$
   Energy in the form of ATP is used in the dark stage of photosynthesis.

8. **a** Tropical forest: a high density of trees and other tropical plants, warm temperatures throughout the year extending the growing season, no shortage of soil nutrients or water, all contribute to the high productivity. Intensive agriculture: a high density planting of crops during the growing season, application of nitrogenous

fertilisers and possibly irrigation, all contribute to the high productivity.
   b Extreme desert and desert scrub: lack of water, lack of soil humus and soil nutrients, all reduce productivity. The last two points are less true of desert scrub.
   c Errors in sampling. Some plant parts may not be collected, e.g. leaves, flowers and fruits may have been lost. Errors occur during dry mass estimates. The range of measurements can vary a great deal within one ecosystem, so average estimates are needed.

9. **a** 10 000 kJ m^{-2} year^{-1} represents 1% of the solar energy absorbed.
   b NPP = GPP – respiration:
   10 000 – 2000 = 8000 kJ m^{-2} year^{-1}.
   c (i) Primary consumer:
   $$\frac{800}{8000} \times 100 = 10\%$$
   (ii) Secondary consumer:
   $$\frac{160}{800} \times 100 = 20\%$$
   (iii) Tertiary consumer:
   $$\frac{16}{160} \times 100 = 10\%$$
   d The secondary consumer.
   e Respiration, excretion, faeces and death.

10. **a** GPP = NPP + respiration:
    x = $(9 \times 10^4) - (5 \times 10^4)$ kJ m^{-2} year^{-1}
    = 4×10^4 kJ m^{-2} year^{-1}.
    b Since sunlight leads to box V, then this box must be a producer (green plant). W = primary consumer, X = secondary consumer and Y = tertiary consumer. Since all arrows go to box Z, it must represent decomposers.
    c There is a net energy loss of 10×10^4 kJ m^{-2} year^{-1}. Since the system is in a steady state (because total biomass and detritus are constant), the total energy input must equal the total energy output. Since GPP is greater than respiration, there must be a net energy loss (as organic matter leaving the ecosystem).

11. **a** (i) 3.3%
    (ii) 63.3%
    b Assimilation efficiency = assimilated food ÷ consumed food:
    $$\frac{34.28}{91.34} = 0.375$$
    c Assimilation efficiency is fairly low. Also only 4% of consumed food ends up in

171

production. So the cow has to spend a lot of its time feeding.

d 1g of beef contains 12 kJ of energy. So 100 g will contain 1200 kJ. As we have worked out in a (i), 3.3% of the energy in one square metre of grass ends up in production. So if 3.3% = 1200 kJ then 100% = 1200 ÷ 3.3 × 100 = 36 363.6 kJ. Since there are 3000 kJ in one square metre of grass, there will be 36 363.6 kJ in 36 363.6 ÷ 3000 = 12.1 square metres of grass.

12 a The cow converts only 3.3% of consumed food into production. This is not very efficient as many herbivores achieve 10% (see question 9).

b Eating plants is cheaper than eating meat.

c A vegetarian diet can support far more people. By cutting down the number of links in a food chain, more individuals can be fed (see Fig. 5).

d The price of food will rise and so more people will have to adopt a vegetarian diet.

Chapter 2

1 a Primary production is the production of organic materials by green plants or by bacteria. Net primary production (NPP) = gross primary production (GPP) – respiration. NPP is available as food for primary consumers.

b Energy enters an ecosystem as solar energy, which is trapped by producers and passed along trophic levels to be released eventually as heat energy. Nutrients, unlike energy, can be released back into the ecosystem in a form that can be taken up by producers and passed along food chains.

2 a Since nitrogen is needed for the production of proteins, shortage will result in stunted growth of plants and chlorosis (yellowing of the leaves).

b The use of chemical fertilisers will help correct nutrient shortage: ammonium nitrate as a source of nitrogen, calcium phosphate and basic slag from steel works as a source of phosphorus, and potassium sulphate for potassium shortage.

3 a Colliery waste has a low pH; in these conditions iron and aluminium phosphates are formed which cannot be used by plants. Many nutrients can be leached out through the free-draining colliery waste. Low humus content also means that there is a smaller pool of nutrients available to plants.

b Tolerant species can survive low pH, toxic metals, lack of water or nutrients and high temperature.

4 a Carbon dioxide enters plants during photosynthesis and leaves during respiration, decomposition and burning.

b Carbon enters animals in their food and leaves as carbon dioxide during respiration and decomposition.

c When plants are compacted eventually to form fossil fuels, and if carbonates, e.g. limestone, are formed in aquatic habitats.

d Bacteria and fungi.

5 Solar radiation passes through the atmosphere and warms the Earth's surface. The Earth radiates heat energy back into space (mainly infrared radiation). Some of this heat energy is absorbed by the greenhouse gases. This heats up the air. Carbon dioxide levels are rising due to increased burning of fossil fuels, removal of large areas of forest and other damage to plant life including phytoplankton.

6 a In their food.

b As waste material and dead bodies.

c Absorption by plant roots, the action of denitrifying bacteria, leaching and run-off into aquatic systems.

d By using nitrogenous fertilisers or by growing plants like clover, peas and beans that have nitrogen-fixing bacteria in their roots.

7 a Water-logged soils inhibit respiration in roots and encourage the growth of denitrifying bacteria. These bacteria can deplete soils of nitrogen and so affect primary production.

b In many ways: by decomposing dead and waste organic material, by nitrogen fixation, by nitrification and denitrification.

8 In tropical forests the rate of decomposition is more rapid due to increased temperature and humidity. Disturbance of the habitat by, say, ploughing, would mean that the rate of decomposition is accelerated and more nutrients could be lost by run-off and leaching.

9 (i) Earthworms are important detritivores that have a significant effect upon the breakdown of buried oak leaves.
(ii) The 0.5 mm mesh excludes earthworms, and results in a large drop in the rate of breakdown of the leaf pieces.
(iii) Although no graph is shown for the percentage disappearance of leaf pieces when all detritivores are excluded, it is likely that the rate of decomposition would be significantly reduced, underlining the key role of detritivores in decomposition.

10 Make a list of the nutrient inputs into the community using Table 4 as a guide. Some items in the table may not apply, e.g. fertiliser application. Then make a list of the possible nutrient outputs focusing upon either the colliery tip or the motorway verge.

11 a In the winter low temperature and poor illumination limit phytoplankton production. In the summer, nutrient shortage limits phytoplankton production.

b A shortage of nutrients and grazing by zooplankton.

c The breakdown of the thermocline, the vertical mixing of the water column, leads to the return of nutrients to the surface waters.

d Temperature and illumination are not as good as in spring, so production is not so great.

12 a Upstream the relatively low phosphate concentrations limit production in the algae. Downstream shows a marked increase in phosphate concentrations leading to greater productivity and a resultant increase in algal numbers.

b Eutrophication, the enrichment of phosphate, could result in such an increase in algal growth that decomposition of dead algae by bacteria would lead to depletion of oxygen and the subsequent death of fish and invertebrates.

13 Algal blooms result from a local enrichment of nutrients; this is eutrophication.

14 a Nutrients (from fertilisers, sewage or detergents) encourage the growth of algae. Some algae do not get enough light and start to die and decay. Bacteria feed upon the dead algae and increased respiration uses up oxygen. Depletion of oxygen kills fish and invertebrates.

b Water abstracted for drinking may have an odour, colour or even be a threat to health. Increased growth of vegetation may impede water flow and navigation. The amenity value of the water may decrease, fisheries may be lost and nature conservation affected.

Chapter 3

1 Grouse shooting occurs almost entirely in areas that have been identified as suitable for coniferous forestry. However, the largest numbers of grouse are shot in those areas that have no, or only a small proportion of, land already planted with conifers.

2 The trees provide a much more suitable habitat for perching birds, with better food supply, nesting sites and protection from predators.

3 a The Institute of Terrestrial Ecology is engaged in all aspects of basic ecological research and has a much wider brief that includes all aspects of grouse biology and ecology. The Game Conservancy is carrying out applied research with the aim of improving the commercial benefits arising from grouse shooting.

   b The Game Conservancy may be seen as having a vested interest as it is funded by landowners. Such a group might be more likely to publish their results selectively and with a bias towards the interests of grouse shooters.

4 A population is a group of individuals of the same species that live in a particular area.

5 Biotic factors are due to other living organisms, and include competition, availability of food plants or prey, parasites and disease-causing organisms. Abiotic factors are chemical and physical influences, and include pH, salinity, oxygen concentration, humidity, light, temperature and wind speed.

6 a Where several factors affect a process, the factor that has the lowest value or of which there is least available will determine the rate of the process and, therefore, will limit the rate.

   b Humans and elephants produce small numbers of young at a time, and these young take a long time to mature before they can reproduce. Bacteria and mice reproduce much more rapidly and thus have a much greater biotic potential.

7 a

Age	% survival
1	100.0
2	48.6
3	28.6
4	14.7
5	9.0
6	5.7
7	4.1
8	2.0
9	1.6
10	0.8

   b The rate of mortality stays fairly constant. Reducing the number of deaths in young birds would be likely to maintain a larger population of kestrels.

8 a A cod population, in which there is a very high mortality in the young fish, would be represented by type III. A human population, in which few individuals die young, would be represented by type I.

   b The kestrel population follows the pattern in type II.

9 a

Time /min	Number of bacterial cells
0	1
20	2
40	4
60	8
80	16
100	32
120	64

   b Exponential, that is the curve gets increasingly steep or J-shaped.

   c For *Daphnia*, at 18°C, the temperature is limiting population growth. After about 13 days, at 23°C some other factor such as nutrient supply is limiting. For flour beetles, food supply becomes limiting in both populations.

10 Choose two (or several) grouse populations living in similar conditions. Treat one population (or half of the populations) with anti-parasite drugs. Record the numbers in the populations over a period of years.

11 a Increase in prey population→Increase in predator population→Decrease in prey population→Decrease in predator population.

   b Regular fluctuation of both prey–host and predator–parasite populations. In each case the peak for the predator–parasite population is later than that for the prey–host population.

   c As the number of prey increases, the reproductive success of the predator increases. The larger numbers of predators accelerate the decline in prey

numbers, but predator numbers only decrease when prey numbers become too low to sustain the predator population.

12 a As the number of seeds sown per pot increases, the number of seeds per plant decreases rapidly and then remains fairly constant at a low level.

   b High density sowing reduces the chance of weeds becoming established between plants, and, up to a point, the yield from the larger number of plants exceeds the reduction in yield per plant. It allows for loss of seeds as a result of failure to germinate and consumption by herbivores. In some crops there may be a reduced chance of wind damage to taller, straighter plants. Disadvantages include the less economical use of seeds and the reduced yields due to competition for resources such as light, nutrients and space at the higher densities.

13 a In the conditions in the culture, species 2 is more successful in competition for the same resources. The population of species 2 rises, whereas that of species 1 declines as it obtains a lower and lower share of the resources. Note that, as a result of the initial competition, the population size of species 2 increases at a lower rate in the combined culture than in the separate culture.

   b Food.

   c One species might directly affect the other, for example by preying on it, or perhaps producing a toxin that kills it.

14 a *Elminius* has the highest biotic potential, and *Semibalanus* has a higher biotic potential than *Chthamalus*.

   b Other environmental factors may limit the growth of the *Elminius* population, such as susceptibility to wave action or desiccation, or shortage of suitable food. As an invading species it might also have lower resistance to disease.

15 The squirrels may be competing for food or for suitable nest sites.

16 As the territories get smaller, the females produce fewer eggs and fewer chicks survive to maturity. Therefore, there will be fewer birds to reproduce in the next generation, and the size of the population will decrease. This in turn will allow males to have larger territories again, and thus be more successful in breeding.

17 a Food and space.

   b At high densities each limpet is likely to obtain less food, grow less fast and reach a lower maximum size. At low densities individuals are able to grow to a larger size. Above a certain minimum population density, the total biomass of the limpets in a given area is more or less constant.

18 a The immigration rate would be high, unless the nuthatch density in the area was already high.

b Food and availability of territories and nest sites would become limiting.

c Density-dependent.

Chapter 4

1 Colonisation is the establishing of a species in a new or different habitat, whereas dispersal is the process of spreading out, which may allow a species to reach a new habitat.

2 A habitat is a particular area within which a species lives, such as a pond or wood. A niche is the specific combination of abiotic and biotic factors within its habitat to which a species is adapted, for example feeding on detritus on the bottom of a pond.

3 a (i) Species A.
(ii) Species B.
(iii) Both species A and B.

b There will be increasing competition for food between species A and B. As species A is at the limit of its range of temperature tolerance, it is likely that species B will be more successful and will displace it from the habitat.

4 No photosynthesis takes place in darkness, so there would be no gross primary production (GPP), and over a period of four months reserves would be continuously depleted by respiration, although at very low temperatures the rate of respiration might be very low. NPP would therefore be very low. As a result few land plants are able to survive in the Antarctic. Overall NPP is also low in the sea, but the richness of nutrients and their circulation by strong currents enable rapid growth of phytoplankton during the long summer daylight hours, thus maintaining a flourishing marine ecosystem.

5 a Species B has the widest, species A the narrowest temperature tolerance.

b (i) As there is no overlap in temperature tolerance range, species A could not transfer.

(ii) Species B could survive at the upper end of the tolerance range for species A, but not over the full range.

c Species A.

6 Air temperature above the snow falls to very low levels, but below the snow surface the greater the depth the less the drop in temperature. Organisms living beneath the snow therefore experience much less extreme temperatures.

7 The short summer growing period makes it impossible to synthesise enough biomass to produce the amount of seeds that would ensure sufficient survive for the following year.

8 The extensive roots provide strong anchorage, and enable the grass to derive water and nutrients from a wide area.

9 Feeding is confined to summer months when the temperature is high enough to avoid freezing. In winter the gut is emptied and supercooling can occur.

10 a A species that completes its life cycle in one season can overwinter at stages in the cycle that are best adapted to survive extreme conditions, such as eggs or pupae.

b By extending the life cycle over several years larger individuals can develop, which may have a competitive advantage, and these can produce greater numbers of offspring, thus increasing the chance of survival.

11 The streamlined shape reduces the amount of energy used in swimming and enables the penguins to make more efficient use of limited food resources. The low surface area:volume ratio helps to reduce heat loss.

12 The restricted range of suitable breeding beaches made them relatively easy to catch and the superior insulation qualities of the fur created a strong demand.

13 a At the level of primary and secondary consumer.

b The sperm whale population is likely to fall as there is less krill for fish and squid to feed on, and therefore less food for the whales.

c The krill population could increase, as the baleen whales were predators. In the longer term this might be balanced out by increases in numbers of other predators, owing to reduced competition from the baleen whales.

Chapter 5

1 Release of pollutants over a large area, as in the case of fertilisers and pesticides, is difficult to monitor, especially as the effects are often additive rather than attributable to one particular incident. Slow percolation of pollutants, for example from a landfill site, may be difficult to pinpoint, particularly if the pollutants emerge in water courses some distance from their origin.

2 Increased tubidity reduces the amount of light available for photosynthesis, and thus reduces the growth of aquatic plants and algae.

3 Individual consumers feed on large numbers of organisms, each of which contains only small amounts of DDT. As DDT is not readily excreted or broken down, it accumulates in the body of the consumer. Tertiary consumers often have long lifespans and as a result accumulate large numbers of doses of DDT from the secondary consumers that they eat. The concentration reaches its highest level in the tertiary consumers, since they have already accumulated relatively large doses from primary consumers.

4 a The minimum dissolved oxygen concentration occurs where there is maximum microbial activity. At the point of discharge the microbial population will not have reached its maximum level. An additional factor may be that the products of microbial breakdown lead to eutrophication, that is the excess growth of algae and plants, and the decay of these further stimulates microbial activity and oxygen depletion.

b Once the effluent has been broken down, there is much less organic material for microorganisms to feed on, and therefore fewer microorganisms to reduce the oxygen concentration. The mineral nutrients released stimulate plant and algal growth, and, provided they are not in excess, they release oxygen during photosynthesis. A flowing river will also absorb oxygen from the air, especially if it is turbulent.

5 Possible sources of error include: incomplete mixing of the water sample; loss of particles that are smaller than the pore size of the filter; incomplete drying in the oven (which can be overcome by further drying and reweighing until a constant mass is reached).

6 a They will increase the BOD.
  b The invertebrate population would decline.

7 High flow rate improves water quality by dispersing pollutants more rapidly, increasing the dilution rate and, especially in turbulent conditions, increasing the rate at which oxygen is absorbed from the air.

8 a The sampling period was restricted to the same limited time in the middle of each day. It therefore failed to record fluctuations outside this period.
  b Sampling should take place at regular intervals throughout the 24 hours of each day. Alternatively, if available, continuous electronic monitoring could be used.

9 a Site 1, biotic index = 79; site 2, biotic index = 18.
  b Site 1, 5.16; site 2, 2.49
  c Site 1 has a greater diversity of species, and contains species that are intolerant of low oxygen concentrations, such as the stonefly larvae. This suggests that the water at site 1 is well oxygenated and not polluted by organic matter. Site 2 has a more limited range of species and these are all ones that are tolerant of low oxygen concentrations. There are, however, large numbers of some of these species, such as the worms, suggesting that there is excess organic matter on which these species can feed.

10 a The change in indicator species from a high proportion of midge larvae and other species that are intolerant to low oxygen levels to ones that are tolerant indicates a high level of organic pollution. The increases in suspended solids and BOD confirm this. The increases in ions are likely to be a result of the decomposition of this organic matter.
  b Worms.

11 The stone loach is much more tolerant of cadmium than the trout. The trout can tolerate almost double the dose of zinc. Both are susceptible to relatively low doses of copper, although it takes longer to take effect in the trout.

12 a Shrimp and limpet.
  b Chironomid fly and simuliid fly.

13 Acid rain can be reduced by reducing sulphur dioxide emissions, e.g. by use of low sulphur fuels, removing sulphur dioxide from factory chimneys, reduced use of fossil fuels by energy saving measures, and use of catalytic converters in vehicles.

14 The fishing industry will have been affected by direct effects on commercial fish, such as suffocation and reduced fertility, and by indirect effects on marine food webs, reducing the availability of food for fish.

15 The population of snails and leeches, which are tolerant of low oxygen levels and organic pollution, have been seriously depleted.

Chapter 6

1 Light intensity, temperature, humidity, wind speed, soil pH, soil water and soil humus should be monitored.

2 Random sampling points do not cover all parts of the grid as in systematic sampling. This could produce distorted results in the sample.

3 Belt transects are usually used for showing zonation along sheltered rocky shores. However, on steep, exposed rocky shores it is not always easy to use quadrats. In this case a line transect is a lot quicker to use over what can be quite a distance.

4 Point quadrats eliminate a lot of the subjective element in frame quadrats. They produce quantitative results and are easy to use on low growing vegetation.

5 a Place a series of quadrats of a suitable size at random across the sampling area. Then use another series of more quadrats, of the same size as the first series, and so on. The total number of species sampled is recorded after each increase in number of quadrats. Eventually a point will be reached where all the common species have been identified and a further increase in quadrat number will not be worth the time and effort required. A minimum number of quadrats has been reached when a 1% increase in the number of quadrats produces not more than a 0.5% increase in the number of species found.
  b Place a series of quadrats of a certain size at random across the sampling area. Then use another series, of the same number but of larger quadrats, and so on. The total number of species sampled is recorded after each increase in quadrat size. Eventually a point will be reached where a further increase in size of quadrat results in only a few extra species being sampled and a further increase in quadrat size will not be worth the time and effort required. The best quadrat size is reached when a 1% increase in quadrat size produces no more than a 0.5% increase in number of species found.

6 Dry biomass measurements involve heating a sample of the species in an oven to constant weight. This is inevitably destructive.

7 a Percentage cover:
  hits ÷ hits + misses × 100:
  $$\frac{20}{150} \times 100 = 13.3\%$$
  b The percentage cover of the weed species is increasing over time, so the rare woodland plant is probably decreasing. A conservation programme may be needed to help the rare plant compete with the weed plant.

8 $P = M \times S \div R =$
  $$\frac{60 \times 50}{15} = 200$$

9 a Fish and other aquatic organisms. Arthropods because they moult their exoskeleton periodically.
  b Births would increase the number of unmarked individuals captured in the second sample (S). This would increase the population estimate. Deaths would decrease the number of unmarked individuals captured in the second sample (S). This would decrease the population estimate.

10 A study in the growth of an aquatic organism, e.g. mayfly nymph. Smaller nymphs would pass through a course mesh.

11 a A line graph shows the numbers of individuals of each species over time. Any trends and differences between the two species can be clearly identified.
  b Competition for scarce resources, e.g. light or nutrients.
  c To establish the normal growth pattern of each species of duckweed without competition.

12 a A bar chart can be used since the fish species can be put into clear categories on the x axis.
  b Overfishing.

13 b A histogram is used since the data (fruit length) are continuous.

14 a There is more vegetation near the natural water course, the man-made water course is very straight, the flow of

water is more tubid in the natural water course.

b There is probably a higher diversity of species in the East Lyn river. The diversity of species in River Rea is probably low due to pollution and loss of pollution-intolerant species, e.g. stonefly larvae.

Chapter 7

1 Fewer young fish will survive to the age at which they are able to breed. The reduced number of breeding fish will affect recruitment and could ultimately lead to the collapse of the stock.

2 Fishery X (underfished):
   (i) The total yield increases as the biomass of the stock increases.
   (ii) The yield per unit effort increases but older fish make catches less marketable.
   (iii) The mean size of fish increases but there is a greater proportion of older fish.
   Fishery Y (overfished):
   (i) The total yield decreases as more young fish are caught.
   (ii) The yield per unit effort decreases as more fishing effort is put into catching fewer fish.
   (iii) The mean size of fish decreases.

3 a The fishery will show a maximum profit at about 30% fishing effort (where the distance between the value and the cost is the greatest). The fishery will cease to be profitable when costs exceeds value, at about 60% fishing effort.
   b Maximum profitability would be at about 40% fishing effort. Minimum profitability would be at about 70% fishing effort.

4 Curve A represents the heavily fished stock. The low biomass is the result of fish being caught too young before they reach their full growth potential.
   Curve B represents the moderately fished stock. The level of fishing enables fish to attain their full growth potential.
   Curve C represents the unfished stock. Young fish are unable to reach their full growth potential because of competition from older, slower growing fish.

5 a The fishery is overfished at point X.
   b Close seasons; protected areas; quotas; gear restrictions; increased mesh size, could all improve the fishery's catch.
   c An increase in the mean size of fish; an increase in the yield per unit effort; an

increase in the total yield of the fishery, would accompany an increase in sustainable catch.

6 Modern nets are made of rot-resistant plastic and appear transparent underwater. This makes them a potential hazard to marine mammals, fish and bottom-living invertebrates for a long period of time.

7

	Trawling	Demersal line fishing
Waste	Wasteful since non-selective so often a large by-catch	Bait and hook size make it more selective so inevitably less wasteful
Efficiency	Method of capture is very efficient However, wastage means that overall efficiency is reduced	Efficient method for catching expensive fish in areas where trawling is not an option
Manpower	Greater mechanisation means reduced manpower	Labour-intensive for baiting hooks and laying the lines
Potential damage to stock and other species	Non-selective nature and efficient method of capture means potential for damage is high	Less potential for damage

8 The advantage to fishermen of implementing a mesh size of 100 mm rather than 120 mm is better short-term profits, due to greater landings because fewer fish are able to escape the net. The disadvantage of the smaller mesh size is that the future of the stock could be threatened because less fish can escape and survive to breed.

9 Fishermen resist the introduction of an increase in mesh size because there will be a short-term loss of yield. Any increase in the minimum mesh size means that more fish escape from the net, leading to reduced landings and reduced profits.

10 a Initially, TACs were not very effective at conserving stocks. However, they had brought about some recovery in the 1980s.
   b Protective measures could have included close seasons; protected areas; quotas; gear restrictions.

11 A minimum mesh size would allow more fish to escape the net, survive to breed and increase the stock. Closing nursery areas would mean spawning fish were not caught, so there would be greater recruitment.

12 Total restriction on over-exploited species; quotas; gear restrictions; close seasons; exclusion zones, could all be used to control fishing effort.

13 Large drift nets would have a greater effect upon fish stocks because they would result in larger landings than long lines.

14 Purse seiners employ advanced and sophisticated fishing technology. They are ruthlessly efficient, with the capacity to remove entire shoals of fish.

15

	Advantages	Disadvantages
Pelagic line	Selective by using specific bait and hook size	Labour intensive
		Can hook sea-birds that dive for the bait
	Can operate where it is too deep or too rocky for trawlers	
	Profitable for expensive species	
Drift nets	Efficient in catching pelagic shoaling species like tuna	Can entangle and drown diving birds, turtles, dolphins and seals
		Many fish can be net-scarred
Purse seine	Very efficient using advanced technology	Ruthless efficiency means that in the absence of control, they have the potential to remove all the pelagic fish from the sea
	Requires low manpower	
	Catches fish in good condition	

16 a The total mass of fish per tank after 80 days when stocked with 500 fish = $0.025 \times 80 = 2.00$ g + 2 g (initial mass)= 4.00 g per fish. $4.00 \times 500 = 2000$ g. The total mass of fish per tank after 80 days when stocked with 1500 fish = $0.01 \times 80 = 0.80$ g + 2 g (initial mass) = 2.80 g per fish. $2.80 \times 1500 = 4200$ g.
   b The average mass after 80 days at 500 density = 4.00 g. The average mass after 80 days at 1500 density = 2.80 g. The fish gain a greater average mass when reared at lower density because there is less competition for food.

Chapter 8

1 b The world average takes into account many less productive areas, whereas highest yields are obviously from the most productive areas.
   c Irrigation; fertiliser application; pest control methods; cultivation techniques; genetically improved crops, could all improve world production.

2 $6CO_2 + 6H_2O$ solar energy $\rightarrow C_6H_{12}O_6 + 6O_2$

carbon dioxide +water →
carbohydrate+oxygen

3 a The main site of photosynthesis is in the chloroplast of the leaf. The greater the leaf area, the greater the ability of a leaf to absorb solar energy, so more light reaches the chloroplasts.

b The leaf area increases as the plant grows. As a result of increased photosynthesis from the greater leaf area, the plant begins to increase in dry mass.

4 a $X = 8.72$. $Y = 0.46$.

b The greater the plant height, the lower the HI.

5 a Protein is used for growth and cell division. Dietary protein is broken down into amino acids that are then used to make structural proteins, enzymes and hormones.

b Harvestable protein is important when a crop is being grown for a particular market, e.g. animal foodstuffs. High protein crops like kale represent better economic value because the conversion efficiency into animal protein is better.

6 Maize has a much greater RGR than barley (2.31 g g^{-1} week^{-1} compared with 0.92g g^{-1} week^{-1} when grown under the same conditions). Therefore the maize was able to add new biomass (which would include grain) to the crop much quicker than barley.

7 a NAR is mainly dependent upon solar energy, so it is greatest in June.

b No, it would not be useful to delay harvesting until later than October. NAR is very low after October and so growth will be low.

c No, the RGR curve would not be the same shape. The increasing plant biomass is due in part to the enlarging sugar beet root, so the growth per unit biomass will decline more quickly than NAR.

8 a NPP = GPP–respiration = 6687

b Energy conversion efficiency = amount of energy in newly formed carbohydrate ÷ amount of light energy falling on the plant:
$$\frac{105.6}{8580} \times 100 = 23.3\%$$

9 a NAR shows the efficiency of the leaf as a producer of new biomass. LAI shows the total leaf area per unit ground area.

(i) If water is in short supply, it affects the opening of stomata, so can affect NAR and LAI.

(ii–iv) Light intensity, temperature and

carbon dioxide all affect the rate of photosynthesis so will affect both NAR and LAI.

(v) Fertilisers can increase biomass so affect NAR, but they may have less effect on leaf area because not all nutrients result in new leaf tissue.

b Water, light intensity and temperature would have the most effect on crop plants needed for dry, hot environments.

10 Winter wheat (sown the preceding autumn) makes little growth during the winter but then has a rapid rise in LAI, keeping pace with the increase in daily solar energy. In contrast, potato is sown much later to avoid spring frosts, which damage developing shoots. Potato reaches a peak in LAI in August/September, well after the June peak in light intensity and day length.

11 a Light intensity is the limiting factor.

b Either some other factor, e.g. carbon dioxide, is limiting the rate of photosynthesis or the increased temperature is affecting the action of photosynthetic enzymes.

12 To evaluate the effects of carbon dioxide as a limiting factor, you must compare increases in carbon dioxide when all other factors (light intensity and temperature) are constant. At a chosen light intensity and at 15°C, an increase in carbon dioxide from 0.03% to 0.13% brings about a large increase in photosynthetic rate. At the same light intensity but at 25°C, an increase in carbon dioxide from 0.03% to 0.13% brings about an even greater increase in the rate.

13 a Given that the minimum daily temperature is 10°C, the growing season is extended by 2 months inside the glasshouse compared with outside.

b Extra heating and lighting would extend the growing season even further.

c Shading and automatic ventilator flaps could help keep the temperature below 28°C.

14 The transportation costs to remote areas would be high. The light intensity would be far too great and temperatures far too high inside a glasshouse in the Sahel. Automatic watering systems would be too difficult to install.

15 a The photosynthetic rate of sorghum increases far more quickly than wheat and reaches a far higher rate than wheat (about double).

b (i) In C_3 plants NAR continues to

increase with increasing light intensity.

(ii) In C_4 plants NAR levels off at relatively low light intensity.

c C_4 plants.

Chapter 9

1 The most appropriate concentration of nitrogen fertiliser is 150 kg ha^{-1}. This concentration results in maximum grain yield. Any less will result in reduced grain yield. Any more will also result in less grain yield and extra expense.

2 At low P, nitrogen is the limiting factor up to about 100 kg ha^{-1}. After that phosphorous is limiting. At high P, nitrogen limits root yield up to about 100 kg ha^{-1}. After that there is a slight decrease which may be due to the lack of some other nutrient such as potassium.

3 b (i) An increase from 0 to 300 kg ha^{-1} results in a percentage increase in grain yield of $2.51 – 2.24 = 0.27 ÷ 2.24 \times 100 = 12.05\%$.

(ii) An increase from 300 to 600 kg ha^{-1} results in a percentage increase in grain yield of $3.84 – 2.51 = 1.33 ÷ 2.51 \times 100 = 53\%$.

c 900 kg ha^{-1}.

d By trying a greater number of different application rates.

4 All farmyard manures have a much lower percentage composition in all three nutrients than NPK fertiliser, so larger amounts of organic fertilisers are needed to achieve the same yield as inorganic fertilisers. However, long-term FYM application achieves comparable yields, as shown in Table 3.

5 b Yield increases with increased application of N fertiliser but the increase is less at high N fertiliser levels.

c 13.6, 8.6, 6.27, 4.8, respectively.

d Yes

e 100 kg ha^{-1} is the most economical. After this increasing fertiliser application does not result in similar increases in yield.

6 a Nitrate levels appear to be higher in the summer months.

b Farm wastes; nitrogen fixation; atmosphere; industry; domestic sewage, are all possible sources of nitrate.

c Root uptake; denitrification, may reduce the nitrate level.

7 a Nitrate gives the highest yield of tomato plants. It is quickly taken up by plant

roots, so there is no need for nitrification as with ammonium.

b Dry mass is more accurate because the water content of plants is so variable.

c (i) Take samples of the circulating liquid and test them for different nutrient levels.

(ii) Use a pH meter or titrate a sample of the culture solution.

8 a The fertiliser recommendations for spring barely are much lower when it is grown after roots compared with when it is grown after cereals. The root crop must use up less nutrients than cereals.

b Winter wheat requires more nitrogen, while sugar beet requires more phosphorous and much more potassium.

c (i) Excess nutrients may leach out of the soil and cause eutrophication in rivers and streams.

(ii) Yields will be reduced.

9 a

	Organic fertilisers	Inorganic fertilisers
Advantages	Overall soil structure is improved, with better aeration, drainage and water retention	High nutrient content and with known amounts
	Organic material acts as food source for soil organisms, and so improves fertility	Easy to store and to apply evenly
	Cycling of organic waste makes good environmental sense	Land does not need period of rest between crops
Disadvantages	Nutrient content is variable and relatively low	Incorrect application can result in loss of fertiliser and environmental hazard due to leaching and run-off
	Nutrients are released slowly by microbial decomposition	Expensive
	Bulky to store and difficult to apply	Over reliance on them can result in lower organic soil content
	May be contaminated with weed seeds and fungal pathogens	
	Sewage sludge can accumulate heavy metals like lead and zinc	

b

Inorganic farming sytems	Organic farming sytems
Rely on mechanisation and large fields of monocultures	Rely on manures and composts, crop residues and off-farm organic wastes
Crops can reach maximum growth potential and guarantee the farmer a good price	Crop rotations include a legume crop to increase soil nitrogen
	This type of farming is very labour intensive

Chapter 10

1 Weeds compete for resources such as water and mineral ions in the soil. They may also overshadow crop plants, especially as seedlings, and thus reduce the rate of photosynthesis. Pests and pathogens harboured by weeds may feed on crop plants and reduce their biomass.

2 a

Crop	Total % loss
Sugar	47.8
Rice	47.1
Maize	35.6
Potatoes	32.3
Fruit	28.1
Vegetables	28.0
Wheat	24.4

b 52.2%

c Disease.

3 Aphids transmit viruses from plant to plant, because they feed by sucking sap from plants. Controlling the aphid population with insecticide prevents viruses being transmitted from plant to plant and stops the spread of viral disease.

4 a The contact herbicide will kill only the parts of the plant above ground and will not affect the perennial root with its food stores. The plant can easily regrow from this root.

b Herbicide residue may remain on the crop. The possible toxicity of this residue would have to be considered. The farmer would have to use a selective herbicide that killed the weeds but not the crop plants. It might also be difficult to apply the herbicide without damaging the crop.

5 Not as much fungicide is used, since it is only applied when needed, which reduces the costs. There is less build-up of fungicide in the environment, less likelihood of it affecting useful fungi such as those in the soil that enhance decay,

and less chance of levels becoming toxic to other organisms. There is also less chance of resistant strains of disease-causing fungi arising as a result of selection due to regular exposure to fungicide.

6 Advantages include: reapplication of the insecticide is needed less often; it may be cheaper since less insecticide is used; labour costs are reduced. Disadvantages include: the insecticide is more likely to remain on crops and be ingested by humans or animals, with possible toxic side-effects; it could affect useful insects in the environment; it is more likely to accumulate in food chains; there is increased chance of resistance developing in pest populations as a result of natural selection.

7 a The concentration of dieldrin in the tissues of the mice increased manyfold (by approximately 50 times).

b The peregrines would feed on many mice and would accumulate large quantities of dieldrin in their tissues. The dieldrin might reach levels that would be toxic to the peregrines or to their young.

8 Broad-spectrum insecticides will have a more severe effect, because they will kill a wider range of non-target species outside the area being treated.

9 a (i) 0.04 kg ha^{-1};
(ii) 0.52 kg ha^{-1}.

b There is an increasing likelihood of reaching toxic or lethal doses for non-target species. The rate of bioaccumulation will also increase, with a greater chance of side-effects in organisms higher up the food chain.

10 Under the strictly controlled conditions in the glasshouse effects can be monitored and measured more reliably. Possible damaging effects on crops or other organisms are more likely to be detected. If the pesticide is hazardous its effects are limited to the glasshouse, and it cannot damage natural habitats.

11 Advantages include: the new crop can become established before weeds have time to grow and spread after harvesting; polluting practices such as stubble burning are avoided; decaying crop remains may help to maintain soil fertility and texture. Disadvantages include: pests specific to a crop are more likely to persist if the same crop is grown again; it may be more difficult to sow seed evenly and at a suitable depth; the season may not be suitable for seedlings to become established.

12 Hoeing uproots or removes the growing shoots of young annual plants before they are able to become fully established or produce seeds. Perennial plants often have underground parts, such as rhizomes, which can regrow and which are not destroyed by hoeing.

13 The fluctuation is a result of predator and prey interactions, as described in Chapter 3, section 3.7. As the population of the pest increases, the numbers of its predators, including the biological control agent, increase. This causes the pest population to fall again and then the predator population also falls.

14 Agents that attack non-target species can cause serious damage to an ecosystem once the pest population has diminished.

15 The biological control agent cannot disperse, and its population can be maintained at a high enough level to control the pest population. There is less chance of the agent affecting natural ecosystems. Environmental conditions are likely to be kept at a favourable level.

Chapter 11

1

	Intensive rearing	Outdoor production
Advantages	Control of diet to ensure high protein content	More natural conditions for pigs
	Control of environmental conditions reduces heat loss and less energy from food is wasted in maintaining body temperature	Meat may command higher price as 'free range'
	Restricted movement reduces energy loss so more is available for growth	Avoids disadvantages of intensive rearing
	Early weaning allows sows to start breeding again more quickly	
Disdvantages	Ethical considerations in terms of the lifestyle of the pigs	Requires larger areas of land for foraging
	Higher capital expenditure on buildings and higher running costs for heating	Some food wasted or eaten by other consumers
	More labour intensive, e.g. feeding and removing faeces	Establishment of social groups leads to fighting and possible injury
	Meat may be more fatty because of restricted movement	
	Use of antibiotics to combat infection may lead to resistant pathogens and residues in meat	
	Increased chance of disease	

2 Anabolic steroid hormones are produced in all animals and are essential for growth.

3 The use of BST can increase milk yield. This could be particularly beneficial in developing countries where there are food shortages; there would be less advantages in the EC where there is already overproduction of milk, although it might help farmers to control milk production. However, the side-effects on humans of BST residues in milk are uncertain, and its use may make cattle more susceptible to disease. In developing countries it would be necessary to balance these factors.

4

Plant growth substances	Animal hormones
Chemical substances	Chemical substances
Have effect on target cells	Have effect on target cells
Produced by unspecialised cells	Produced in special tissues or glands
May be produced at site of activity	Transported widely around animal
Not specific	Target specific cells or organs
May affect different tissues and organs in contrasting ways	Usually have particular effects on target cells or organs

5 The root meristems must produce much lower concentrations of IAA than shoot meristems. The IAA produced in relatively high concentrations in the shoot must not be distributed to the roots, otherwise root growth would be inhibited.

6 Synergistic, since together they promote cell division.

7 a Addition of ABA inhibits the production of α-amylase. At low concentrations of gibberellin production of α-amylase is almost totally stopped by the addition of ABA; at higher concentrations production does occur but at a reduced rate compared with when ABA is absent. In barley seeds α-amylase causes the breakdown of starch reserves to maltose, so the production of ABA will prevent this happening.

b During germination starch reserves need to be broken down so that the sugars can be used in respiration and for the synthesis of cellulose and other compounds for growth. The concentration of ABA might be expected to fall so that gibberellin can stimulate α-amylase production and allow this break down to occur.

8 a Increasing ethene production promotes ripening of the tomato fruit; as the tomato ripens it becomes less firm.

b Ethene stimulates fruit to ripen and therefore decreases their shelf-life. Production of ethene by some fruit may speed up the ripening process in others.

Chapter 12

1 Since asexual reproduction produces genetically identical offspring, desirable characteristics are preserved. Therefore, the quality of the crop products is consistent. This is particularly valuable when new varieties have been produced, for example by hybridisation. It may be the only way of reproducing infertile hybrids. Often one plant can be used to produce many offspring asexually, and this process is much quicker than waiting for plants to flower and produce seed.

2 a The frequency of the 'tight ear' allele in the population would increase and the frequency of the 'loose ear' allele would decrease.
   b An increasingly high proportion of the crop would have 'tight' ears.

3 Dwarf wheats are less likely to be knocked over by heavy rain or high winds. This makes harvesting easier. Since less energy is used in producing the stalks the yield of harvestable grain is likely to be higher.

4 The area for light absorption is large, thus giving an overall high rate of photosynthesis. More photosynthetic product is available for growth, and yield is greater.

5 9/16 (56.25%).

6 a After 3 backcrosses: 93.75% V, 6.25% W. After 4 backcrosses: 96.875%V, 3.125% W.
   b The proportion of wild genes decreases, but the rate of decrease declines, so some genes from the wild parent tend to persist for many generations.

7 Homozygous genotype, inbreeding.

8 There will be fewer different alleles in the gene pool from which to select. The possible range of features that can be selected for is much reduced. It is difficult to breed varieties with new characteristics.

9 The increased rate of mutation in micropropogation produces new alleles. These may produce new phenotypes which have advantageous characteristics. Plants with these phenotypes can be selected for further micropagation, just as individuals with desirable features are used in selective breeding.

10 In a breeding programme cows with high milk yields would be used for breeding. Their embryos can be split to yield several embryos. Each of these can be inserted into the womb of a less valuable cow. Therefore, the high-yielding cow can be bred repeatedly and large numbers of calves with its genes can be raised simultaneously. This speeds up the breeding programme considerably.

11 a Plants need nitrogen to synthesise proteins (and in smaller quantities such compounds as nucleotides). This is taken up as nitrate ions.
    b Yield could be greatly improved without the use of expensive fertilisers.

12 The rate of carbohydrate production by photosynthesis would not change. More of this carbohydrate would be used as respiratory substrate in nitrogen fixation and less would be available as food reserves in the cereal grains.

Glossary

abiotic components are all the non-living parts of a system, including rainfall, temperature, mineral nutrient status, etc. 7

abscisic acid is a plant growth substance. 151

abscission is when plant leaves, fruit or flowers fall. 151

absorbed means taken up by, and used by a body. 12

acid rain is any precipitation with a pH below 5·6. 70

active substance is the substance that has the effect on the biochemistry of an organism to produce an observable change in growth or behaviour. 148

acute is an event which occurs quickly, lasts a short time and typically has a large, immediate effect. 69

adsorbed means attracted to, and held on, the surface of a body rather than being absorbed into it. 62

afforestation means that the land is planted and then managed as forest. 32

algal blooms are rapid growths of algae, typically occurring during the summer months. 30

alleles are a form of a particular gene, so a gene for height in plants may have two alleles – tall and short. 157

Allen's rule states that parts of the body that stick out, such as limbs and facial features, are smaller in species living in colder regions than species living in warmer regions. 56

ammonification is the breakdown of dead and waste organic matter by bacteria and fungi to form ammonium ions. 25

anabolic steroids are hormones that encourage the production of body mass, particularly muscle growth. 144

androgens are hormones that promote the growth of male secondary sexual characteristics. 144

annuals are plants that complete their life cycle within a single season. 53; 128

antagonistic substances tend to reduce the effect of each other. 61,147

antisense technology uses antisense strands of plant genes and bacteria plasmids to alter the genetic make up of plants. 166

aquaculture is fish farming. 98

arable land is land used for crop production. 119

arthropods are a group of animals with jointed limbs including mites, millipedes, woodlice and insects. 128

artificial insemination involves transferring sperm from a male to a female without sexual intercourse. 144

artificial propagation involves producing new individuals by cuttings or grafts. 161

artificial selection is the deliberate selection and breeding of organisms with desirable characteristics. 157

asexual reproduction is reproduction that does not involve fusion of gametes and produces offspring that are genetically identical to the parent. 156

assimilated food is used to produce new growth. 15

assimilation efficiency is the proportion of assimilated food to consumed food. 15

autotrophs are able to make their own complex organic molecules (food) from inorganic mineral ions and a source of energy. 8

auxin is a plant growth substance. 147

backcross is crossing a plant with one of its parents. 160

basal metabolic rate (BMR) is the minimum metabolic rate of an organism that keeps it alive. 51

beam trawl uses a large wooden beam to drag a net over the sea bed and was the main type of trawl when vessels were sail-driven. 93

belt transect is a narrow strip of the study area chosen to cross regions where changes can be seen with the naked eye. 78

Bergman's rule states that animals of the same genus tend to be smaller in warmer regions and larger in colder regions. 56

bioaccumulation is the tendency of certain compounds to be concentrated as they pass up the food chain. A number of synthetic pesticides show bioaccumulation so that the concentration of the chemical in a top carnivore is much higher than the concentration of the same chemical in the environment. 63; 132

biochemical oxygen demand (BOD) is a measure of the oxygen required by a body of water, typically organic pollution raises the BOD of a water course. 64

biodegradable wastes can be broken down by animals and microorganisms into simple, inorganic compounds. 62

biological control is a method of pest control that does not involve chemicals. 138

biological monitoring uses living organisms to monitor the conditions in the environment. 67

biological yield is the total biomass of a crop which may include material that cannot be harvested and so does not contribute to the harvestable dry matter. 105

biomass is the total mass of all living organisms per unit volume or area, at a particular time. 11; 89

biotic components of an ecosystem are formed by the plants, animals and microorganisms present. 7

biotic indices are based on the relative tolerance of invertebrates to organic pollution, in particular their response to environmental stresses such as low oxygen levels. 67

biotic potential of a population is the maximum rate at which it can reproduce given unlimited supplies of nutrients and space. 34

biotransformation occurs when chemicals discharged into the environment are transformed by living organisms. 63

birth rate is the rate at which young are born in a population. 34

broad-spectrum pesticides have an effect on a wide range of organisms and so can damage both pests and useful organisms. 130

brood fish are fish that are used to produce a population of fish for farming. 99

by-catch are fish of the wrong species or fish that are too young or small that are caught accidentally while fishing for the target catch. 94

C_3 plants are plants that capture carbon dioxide and build it into an intermediate compound containing three carbon atoms before they produce glucose. Most crop plants that have evolved in a temperate climate are C_3 plants. 112

C_4 plants are plants that capture carbon dioxide and build it into an intermediate compound containing four carbon atoms before they produce glucose. Many tropical plants and high yielding grasses are C_4 species. 112

callus is a mass of undifferentiated plant tissue. 163

carrying capacity of the environment is a measure of the maximum number of a species that can be supported in a habitat. It is often abbreviated to K. 35

castrated animals have had their testicles removed to make them easier to manage. 144

chemical monitoring involves sampling and monitoring the environment using chemical techniques. 64

chemical transformation occurs when chemicals discharged into the environment react together to form new chemicals. 62

chi-squared test is a test used to compare two populations or distributions to measure the likelihood of any differences between them being due to chance alone. 86

chronic is an event which occurs over a long time but typically having a lower impact than an acute event. 69

climax community is the final community in a succession. The climax community will not change into another community unless environmental conditions change. 16

clones are a group of organisms with the same genetic constitution. 161

coleoptiles are the shoots of young plant seedlings. 147

colonisation is when a species survives in a new or different habitat. 47

community is the collection of plants and animals typically found in an area, for example a grassland community will have a characteristic collection of plants and animals. 7

competitive exclusion principle states that no two species in an ecosystem can occupy the same part of the habitat (niche) at the same time. 42

conservation means to keep something whole and undamaged but allowing for natural changes. 76

consumers are organisms that cannot produce organic matter from simple inorganic compounds. 8

contact herbicides act only on the part of the plant where they are applied. 130

continuous belt transect records the species present within the whole of the transect. 78

corpus luteum is sometimes called the yellow body and consists of the remains of the follicle after the egg has been released. 145

cost–benefit ratio is the value of the yield return divided by the cost of applying the fertiliser chosen. 119

countercurrent heat exchanger system is a system of blood vessels in the flippers and legs of penguins whereby the heat from outgoing arterial blood is transferred to venous blood returning from exposed parts. This reduces heat loss from the body core. 57

crash is a very rapid decline in numbers when applied to biological populations. 35

crop rotation involves planting a different crop in a particular field every year. Typically a rotation uses a three or four year cycle of crops. 137

cross-pollination is when gametes from two unrelated plants fuse. 158

cytokinins are plant growth substances. 150

death rate is the rate at which death occurs in a population. 34

decomposers break down dead plants and animals or other organic remains (e.g. manure) to simple inorganic forms. 8

demersal fish live on the sea bed. 93

denitrifying/denitrification is the process that converts nitrates and ammonium ions into nitrogen gas. 25

density-dependent describes anything that depends on the density of one or all of the populations involved. 43

density-independent factors are not affected by population density. 44

deoxyribonucleic acid (DNA) is the molecule which codes the genetic information for individuals. It has a double helix structure. 157

detritivores feed upon fragments of dead organic matter called detritus. 8

detritus is fragments of dead organic matter. 8

dilution is making a substance less concentrated by adding more liquid. 62

direct killing occurs when a pesticide causes the death of humans, pets or domestic animals by direct contact. 134

direct sowing involves planting the seeds of the next year's crop into the soil through the remains of the current year's crop after harvesting but without any other soil treatments such as ploughing or harrowing. 137

dispersal is the spread of species to different areas. 47

diversity is the variety of species in an area. 58

diversity index measures the species diversity of a particular ecosystem. 67

dormancy is a period of time when an organism's BMR is reduced and growth ceases. Dormancy is often used to avoid stressful environmental conditions, for example low temperatures. 51; 149

drift nets are large nets suspended by floats which hang vertically like a curtain in the water and can stretch from 5 to 50 km in length. 96

dry mass is the mass of an organism with the water removed, usually used with plants and involving heating the sample in an oven at 110°C to a constant mass. 11

dynamic study looks at the way factors change over time, so an ecosystem is a dynamic system because it changes over time. 7

ecology is the study of how organisms interact with each other and their environment. 7

economic yield is the part of crop biomass which is useful and so has economic value, for example the grain of barley. 105

ecosystems are made up of biotic, the living, and abiotic, the non-living, components in an area, and the interrelationships between them. 7

ectothermic animals depend almost entirely on the environment for their body heat. Many have evolved behavioural strategies to try to regulate body temperatures, for example some lizards control heat input from the Sun by moving in and out of the shade. 51

effluent is the outflow from a sewage plant or industrial site into a stream or river. 61

Eltonian pyramid of numbers plots the numbers of organisms as horizontal bars to show the reduction in the number of organisms at each trophic level in an ecosystem. 10

embryo transplantation involves taking fertilised embryos from one animal (the donor) and transplanting them into the uterus of another (the recipient). 144

emigration is the movement of individuals out of a population. 34

endothermic animals generate their own body heat to provide the warmth needed to maintain their body temperatures at a constant figure, usually above the environmental temperature. 51

energy budgets describe the amounts of energy entering, being retained and leaving animals or plants. 15

energy flow is the name given to the transfer of energy from one trophic level to another. 12

environment of an organism consists of all the conditions that affect it including other living organisms and the physical surroundings. 7

environmental resistance is the sum of the abiotic and biotic environmental factors that prevent a population from growing indefinitely at its maximum theoretical rate. 34

epilimnion is the less dense, warmer upper layer in a body of standing water. 28

equilibrium catch is the biomass of fish that exactly equals the natural yield of the stock. 90

essential trace elements are nutrients that are needed in very small quantities. 20; 116

ethene is a plant growth substance. 152

eutrophication is the enrichment of waters by inorganic nutrients such as nitrate and phosphate. 28

evolution is the process by which living organisms change over time. 47

exponential growth is when the size of a population repeatedly doubles. 37

fertilisers are mixtures applied to the soil or directly to plants that contain mineral nutrients for plants and so encourage growth. 116

food chains show the passage of energy through an ecosystem in terms of what animal eats what. 7

food webs show a selection of the food chains in a particular area to give a better picture of the feeding relationships in an ecosystem. 8

freeze–thaw cycle is the constant freezing, melting and refreezing of water. 51

freezing susceptible organisms are damaged by freezing and so have to avoid ice formation in their cells and tissues. 53

freezing tolerant organisms are not damaged by freezing and so can tolerate the presence of ice in their body cells. 53

fundamental niche is the potential niche an organism could occupy in the absence of any competitors or predators. 48

fungicides are pesticides designed to kill fungi. 130

gametes are specialised cells produced for sexual reproduction containing half the number of chromosomes of normal body cells. 157

gene pool contains all the genes available in a local population. 157

genes are sections of DNA which code for particular inherited characteristics. 157

genetic engineering involves artificially changing an organism's genetic make up. 164

genotype is the genes present in an organism. 156

gestation is the time between the fertilisation of an egg and birth. 143

gibberellins are plant growth substances. 149

global warming is the observed rise in global mean temperatures over the last few centuries. 23

Green Revolution is a general term used to describe changes in the way farmers work when they start to use scientific knowledge to help increase food production. 104

greenhouse effect attempts to explain the observed rise in global mean temperatures in terms of gases in the atmosphere reflecting heat back towards the surface of the Earth. 23

gross primary productivity (GPP) is the rate at which photosynthetic products accumulate in plants. 13; 104

growth curves show the predictable patterns of growth and decline of some populations. 37

growth overfishing occurs when too many young, small fish are caught so that the yield of fish biomass is low. 91

habitat is the physical space where a particular organism lives. 7

harrowing involves breaking up the top layer of soil, often by dragging a metal frame over it, before planting seeds. 137

harvest index is the proportion of the biological yield that makes up the economic yield. 105

harvestable dry matter is the proportion of dry mass that can be harvested from a crop. 105

harvestable protein is the amount of protein available from a crop. 106

Hatch–Slack pathway is the series of reactions in the light-independent reactions of C_4 plants. 113

heavy metals are metals with an atomic number greater than 20, for example lead, nickel, cadmium, zinc, copper and mercury. 62

herbicides are pesticides designed to kill plants. 130

heterotrophs cannot make their own food; they have to take food into their bodies in complex organic form. All animals are heterotrophs. 8

heterozygous organisms contain two different alleles for a particular gene, for example tall-short for height in plants. 158

hibernation is a form of dormancy where animals sleep through cold periods. 51

hoeing is digging up the soil around plants to kill off any weeds starting to grow around the crops. 138

homeothermic animals maintain a constant core body temperature, usually higher than the environmental temperature. 50

homozygous organisms contain two copies of the same allele for a particular gene, for example tall-tall for height in plants. 158

hormones are chemicals secreted by glands that control body processes. 143

host organisms carry parasites. 35

humus is decaying organic matter in the soil that acts as a pool of nutrients that plants can use. 21

hybridisation is crossing two different varieties of a plant to produce offspring with characteristics from both parent strains. 158

hydroponics is a technique that involves growing plants in mineral solutions without soil. 122

hypolimnion is the colder, denser layer of water below the thermocline that can develop in standing bodies of water. 28

immigration is the movement of new individuals into a population. 34

inbreeder is a plant species which typically carries out self fertilisation and so does not need another individual to produce viable seed. 158

inbreeding depression is loss of vigour in plants produced by inbreeding normally outbred plants over a number of generations. 158

indicator species are species that are used to indicate the quality of the water, indicator species used in water-based work are typically invertebrates. 68

inorganic compounds do not contain carbon and hydrogen atoms. 8

inorganic fertilisers are sometimes called artificial fertilisers and consist of carefully controlled mixtures of pure substances produced by chemical processes in factories. 116

insecticides are pesticides designed to kill insects. 130

integrated pest management is a system that uses a variety of techniques (chemical, cultural and biological) to reduce damage done to crop plants by pests. 140

interspecific means between species so an interspecific hybrid is the offspring of a cross between two different species. 159

interspecific competition occurs between individuals of different populations. 41

interspecific interactions take place between members of different species. 40

intraspecific competition is competition between individuals of the same population. 41

intraspecific interactions take place between individuals of the same species. 40

J-shaped growth curves are characteristic of a 'boom and bust' populations. 37

krill are tiny shrimp-like organisms. 58

lactation is milk production by an animal to feed its offspring. 145

ladder transects sample every metre along a transect so that gaps are left in the coverage. 78

law of diminishing returns is an idea concerned with the effect of increasing a factor in a process to the point where any additional rise in that factor produces a smaller and smaller effect on the whole process. 116

leaching is the loss of nutrients due to water washing them away as it passes through the soil. 20; 118

leaf area index (LAI) is the ratio of leaf area of a plant or the whole crop to the area of ground covered by the plant or crop. 108

legumes are plants from the pea family. 117

lethal concentration (LC$_{50}$) or lethal dose (LD$_{50}$) is the concentration or dose of a substance required to kill 50% of the population. 69

ley is a grass/legume mix that can be grazed by livestock. 125

lichens are organisms formed by algae and fungi living together in a mutualistic relationship. 53

life cycle is the series of changes that occur during the life of an organism. 50

limiting factor is a factor which is acting as a limit on a process. Increasing the limiting factor should speed up the process until it, or another factor, becomes limiting. 21; 109

Lincoln Index is a measure of population size used with mark, release and recapture. 81

line transect is a tape laid across the sample area, and the species that touch or are covered by the tape are then recorded. The species can be recorded all the way along the tape or at regular intervals. 78

lodging occurs when the stems of wheat or other cereals collapse so that it lies on the ground. This makes harvesting the crop much more difficult. 150

long lines are the commercial equivalent of the angler's line. 93

loop of Henle is a part of the kidney tubule concerned with absorption of water from urine. Animals adapted to living in dry environments typically have long loops of Henle. 52

macronutrients are nutrients needed in relatively large amounts, for example nitrogen, phosphorus and potassium. 20; 116

malate is a compound containing four carbon atoms. 112

mark, release and recapture (MRR) is a method of estimating the population of animals in an area. 81

maximum net yield is the value of the increased yield due to the fertiliser application minus the cost of the fertiliser application. 119

maximum sustainable yield (MSY) is the maximum yield that a fishery will support without being over-fished and so lead to population falls. 90

mean is found by adding the values together and dividing the total by the number of values. 86

meristem micropropagation uses the growing point or meristem of a plant along with a few small leaves as the starting point for micropropagation of plantlets. 163

meristems are regions of actively dividing cells in plants. 148

microarthropods are common in the Antarctic and have smaller wings and body size than arthropods elsewhere in the world. 55

micropropagation is growing plantlets from small samples of plant using tissue culture techniques. 162

migration is a seasonal movement of a population from one habitat to another. 51

mobilisation is the conversion of insoluble compounds into soluble ones so that they can pass more easily through the environment. 62

monoculture involves the growing of the same crop on the same land, year after year. 123

mulching involves covering the soil with material to prevent light reaching the surface and so killing any weeds growing there. Organic mulches like manure also help to add mineral nutrients and retain moisture. 138

mutualistic relationships between two organisms benefit both organisms. 25

narrow-spectrum pesticides have an effect on a narrow range of organisms and so leave other organisms unharmed. 130

natural yield in fish populations is the increase in biomass if no fishing takes place. 89

net assimilation rate (NAR) is the increase in plant dry mass in a given period of time divided by the leaf area of the plant. NAR gives a measure of the efficiency of the photosynthetic equipment of the plant. 106

net primary productivity (NPP) is the net gain of dry mass stored in the plant after respiration has used up some of it. 13; 104

nets are simple pieces of equipment used to catch animals or insects alive. 82

niche includes both the position where an organism lives in the habitat and the role the organism has in the ecosystem. 48

nitrifying / nitrification is the conversion of ammonium ions into toxic nitrite ions. 25

nitrogen fixation is the ability of some bacteria to extract nitrogen gas from the air and use it to build organic molecules. 25

nitrogenase is a bacterial enzyme essential for the fixation of gaseous nitrogen into nitrogen-containing compounds that bacteria can use. 167

nodulation is the production of nodules by *Rhizobium*. 167

non-selective pesticides will kill any pest, weed or disease. 130

non-target species are species damaged by pesticides even though they are not pests or are not targeted directly in a pesticide treatment. 134

NPK value is the ratio of the three macronutrients nitrogen, phosphorus and potassium in a fertiliser that will produce the largest increase in yield for that crop. 117

nutrient budget is a statement of the nutrient inputs and outputs of an organism or ecosystem. 26

nutrient cycles show the use and re-use of nutrients in the environment. 20

nutrient film technique is a soil-free culture technique that uses a flowing solution that provides the plant roots with water, mineral ions and a good supply of oxygen. 122

oestrogens are hormones that promote the growth of female secondary sexual characteristics. 144

oestrus is the time during a female animal's life when she can become pregnant. 144

oligotrophic lakes are lakes with low levels of key nutrients. 28

organic compounds are compounds that contain carbon and hydrogen atoms. 8

organic fertilisers are sometimes called natural fertilisers and consist of organic materials such as animal manures, composts and sewage sludge which have a wide range of chemicals in them. 116

otter trawl has boards called otter boards attached to the sides of the net which draw the mouth of the net open as it is pulled through the water. 94

outbreeder is a plant species which typically carries out cross fertilisation and so needs another individual of the same species to produce viable seed. 158

oxaloacetate is a compound containing four carbon atoms. 112

parasites are organisms that feed off another species, called the host, without killing it. 35

parthenocarpy is the development of fruit on a plant without fertilisation. 150

peat culture is a technique that involves growing plants without soil in peat, the most familiar example is amateur gardeners using grow bags. 122

pelagic fish live in open water and swim in large groups called shoals. 93

perennation is the practice of spreading the life cycle over a number of seasons. 53

perennials are plants which take more than one year to complete their life cycle. 53; 128

persistence is the ability of a compound to remain unchanged within the environment for long periods of time. 62; 132

pest replacement occurs when a new pest replaces a pest that has been killed off by pesticides. 135

pest resistance occurs when a pest species is not affected by the application of a pesticide which would previously have been fatal. As pests develop resistance the farmers typically increase the dose of the pesticide or switch to another type. 134

pest resurgence occurs when a pesticide kills both the pest and its natural predators. When the effects of the pesticide fade away the pest population rises more rapidly than the population of its predators and so reaches levels that are higher than the levels prior to pesticide application. 135

pesticides are chemicals designed to kill pests, weeds or diseases of crop plants or domesticated animals to increase economic yield. 130

pests are any organisms that reduce the yield of a crop. 128

phentotype is the appearance of an organism. 156

photosynthetic efficiency is a measure of how well a plant captures energy. It is the amount of energy stored in newly formed carbohydrates divided by the amount of light energy that falls upon the plant. 13; 107

photosynthetically active radiation (PAR) is the proportion of sunlight that can cause photosynthesis in a plant, plants do not usually absorb all of this energy. 13; 107

phototropism is the response of coleoptiles to light. 147

phytoplankton are small plants living in water. 11; 27

pituitary gland is a small gland at the base of the brain which secretes a range of hormones. 146

plant growth regulators (PGR) are synthetic versions of plant growth substances. 147

plant growth substances (PGS) alter the growth and development of plants when present in small amounts. 147

plantlet is a small plant produced by tissue culture. 162

plasmids are small ring-shaped DNA molecules in the cytoplasm of bacteria. 165

poikilothermic animals allow their temperatures to fluctuate with the temperature of their environment. 50

point quadrats are spikes used to indicate the area of study when carrying out certain measures of abundance in plant ecology. 78

pollution occurs when humans introduce substances, pollutants, into the environment that are likely to cause damage to the biotic and abiotic environment. 61

population is a group of individuals of the same species living in a particular area. 7

population density is the number of individuals per unit area in a population. 34

population dynamics is the study of the factors influencing changes in a population. 33

population ecology is the study of populations in their environment. 33

precipitation is water that forms in the atmosphere and falls to the surface of the Earth. It includes rainfall, dew and snow. 52

precipitation occurs when a substance comes out of solution or suspension to form a solid. 62

predators are animals that eat other animals. 35

preservation involves keeping something the same without allowing for change. 76

prey animals are eaten by predators. 35

primary consumers are herbivores, they feed upon green plants. 8

primary production is the production of biomass by the producers. 12

producers are green plants which use sunlight energy to build complex, organic matter (food) from simple inorganic matter. Producers are the only source of this organic matter for all other members of the community. 8

productivity is the rate at which materials are produced or used up per unit time. 11

progesterone is a hormone produced by the corpus luteum which helps to control the oestrous cycle of many animals. 145

prostaglandin F2α is a hormone secreted by the uterus which helps to control the oestrous cycle. 145

protectants are chemicals that help to protect against damage by preventing infection by a pest, weed or disease. 131

protein conversion efficiency is a measure of the proportion of protein in an animal's diet that is converted into protein in the animals body. 143

protoplasts are plant cells which have had their cell walls removed by enzyme treatment. 165

purse seiners are fishing boats that use purse seines which are large nets that can be drawn around a shoal of fish and then closed to catch all the fish. 97

pyramids of biomass plot biomass as horizontal bars to show the reduction in the biomass at each trophic level in an ecosystem. 11

pyramids of energy show the productivity or the rate of energy flow at successive trophic levels in a given area or volume, over a fixed period of time. 11

quadrats are frames used to mark the boundaries of the sample area. 78

qualitative approaches study the qualities or characteristics of the parts in a system. 7

quantitative approaches are concerned with the quantities, the relative amounts, of the parts in a system. 7

random samples are samples taken, typically in plant ecology, following a random placement of quadrats. 77

realised niche is the niche that an organism actually occupies in the presence of its competitors and predators. 48

recruitment is the addition of new individuals that are either born into the population, or join it from elsewhere. 89

recruitment overfishing occurs when too many fish are caught before they can spawn. 91

relative growth rate (RGR) is the increase in plant dry mass over a certain length of time divided by the total mass of the plant. It provides a measure of the rate at which a plant grows. 106

rockwool slabs are slabs made of a mineral fibre. They are used in a soil-less culture technique by commercial growers. 122

S-shaped growth curves are characteristic of populations that encounter environmental resistance as they start to grow. 37

samples are used to provide a picture of the whole by studying a smaller part (the sample) in detail. 77

secondary consumers are carnivores, they feed upon primary consumers. 8

secondary production is the energy conversion from biomass in producers into biomass in the bodies of primary consumers. 14

sedimentation occurs as solids settle out of liquid. 62

selective pesticides will kill only certain pests, weeds or diseases, 130

senescence is the ageing of all tissues, but is applied particularly in leaves prior to leaf fall. 150

sexual reproduction involves the fusion of specialised cells called gametes which produces offspring that are different from their parents and different from each other. 156

shoals are large groups of fish. 93

significance is a measure of whether a result has occurred because of chance or because of an underlying relationship. 86

somatotrophin is a hormone secreted by the pituitary gland which helps to control growth. 145

spawn are fish eggs. 91

species is a group of organisms with similar features that can interbreed to produce fertile offpsring. 7

species diversity is the number of different species in the same community. 17

standard deviation is a measure of the spread of data around its mean. 86

standing crop is the total mass of all living organisms per unit volume or area, at a particular time. 11

succession is the natural changes that convert one community to another, e.g. grassland to woodland. 16

supercooling is cooling of a liquid below its freezing point but without allowing it to freeze. 55

surface area to volume ratio as the volume of an organism increases, the surface area increases by less, so the surface area to volume ratio decreases. A larger volume means an organism can store more heat within its body. 56

survivorship curve is drawn for a sample of individuals, perhaps a thousand, that is followed from birth and, at regular intervals of time, the total number of survivors from this thousand is plotted. 36

symbiotic is a relationship in which one organism usually provides a habitat for another, different organism. 25

synergistic substances tend to increase the effect of each other. 61; 147

synthetic compounds do not occur naturally but have been synthesised in laboratories. 132

systematic sampling are samples taken, typically in plant ecology, by covering the whole area with equally spaced samples. 77

systemic herbicides are transported through the plant and so have an effect throughout the plant. 131

target species are the species a pesticide is designed to kill and is the main reason for the application of the pesticide. 134

target catch is the fish that are meant to be caught. 94

territories are the areas that an organism defends from other organisms of the same species. 34

tertiary consumers are carnivores that feed upon secondary consumers. 8

thalli are large leaf-like structures found in lichens. 54

thermal pollution causes a change in the normal temperature of an area, often in a river as a result of hot effluent. 61

thermocline is the region where the upper, less dense warm waters rest on top of lower, denser cold waters in a standing body of water like a lake or reservoir. The thermocline shows a rapid change in temperature over a small vertical range. 28

thermoregulation is the control of body temperature to keep it within certain limits. 50

tillage is working the soil to improve it. Primary tillage involves deep ploughing; secondary tillage involves harrowing. 137

titration is a method of determining the concentration of one solution using another solution of known concentration. 65

tolerance describes the range of an environmental factor that a species can survive. 50

toxic means poisonous. 21

transects are a type of systematic sampling, typically used in plant ecology, where the samples are arranged in a line across obvious changes in the area. 77

transgenic organisms contain genetic material from other species. 165

traps are simple pieces of equipment to catch animals or insects. 82

trawling involves dragging a tapering bag of netting over the sea bed to enclose fish living on the sea bottom. 93

trophic level for an organism gives the position of that organism in a food chain. So, primary producers are at trophic level 1, primary consumers are trophic level 2 and so on. 7

turbidity is a measure of the cloudiness of a water sample. 30

upper and lower lethal temperatures are the temperatures that mark the boundaries of the safe range for an organism. 49

vegetative propagation involves producing new individuals without sexual reproduction. 161

weeds are any plant growing in the wrong place or at the wrong time which appears to have no use and may compete with more useful plants for space and nutrients. 128

wet mass is the mass of an organism in its natural state, i.e. fully hydrated. 11

xerophytes are plants that have adapted to survive habitats with very little available water. 53

yield return is the value of increased yield produced by a fertiliser application. 119

zooplankton are small animals living in water and feeding on phytoplankton. 11

Index